ELECTRIC VEHICLES
Design and Build Your Own

first in a series by
Michael A. Hackleman

Book Design and Production by Vanessa Hackleman
Another Earthmind/Peace Press Publication

9 8 7 6 5 4 3 2

Library of Congress Cataloging in Publication Data
Catalog Card No.: 77-6158
Hackleman, Michael A.
Electric Vehicles.

"Another Earthmind/Peace Press publication."
Bibliography: p.
1. Electric vehicles--Design and construction.
I. Title.
TL220 .H3   629.22'93   77-6158

ISBN 0-915238-17-9

Other books by Michael A. Hackleman:
WIND AND WINDSPINNERS
    A Nuts and Bolts Approach to Wind/Electric Systems
THE HOMEBUILT, WIND-GENERATED ELECTRICITY HANDBOOK

Additional single copies of these three books may be obtained from:

EARTHMIND
XXXXXBoyexXRxxxX   4844 Hirsch Road
Mariposa, California 95338

for $8 (includes book-rate postage and handling) or $10 (foreign
or $10 (foreign orders)
California orders add 6% sales tax.

EARTHMIND is a non-profit corporation pursuing alternative
energy research in these and related areas. For more information
about us and our other publications, send a stamped, self-
addressed, long envelope and 50¢ (cash or stamps) for our
current publications list. Please use an SASE when corresponding
with us, for whatever reason. Thank you.

For wholesale and bulk ordering information contact:

PEACE PRESS
3828 Willat Avenue
Culver City, California 90230

INTRODUCTION

Designing and building an EV is akin to writing a book. Even this book. It's a process of integrating what you know and have, finding out what you don't know, trying to put it all into a proper sequence. The order-of-importance idea doesn't work here, though. There is no part of an EV, or most anything else, that's not important. If it wasn't part of the whole, it wouldn't be there. You might be killed in an automobile because of its poor design or because a cotter-pin fell out of a steering knuckle.

So, it becomes a process of talking about things, describing their association with other things, without having it all become too complicated to comprehend, much less to make decisions from. The design changes as you go through the process. This is not so much a matter of compromising, but of simply coming to understand yourself and what you want or need, and what you know, and don't know.

You should understand that I am an advocate of smaller vehicles on the road --- electric or not. When you boil down all the controversy about big vs. small cars, you're left with one nasty bit of residue: big cars are preferred because they give the driver a good chance of surviving a crash with a smaller car. I don't like that attitude. One, it automatically means that you're deciding against the other guy --- you don't get creamed, but he sure does. Second, it makes you careless; if you don't worry about accidents, you drive that way. Me? I don't want to cream anybody. And, admittedly, I don't want to get creamed. I want to avoid a collison, not prepare for one. I'll trade agility for mass anyday; I want to be difficult to hit. Sure, I've got to do a lot of defensive driving but, then, what else should a driver be doing?

I think small is nice because it means ecomony, range, and less dead weight to haul around. I don't have money to flaunt, so it stays simple, fixable, and easy to operate. I'm not trying to impress anyone with my vehicle; I'm not itching to compete with, or look like, gas-guzzlers or space-hippie vans. I don't carry a circus around with me; at the most, I've got my ladyfriend. I save acceleration and power for emergencies; I like to leave the rubber on my tires, not on the road. I'm not trying to break any EV land or air speed records. I'm a high-energy person, and I don't like to move slow, but safety keeps telling me to slow down. So, I do my designing with that in mind.

Whatever _you_ decide to do, I hope this book gets you a lot closer to it; that was my intention in writing it and, looking back through all these pages, that's the way it feels. Good reading!

FOREWORD

A few people have made it very pleasant for me to write this book. Our typist,
who wishes to remain anonymous, deserves many thanks. There's Hendrik Rienks;
he hasn't helped directly, but has done all of those things around the farm
that demand our much-divided attention, and it liberated our time to give this
book the energy it needed. I thank Megan Dehn for her efforts, proofreading
and catching hundreds of tinky typo, syntax, and nonsense errors; as well, she
has worked along with Hendrik, handling everything else. And in the midst
of the turmoil there was the quiet gentleness of Will Evans, building, digging, planting, mending, and cheering us on; his month-long visit was all
too short.

Help came from afar, too. Again, one of my books is laced with cartoons from
Jim DeKorne of El Rito, New Mexico; these are always a nice surprise. And, of
course, Mark Dankoff couldn't help but do some <u>very</u> butterfingery electronic
drawings, turning pumpkin sketches into royal schematics. Mary Leonard took a
few moments away from the gas pumps and other sundry chores to whisk out some
fine mechanical illustrations for Chapter 4. And, from Jim Dunn and the
other folks at Taylor-Dunn Manufacturing Company in Anaheim, California,
came permission to reprint drawings from several of their industrial electric
vehicle service manuals (notably Figures 2-11, 2-12, 2-20, 4-8, 4-17, 4-18 and
4-19). Most grateful!

And, the best saved for the last, I appreciate the work of Vanessa Naumann,
my ladyfriend and this book's designer. Layout, proofreading, arrangement,
cover, cartoons, and photos, by critic, advisor, and friend --- all in a
little more than a hundred pounds of warm human being. The words seem some-
how inadequate.

I dedicate this book to Kuby. She might try to deny it, but she had a lot to
do with me being here in the first place, to write this book.

Table of Contents

3---ELECTRICAL POWER

(cont.)

5---VEHICLES

The world's first electric vehicle

FUNCTIONS

The only answer that I can come up with when someone asks me, "Why an EV?" is "Why not!" Which, I must admit, is not very original or information-filled. If I got very philosophical and serious about it, I'd probably just answer that question with a stare and walk off and sulk. First thing you ought to know about me is that I don't want to convince anyone that they should build or buy an electric vehicle. There are enough people walking around who are excited about EVs but aren't doing anything about it!

But, if I got involved in a friendly discussion with someone who seems very interested in the subject, I might soften up enough to give what I thought were some advantages to owning an EV. One --- the little critters are fun to own, operate, and fiddle with. Two --- they are quiet when they run. From a technician's standpoint, that means that energy is not being wasted in making noise. From a person's standpoint, that means you don't get a headache and don't give others a headache. Three --- they're usually small. They park easier, can skooter around in slow-moving traffic better, and you're not consuming energy trying to push around a lot of extra mass. Four --- they don't usually go very fast. This is a good point because it means you're conserving energy, you're not caught up in the frenzy of getting somewhere, you've got good control of the vehicle, you're less likely to hit another vehicle, and you're not going to do much people or property damage if you do. Five --- you're less likely to hit and kill little animals. Six --- they don't pollute. Seven --- you don't waste energy at a light or stopsign, waiting to go. Eight --- you don't wait in line at the gas pumps. Nine --- if you have wind-generated electricity at home, like I do, you aren't depleting natural resources in operating the EV. If you have to plug your EV into the wall socket at home, you'll find that it costs you only a few cents per mile to operate. Ten --- you're less likely to make a <u>lot</u> of trips with an EV, because it won't take a 'quick' charge like the gas tank of a car will. That saves on resources, wear and tear on the vehicle, and liberates you to do other things.

I could go on and on, but let's look at the possible disadvantages. I say 'possible' because they only apply to some folks and to some ways of thinking. One --- EVs require a large initial investment. Since it's generally less than what you'd pay for a regular car of equal value, this may go out the window as a disadvantage. Two --- you have to replace the battery pack once every 2-5 years, depending on how you drive. Well, I've got a few responses to that. First, it will teach you how to drive. And second, you can add on the cost of several battery replacements and <u>still</u> not touch the original cost of the IC (internal combustion) engine'd car (plus the maintenance and repair on it during that same time period). Three --- most EVs don't have more than 45 MPH top speed and few exceed 75 miles range under the best of conditions. True. Four --- if I'm not careful, I might end up out in the boonies with dead batteries. True. Five --- they don't accelerate at a very good rate. True. Six --- most of them don't have air conditioning. True. Seven --- I have a better investment if I buy a new car every other year. I don't know. Eight --- They're uncomfortable. False. Nine --- I don't see an awful lot of models to choose from. True. Ten --- if someone hit me in that thing, I wouldn't have a chance. True.

Well, there you have it. Ten for and ten against. Check the appropriate ones which apply to you and tally them up. If it's against an EV, you can still send this book off to a friend for his or her birthday. If it's in favor of the EV, or even a tentative maybe, you and I have some communicating to do.

dEsiGN pROCESS

Process means progress. In transforming the fantasy of owning an EV into the one parked out in your driveway. In deciding that you can own one. That you more than want an EV, that you need an EV. And exploring all the ways of getting from here to there. Let's go down that path now.

TYPE OF EV

While it's important that you know the type of electric vehicle that you need or want, this may be the last thing you decide. Why? Because we don't always know what we want or need. If you only want to gratify an irresistible urge to own or drive an electric vehicle, you must develop the patience required to fashion that very specific vehicle; not just any ole electric vehicle is going to satisfy you. If you need something to get you into town, to buy a few groceries, to visit friends, it's a reasonable request. If you need a rugged, tough, farm vehicle, you can have it! If you want something which will do all of these things, you may be asking for too much. Or if you want any or all of them done with the power and speed you're used to 'getting' from another type of vehicle, you are being obnoxious. But, then, who wants to take a leisurely Sunday drive in the country in the same vehicle in which you hauled cow manure just this morning!

Versatility in any vehicle is nice, but it's lousy for efficiency. That is, if you've got a vehicle that allows you to carry a week's worth of groceries, half the neighborhood's kids, take a couple of goats to the veterinarian, and go to a movie with your honey, you have it for a price. A high gas (or electricity) bill. That's lots of dead weight you're lugging around. It's the same as packing a month's worth of stuff for a weekend journey. Compromise it only a little bit, and now it does nothing well. Not long enough for the sheet of plywood you need. Not beefy enough for this load. Still too big for you to corner your reluctant sweetie at the drive-in.

A specialized vehicle is the answer. But if you need a vehicle for six different kinds of jobs, six vehicles is a bit absurd. This is where you pull back on your fantasies, and get something which will do at least one job beautifully as opposed to a vehicle that does six poorly. Make it the job that you do most often. If it's farm work, build a rugged electric Ox. If it's for Sunday drives, shame on you; those should be done in the open, like on a bi-

2

cycle. If you live where it's suicide to venture out onto the roads on a fragile bicycle, you've put off that decision to move too long. But maybe you do need a vehicle to go into town, or to do some shopping, etc. You don't have to write me and say what you'll use it for, but be honest with yourself. Decide what you really need, and build it --- you won't have to make any excuses. They laughed at Noah, you know!

LOCAL vs DISTANT TRAVEL

Will the EV of your dreams be a homebody, or a traveler? If you can make this simple decision soon, all kinds of things are decided about the EV. Which is good because it's all the fewer decisions that you must make. By local, I mean around the place (a 40-acre farm) or maybe you live in the city and just a few blocks away is the furtherest you venture in the jungle. By distant, I mean to visit a friend that's 10-50 miles away. Or up and down some mountains, or around your 4000-acre tax-deduction out in Arizona.

THE UTLEV AND THE PASEV

Sounds like a Russian novel, but I've coined these two words to help describe the two basic types of EV that I envision people building. The UTLEV is very short for UTiLity Electric Vehicle and PASEV is a lot less writing than PASsenger Electric Vehicle. A little rough to pronounce, but it's the transistorized version of the three-word phrases, and it's my book, so that's that. Since my distinctions between the UTLEV and PASEV may not conjure up spitting images of what I mean, I'll elaborate.

The PASEV should satisfy the decadence in all of us. It's the result of breeding a sedan to a bicycle. Lightweight but tough; this way a goodly percentage of the vehicle's traveling-down-the-road weight is that of the people in it. Likewise, a solid chunk of the batteries' energy is moving your carcass; in today's cars, you're a dust mote on the steering wheel, for all the engine knows. The PASEV can obtain good speeds and good range, but (as you will soon discover) not necessarily both. The framework is designed primarily for driver/passenger protection. What it can't provide for in safety should a collision occur, it tries to make up for in a low center of gravity for sure control, snappy maneuvering, and responsive steering. Also --- a cushy suspension for comfort and minimized fanny-fatigue. A built-in battery charger for that away-from-home plug-in. A good monitor/display panel so, among other things, you know when the batteries are nearing 'empty'. After-darkness equipment --- headlights, turn signals, dashlights, emergency flasher, backup lamps, etc. --- for when your honey says "how 'bout one more for the road", and keeps you later than dusk. Streamlined design to impress your friends, and, at the same time, plow majestically through swarms of killer bees.

The UTLEV is the broken-mirror image of the PASEV. It's what you get when an ox meets up with an electric fence. An electric Ox. Doesn't have to be light, but assuredly tough. You might take along a friend when you're spiriting about, sightseeing, or showing off the place, but the UTLEV is designed for work, work, work. You get generous with the weight because you don't want the skeleton to collapse under the load. Don't worry about the batteries' energy. You won't go far in the UTLEV and you won't go fast. A tiller will do for steering and it gets a stiff suspension for control; you're lucky if

you get a padded seat as the driver. Low gears, high ratios, not pretty,
but mean. No fringes; that means a spotlight at the most for darkness work.
Ugly, ungainly, unsightly --- but _real_ practical.

THE big five

If you want to know what works and what doesn't when you build a PASEV or UTLEV,
you need to know the interplay of five major factors, all of which you can't
see. So, ghosts they are, and they'll act like them, too. They will haunt
you at every stage of the EV's design. And they do a lot of interrelating, so
you're not going to diminish their importance by taking them one at a time.
Their names? Torque. Speed. Weight. Range. And power capacity. First,
one at a time. Then, together.

TORQUE

Torque is both a physics word and an automotive word. If you've ever handled
a torque wrench, you'll know it's calibrated in foot-pounds. So, it should
be understood that torque means force through a distance. Leverage. Or a
lower gear. Or a higher ratio. Which also translates into a lesser rate of
energy transfer (speed) but the capacity to climb walls. Or moxie. It's what
Sampson got from his hair. Or Popeye from his spinach. Krietaslam. Mechanical
advantage.

If you want to learn more about torque, do your homework. Pull out that dusty
copy of Physics I. Study gear ratios. If you've got a UTLEV in mind, it's
got to have torque. You won't go anywhere very fast, but it'll haul the big
load. If you have a high-speed PASEV planned, torque can be sacrificed a bit,
depending on how fast you want to go. If it's faster than 25mph, you're going
to need a two-speed gearbox to get the vehicle started and still not be
screaming the motor at higher speeds. The only importance torque will have in
a high-speed PASEV (other than simply achieving a given speed and the initial
starting) is acceleration.

SPEED

Speed is the rate of distance covered in a given time span. If we want in-
stantaneous readings, we look at a speedometer. If we want the average over
the last hour or day, or for the just-finished trip, we take the difference
in odometer readings, divided by the difference in time of stand and time of
end, and we have the average speed. For the PASEV, our chief concern is the
difference between creeping along and holding our own on the freeway. Well,
not really. Most homebuilt EVs don't stand a chance of getting licensed for
the freeway, but no matter; no self-respecting EV owner would want all of
that noise and pollution.

Higher speeds are difficult to achieve in the PASEV without really, really
sacrificing range! It takes power to move anything through a 30, 40, or 50
mph wind. Streamlining becomes a must, the effect of the rolling friction
of the wheels is absurdly high, a high-quality two- or three-speed gearbox

becomes a necessity, and engineering problems are as frequent as your pulse.
If you're not convinced yet, read on; it's going to become much clearer!

WEIGHT

Weight equates to drag in an EV. You don't want it. Assuredly, you will
have some that's unavoidable, such as that of your own carcass. But it's
going to be an all-out, no-holds-barred fight to keep it down. The more
weight you have, the greater the rolling friction. Yes, you must have some,
or your wheels will spin. I can, however, assure you that too little weight
will not be your problem. You'll learn some things in this book which will
help to lessen the effect of the weight the EV might have, but watch out!
If you start reducing the coefficient of friction, you might lose traction.
The final decision or situation is usually a compromise between the power-
gulping friction and safety, but you help both situations if you keep the
weight to a minimum.

We will experience different kinds of weight in the EV. First, and inescap-
able, is the battery weight. It boils down to so many watts of power for so
many pounds of battery. There will be times when you wish you could add just
a few more batteries to get a little bit more speed, range, or torque --- but
even if there is some room to put them, the additional energy must go as well
toward carting around the additional weight.

The second kind of weight is the vehicle weight, stripped of batteries, load,
people. Just sittin' there by its lonesome. I call this 'box' weight (see
Frame Works, Chapter 4). This is the only place you can really keep weight
down, but you'll have to work at it hard. With a low budget, weight reduction
invariably equates to strength reduction, so it's a compromise. Good luck!

The last two major weights to consider in the EV are the load and the people.
In the PASEV, the 'load' is the people --- a driver and maybe a passenger---
and whatever they have brought with them. In the UTLEV, the 'load' and the
'people' are different. Just so that we can keep things straight, we'll
consider the people as being the 'bodies' and the load weight as applying only
to the UTLEV's cargo; let's refer to it as 'booty'. The load weight in the
UTLEV can be variable; it can be adjusted to meet overall EV performance,
taking more trips by taking less of a load on any one of them. For the PASEV
we're stuck with whatever you (and your passenger) weigh. EV owners diet
frequently or pick their friends by their slenderness!

To keep things tidy, then, there's battery weight, frame weight (emptied),
people weight, and load weight. Just so that we can account for something
extra brought along --- like the family pet, an overnight bag, a potato plant,
etc. --- we'll add one more category wheich we'll refer to as 'baggage'. If
we want them all combined, we call this 'operational' or 'driving' weight. If
we are talking about everything but the people weight, that's called the 'curb'
weight. Confused? Proceed!

RANGE

If you're designing a true PASEV, this is your goal --- range. It's defined
as starting with a full charge and going until the EV crawls to a whoa.
You'll want to know this number of miles. Otherwise, it may be about 5 miles

short of where you could have recharged overnight. And nary an extension
cord in sight. Unless you've got a separately-fueled battery charger on
board, exactly one-half of this range is the point where you turn around and
come back to where you <u>do</u> have a charging station.

Range will vary with conditions, so it should be defined in parameters other
than just miles. At what speed? Continuous running or stop-and-go? Level
road or up and down hills? With what load and how many passengers? Hot or
cold weather?

Torque, speed, and weight will all affect range. The higher you go with any one
of them, the more range you'll lose. If you can cinch up on any one of them, EV
range will increase.

POWER CAPACITY

While the power capacity of the EV is the subject of first discussion in the
chapter on electrical power, it also belongs here. The only battery with any
decent cost/benefit ratio is the lead-acid battery. For any type of battery,
though, additional batteries will bring in the same watts per pound. What
you have going for you is that doubling the battery complement (and capacity)
does not bring about twice the EV weight. Hence, you can do a little bit
better by adding some batteries. But the gain diminishes with other considerations until, finally, any additional batteries, along with the booty,
baggage, bodies, and box, will be too much.

INTERRELATIONSHIPS OF THE BIG FIVE

Portions of the functions --- torque, speed, weight, range, and power capacity
--- will complement or combat one another, depending on whether you're
building a PASEV or a UTLEV or a combination thereof. Let's begin with the
UTLEV.

The UTLEV needs torque. To tote that barge and lift that bale. To climb
steep slopes with heavy loads. It'll need power capacity, too. It gobbles
up energy in proportion to the job that's asked of it. And it's going to have
weight; that comes from the load, batteries, box, and driver. The frame will
need to be built strong to keep from collapsing under the load and terrain
conditions. With these three --- torque, power capacity, and weight --- all
at maximum, you're not going to have any range or speed. But who cares? By
definition, a UTLEV is not intended for speed. As well, it's probably not
going to be street-legal, so it won't have far to go. You're at home or on
the range. And there's only so much that you can do during one day. So the
ole electric OX will get a chance for some nightime R&R (rest and recharging)
before starting anew. If you need more from it than it seems capable of
doing, you could design your battery housing to be detachable. And with two
battery packs, there's one for the morning and one for the afternoon.

The PASEV doesn't have it so lucky. In fact, it has everthing working against
it, or so it seems. Range is probably (but not necessarily) the highest
priority in the PASEV, and speed is a close second. But, even without any
consideration for the other factors, these two will fight each other. It

takes power to make speed --- to overcome system efficiency losses, rolling resistance, and air resistance --- and to accelerate. Range, however, means the conservative use of the power you do have. Increasing the power capacity may slightly increase the range and speed, but it's a bit tough on the pocket book. Maybe you were just squeezing by with that two-speed transmission and now you must go a three-speed tranny. The _need_ for a pocketbook is looking dim with those expenses!

With the problems inherent in designing and building a PASEV it's little wonder that there are more UTLEVs (electric forklifts and small industrial trucks) made today than PASEVs. Of course, this will change; electric vehicles are 'in' and nothing is sacred to the eye of Progress. Light-but-tough alloys and plastics will reduce 'box' weight, new and improved batteries will deliver more watts per pound, and precise engineering will . . . well, maybe!

SOURCE

So far, it may seem like the only option that you have if you want an EV is to build one. Not true. Electric vehicles are not new. In fact, they were being manufactured as early as 1897. By 1912, there were several scores of companies manufacturing and selling electric vehicles of all types --- private cars, trucks, etc. --- and there were tens of thousands of the things on the road. That died out as the IC engine came into prominence, but there have been many applications where the IC engine is hazardous or inconvenient to use. Like in coal mines. Or inside buildings, moving things about. Or, where you need little speed but lots of quiet.

On the other hand, you won't find electric vehicles under cabbage leaves. Big cities --- like Los Angeles, San Francisco, New York, Chicago, etc. --- usually have a number of companies selling electric vehicles. Unfortunately, few offer 'street-legal' vehicles (it's an upcoming section, so hang in there); most deal exclusively with industrial trucks or golf carts. That will, of course, change. Electric vehicles are one very good answer to many problems.

The commercially-made, store-bought EV is convenient, quickly-built, and utilizes most of what everyone wants in a vehicle. It will be a compromise of many factors but it will generally have range, power, speed, comfort, and safety. It's made for people who don't have the time to build their own, wouldn't know how to do it if they did have the time, or have lots of money to spend. It's also made so that you don't have to think about what you want or need; some one else has done this for you and you can be on your way.

Those companies which do sell 'passenger'-type EVs are trying very hard to make them competitive with regular cars in terms of speed, and that puts their price tag way up there. If that's the only way you'd go, having no desire or ability to build your own, this book's information will go a long way toward insuring that you get everything you want in an EV.

Another alternative in acquiring an EV is to convert an IC-engine'd car into an electric one. This is frequently done. After all, the vehicle you'd convert is usually licensed and everything else in it is 'street-legal', so it's a good bet. And you don't have to look too radical to the neighbors, although they'll probably wonder how it is that you can coast up your driveway! And you can have all the comfort the original vehicle offered, though all the extra spaces will be consumed in a sea of batteries.

The final decision is yours, but I don't go along with converted vehicles. That's because there's just too much that you have to compromise. By the time you've chopped to fit, removed extraneous weight, and mated a DC motor to the existing powertrain, you might as well have built one from the ground up. Sometimes, trying to transform a vehicle that you happen to have 'around' is like trying to make a ballerina out of a hippopotamus. Sure, Disney could do it, but he used magic, mirrors, and animation.

Homebrewing an electric vehicle must be considered as seriously as these other alternatives. Provided that you have access to tools and the equipment needed, it may be the only way to get exactly what you want or need. Don't decide to do this until you have a firm grasp of everything involved, or you're headed for trouble. As well, assess yourself. Are you discouraged easily by mistakes or miscalculations, or the other problems that inevitably arise during construction? What's your attention span? Do you complete projects you begin? How much patience do you have? Think about it.

THE OWNERBUILT EV

After reading the last section, you might have an inkling about which way you will go. The purpose of this book will be to discourage you from building your own. Now you ask, "Am I kidding?" Nope. That's what giving you the straight dope is all about. If you can survive learning about everything related to building your own, only then are you ready to do it. De-mystifying something often has the effect of turning people off. The process of building your own electric vehicle does not start with your deciding to build your own. It starts by admitting that, despite your relative inexperience, you're intrigued by the idea of building your own EV and you want to explore that possibility until it becomes clear, one way or the other, as to your capacity to do so.

A few words of caution. Unless you've a lot of time on your hands and a willingness to engage in some fancy engineering work, there's no sense in re-inventing the wheel. Get as many of the parts out of the local junk yard or off the shelf. The 'shelf' is a term which connotes that somebody makes just the thing you're looking for. That's usually the case for anything you may need, or think of, but the problem comes in finding that 'shelf'. Visit surplus yards. Get surplus catalogs (see Sources); you would not believe all the stuff they have! Look up the items you need in the Yellow Pages. Call distributors, briefly describe what you need, and ask for catalogs. Don't be afraid to send a dollar or two away for some of these; you may be pleasantly surprised to have the money returned when they send the catalog. And, even if you don't get the money back, you may get some fast service, and that's worth a dollar any day.

Here's a caution on top of a caution. Move slowly and be skeptical when you have uncovered a potential EV 'sub-system'. A 'sub-system' is something which works as a whole in your EV's design; the front assembly, steering, brakes, mounts and suspension --- all are sub-systems. If it's not <u>exactly</u> what you wanted, don't just assume that you are willing to compromise. Stop for a moment and ask yourself. No matter how easily you might convert or modify it to your design, is it what you want? Stick to your guns!

STREET legal

An essential first decision about your electric vehicle is whether or not you wish to drive it on the street, highway, or any public road. Now, or at any time in the future. The kids have a name for this: being street-legal. There is no aspect of design which is not affected by a decision here. If you decide to operate your EV exclusively on your own place, you will <u>not</u> be governed by any laws, regulations, or rules. But, if you even cross a public road, street, or highway, you are breaking the law if the vehicle isn't registered, licensed, titled, or otherwise in full compliance with the vehicle code for the state. Of course, you might not get caught, but I can't think of anything more ridiculous than trying to outrun the law in your EV. If you're modifying a vehicle which is already registered, licensed, etc., you shouldn't have much difficulty in maintaining the status. However, if you're building it from the ground up, don't ignore the codes; you'll never get it 'verified' if it's not up to snuff.

Each state has available, at its Department of Motor Vehicles, copies of the Vehicle Code for that state. These are available for $1 and, for the information that they contain, probably one of the few good buys left for a dollar. I obtained a copy of the California book and found it informative, understandable, and easy to refer to. I doubt that you'll spend less than an evening perusing its contents for vital information, but do it! The codes that I will quote in this book are taken from the California version of the Vehicle Codes, but there are unquestionably a few differences between different states' codes.

Okay, let's look closer at what 'street-legal' means and to whom. If you've got a Detroit car, street-legal is going to mean that you 'appear' to be street-legal. In order for the vehicles to be sold in this country in the first place, they must use approved equipment and otherwise comply with the Federal Safety Standards, which is a process that occurs between the manufacturers and the government. So, unless you've added some accessories that might not conform to the Highway Patrol standards for your state, they're going to assume, at the very least, that you're sporting approved equipment.

Now, the question is: "Does that equipment work and work well?" This is what I mean also by saying that you 'appear' to be street-legal. If the Highway Patrol pulls you over because your license plate is dangling by one bolt, you've just violated section 5201 of the California Vehicle Code, to wit, "License plates shall at all times be securely fastened to the vehicle for which they are issued so as to prevent the plates from swinging and ... etc."; you'll get a warning or a citation for an equipment violation, at least. If you're well-mannered, have a clean car, and there are no other obvious discrepancies, the officer is not going to take it any further. And you'll breathe a sigh of relief, because just last night you noticed that one of your sealed beams was out, or that your windshield wiper was smearing the window instead of clearing off the water. These, too, are violations of the code, but they, at least, don't 'appear' to be malfunctioning right then.

If you get pulled over for the same initial violation, but your vehicle is splotchy with five different colors of primer, you're abrupt, and the vehicle doesn't look like it could go over a few bumps without leaving some of its innards on the road, you've got trouble. Odds are pretty high that the officer is going to ask you to demonstrate the proper functioning of any number of things he can think of. Okay, this is discrimination, but let's face it: something is not <u>necessarily</u> safe if it looks it, but if it <u>doesn't</u> look it, it probably isn't!

All right, what's this got to do with electric vehicles? Just this: you will not only have to appear street-legal, you will have to <u>be</u> street-legal. If your vehicle needs to be registered or licensed, it mus<u>t</u> be verified by a certified "Vehicle Verifier". So, let's get things off to a good start. Try to appear street-legal. If the inspector doesn't like what he sees right off, it's probably not going to get approved. At the very least, you're going to have to fight that prejudice throughout the inspection, and communication is going to break down into feeling attacked or being defensive. Be aware that, while the Vehicle Codes are fairly specific, they also have allowance for specific circumstances and interpretation at the local level. Your Verifier is putting his job on the line; if he thinks it's unsafe, it's unsafe. He'll probably find something to pin it on, but even if he doesn't, realize that he doesn't have to <u>prove</u> your vehicle is unsafe. He can always throw it back on the Federal Safety Standards and <u>you do not want this to happen</u>! This may mean that the vehicle's welds will need to have been made by a Certified Welder or, if not, magnafluxed to prove they have no flaws. Or, you'll have to show that the brakes won't fade, lock, or cause the vehicle to swerve on four or five consecutive stops. Etc., etc., ETC. This will cost you --- time, money, and involvement --- and turn a relatively straightforward process into a nightmare.

Don't get too worked up over the thought of having to go through a process getting your EV verified. If you've followed the codes and planned all along to get it street-legal, it'll just be a process. If you don't pass all the tests, you can regroup, rethink, redo, and take 'em again. If you didn't decide to make it street-legal until after you did some design and construction, you take your chances; if the deficiency is basic to the design, it may be too involved or costly to change, and you'll have to scrap it, or just use it around the farm.

Now that you've been scared and reassured, let's figure out what your vehicle is going to be. It'll certainly be a Section 430 (a new vehicle), a Section 580 (a specially-constructed vehicle), and a Section 465 (a passenger vehicle, if you've so designated it). But what else?

Well, that depends. Are you trying to come up with something that's just a miniature piece of the Detroit iron? Well, with that kind of speed, acceleration, and bulkiness, you're going to stay with four wheels, and subject your vehicle design to the same codes that apply to any other car on the road. The equipment (windshield and wipers, two headlites, two taillites, backup lites, brake lites, brake requirements, mirrors, reflectors, horn, etc.) and rules of the road (turns, U-turns, maximum speed, etc.) will be the same. And you'd better get hold of some good books on automotive chassis, suspension, steering, braking, drivetrain, etc., because you're going to need them; there is a <u>lot</u> of engineering that goes into handling these massive objects hurtling along our highways. You must be equipped to handle these forces, polar moments of inertia, and other stresses.

Of course, many folks will consider the conversion of that old Renault that's been sitting behind the shed. Or a VW, or a Corvair or ? In the eyes of the law, that's no different --- the codes apply. If you live in California or any other state which might have provisions for the same specific codes, you have an option to the relative hassle of verification, registration, licensing, and the equipment requirements for regular vehicles. That is, if you are willing to sacrifice speed, acceleration, roominess, and versatility of the completed vehicle. Interested? Then look at this code section!

<u>THE MOTORIZED BICYCLE</u>

Section 406 (or the equivalent, in another state, of this California code) states:
> A "motorized bicycle" is any two-wheeled or three-wheeled device having fully operative pedals for propulsion by human power, or having no pedals if powered solely by electrical energy, and having an automatic transmission and a motor which produces less than 2 gross brake horsepower and

11

is capable of propelling the device at a maximum speed of not more than 30 miles per hour on level ground.

This is quite a blockbuster, for what it represents in and of itself, but even more so when the equipment requirements for this vehicle are followed through-out the Vehicle Code book. In essence, such a vehicle requires only that equipment which is expected of bicycles --- relectors, a single headlight if operating the vehicle during darkness, etc. --- and it does not need to be registered or licensed. It can operate on any street or highway (not to in-clude freeways or freeway-type roads) and may use the special bicycle lanes now springing up all over. It must assume the role of being a bicycle, keep-ing to the right, not impeding traffic (which is 5 or more vehicles stacked up behind you), and generally maintaining the attitude of a slow-moving vehicle. A motorized bicycle (hereafter referred to as an MB) must display a slow-moving emblem on its posterior. But it needs no brake lights, turn signals, or wind-shield and wiper.

Section A of the Cubbyhole (at the back of the book) provides you with a de-tailed accounting of ALL the codes that apply to electric vehicles in the MB, BC, and MV classes, for the state of California. Motorcycles are excluded, for reasons that I will shortly explain. The Cubbyhole will often be referred to as you proceed through the book; it's where I stick all those things that would break into your reverie as you read the text. I've got one in the office for all of the otherwise unlistable things; why can't I have one in the book?

If you don't live in California, get your state's Code and bone up on it. Read and heed. So that you don't have to read the bloody thing several times (it IS a long book!), circle the applicable code numbers (even for possibly-applicable codes) and also circle the page number. Or underline them in the table of contents. By doing this, you can find things quickly. May I suggest one more thing? Cut out the applicable codes and, using your trusty Glue-Stick, paste them onto sheets and then xerox the critters. If you have some codes back to back in the Vehicle Code book, buy two books so you can lay them out intact. You would not believe how much this will simplify things as you design your EV.

There are several ready-made classes under which your EV will fall, by design or by fate. Almost everything comes under motor vehicles (MV); see code #415. If something doesn't fall under that class, it will fall under one of only a few other classes. Bicycles (BC) is one, but they're usually non-motorized. Motorized-bicycle (MB) has been defined and discussed. The remaining two are specialized vehicles (SV) and motorcycles (MC). Maybe you can get into the Special Vehicles class, but what you'll do there, I don't know. You may be re-quired to meet any number of codes from other classes and you may be exempted from others. Motorcycles are code-defined as two-wheeled devices. However, I have seen one exception to that; a four-wheeled vehicle was supposedly defin-ed as a motorcycle. How the manufacturer wrangled that, I don't know. Maybe it was a special class designation which meant compliance with those codes applicable to motorcycles. Anyhow, find out what you can do (or get away with) before you incorporate that information in the design, or you'll be in trouble.

THE THREE-WHEELED EV

Four wheels on a vehicle is like one sun rising in the morning. The way it should be. Except to us malcontents. If you have two wheels, you're a glorified bicycle or a motorcycle. Go to one, and you're a unicylist. But three! The magic number. Three forms a triangle, and it's the first geometric configuration that can enclose a space and the only one that has its own structural integrity, irrespective of how tight the connectors joining the pieces are. Makes you stop and think.

I'm not attempting to change your thinking on matters, but if you want to get your EV classified as a motorized bicycle (MB), you must have two or three wheels. Four wheels don't make it here. And, as the code sections indicate, you don't have nearly the equipment requirements. But if you go for three, there's a few 'quirks' that you should be aware of, and a few arrangements to consider.

There are a number of ways to arrange three wheels, but there are only four worth mentioning, and only two of those will work (see Fig. 4-1 in Chapter 4). So, you end up with twin wheels up front for steering and a single-drive wheel in the rear, or you have a single, steerable wheel up front and twin drive wheels aft (Navy talk for "that which follows"). While the Steering section of Chapter 4 details single- and twin-wheel steering and the Transaxle section of Chapter 2 details the attributes of single- and twin-wheel drive, this section focuses primarily on which arrangement might easily lend itself to the UTLEV or the PASEV.

A THREE-WHEELED PASEV

Outright, I recommend the C design for the PASEV (see Fig. 4-1), and stoically vote against the A design. This is supported by the following reasons:
1. The C design eliminates the need for a differential, which is essential to the high-speed operation of a rear drive of two wheels (see Transaxle, Chapter 2). This cuts down EV design complexity, weight, and cost.
2. The C design has two (front) steerable wheels. I feel this insures positive EV control and also guarantees the 'automatic' steering function without the tremendous 'rake' required if a single steerable wheel is used.
3. The C design assures positive braking on the higher speed EV. As braking occurs, most of the EV's weight is shifted forward. With two wheels up there, the load can be handled. With only one, it's going to be a strain.
4. With the power train clustered about the single, rear-drive wheel, and most of the driver/passenger weight located rearward, the natural place for the batteries is forward. The twin front wheels will help distribute this load. As well, the batteries are located at some distance from the power train. This makes it easier to keep the explosive gases the batteries might emit away from the motor and its spark-producing brushes.

There are more subtle reasons for using the C design with the PASEV, but I must admit that they are my own prejudices, and I'm trying not to influence you one way or the other. So that you can see why the C design may not work for the UTLEV, let's look at the UTLEV's requirements.

A THREE-WHEELED UTLEV

I recommend the A design for the UTLEV. Again for reasons. And again a list:
1. Most loads 'follow' the driver. If they were up front, the driver would need to be high enough to see over them. Unless, of course, you spend most of your time backing up. But, if the driver is up front and the load is in back, that's where the two wheels should be: helping to support the load.
2. Since traction is affected by weight, and braking demands good traction, two wheels under the load will do a better job than one. Non-skid braking is just as important to the UTLEV as the PASEV, but with the lower speeds achieved in the UTLEV, less weight is shifted forward, so the braking wheels should be in back.
3. Lots of tire surface area aids traction and that means better hill climbing ability in a twin-wheel, rear-driven UTLEV. Low gear ratios are good too, but surface area keeps it non-slip under a heavy load heading skyward.
4. Since the UTLEV will be operating off-road, it can more easily break traction in the curves with a straight, locked-axle rear drive. A differential would be nice here, but it doesn't have to be used on the 'forgiving' loose surface.
5. If a transaxle is used, it will probably come equipped with single-tailing brakes (see Brakes, Chapter 4) and this insures good braking in both directions on the two wheels that can do the best job of braking.

These arrangements --- the C design for PASEVs and the A design for UTLEVs --- do not automatically 'fix' everything for you. They just do the ground-clearing. You will still need to devote much of your meditation to 'balancing' the EV. That means figure the weight distribution so that you don't look like a submarine on a crash dive or a Nike missile ready for launch. Don't forget where whe weight (or how much of it) goes when you slam on the brakes. Having the front wheel(s) burst in a panic stop is undignified. The same goes for turns. If you are tailheavy (the EV, that is), and you negotiate a turn, you might suddenly find your EV's rear end in front of you. Or, if you weren't able to track that event with your eyes, you'll suddenly be looking backward. Very embarrassing! If you're normally front-heavy, you might lose steering traction, merrily maintaining a straight line despite the curved road. This is not conducive to enjoying an outing in your EV.

EV CLASSES

What applies to a small EV doesn't necessarily apply to a large EV. So that I could maintain some semblance of sanity in writing this book, I've set up a number of EV classes. And, realizing that this move was more to my immediate benefit than yours, I've tried to correct that. I will list here the six classes of EVs that I will frequently refer to throughout the book. So that you don't have to keep flipping back to this page, I've also listed them in the back of the book; check the inside of the back cover. Back there, they are listed so that you can, by carefully cutting along the dotted line, cut the informative listing from the book. Then, it becomes a book marker, as well as a quick-reference sheet for the multitude of abbreviations I use. Sorry, the dotted lines aren't quick-rip perforations, but there's no sense in making all of this a headache for our printer/publisher, too!

Notice that there are six listings, and that they are all described in terms of the number of wheels used, and the <u>probable</u> weight, speed, and type of vehicle, and what vehicle code designation is being sought. I've tried to cover the whole area, but I'm sure that someone will write me in the years to come with one that doesn't fit in one of these classes. Proceed.

Class One --- This is a four-wheeled, 2000 pound-plus monstrosity designed for speeds in excess of 30 mph. While it's possible that an exceptionally heavy-duty UTLEV might fall into this category, it's one that I think will be reserved for the biggest-and-best of the PASEVs, bombing down the freeway, boasting of its electrification. Commercially-built for the conspicuous consumer, or a converted Detroit guzzler.

Class Two --- This is the economical, sane substitute for the Class One EVs. Same speeds attempted (30 mph plus), and still four wheels. But under 2000 pounds. A humble, manufactured EV, an ingenious conversion, or a homebuilt model. UTLEV or PASEV.

Class Three --- This is the three-wheeled version of a Class Two EV. One to two thousand pounds operating weight, capable of speeds around 30 MPH. Manufactured or homebuilt and using a motor that <u>doesn't</u> permit a motorized-bicycle classification (but the owner gets an ecology button for Earthmindedness).

Class Four --- This is the first of two vehicles under the MB (motorized bicycle) classification. Definitely under 1000 pounds operating weight (box, bodies, booty, baggage, and batteries), if it's a PASEV striking for just-under-30mph speeds; or under 1500 pounds for a basic-essentials UTLEV that can do 15 mph flat out downhill.

Class Five --- Also under a MB classification, this EV will weigh less than 500 pounds and resemble a beefed-up, adult tri-wheel bike. No power or strength to be a UTLEV, this is strictly for PASEV-type operation. Speeds over 15mph normally and maybe 25 tops, but safety will insist on low speeds for this fragile unit.

Class Six --- This is the modified-bicycle EV. It's a two-wheeler that's got a motor-assist. It may have to live up to the code requirements of the motorized bicycle, but its weight will probably not exceed 250 pounds and it will not surpass speeds of 20 mph, with 15 mph as the probabilistic norm. Also strictly PASEV.

Maybe my class distinctions seem picky-picky, but I think the subject of this book will reinforce my breakdown (of the classes). Even if you don't want to pigeonhole your EV, the classifications helped me.

2 MECHANICAL POWER

This is the heart and soul of the EV. You squiggle back into the seat, cinch
the seatbelt, unlock the parking brake, shove the fwd-neutral-rev switch into
forward, and, with a firm grip on the wheel (or the tiller, if you're a grass-
roots'er), nudge the accelerator pedal down an inch or so. And you've just
liberated all those wonderful amperes. In wild frenzy, they surge through the
field coils and armature, punishing the driveshaft into motion. The wheels
grab, rocking the vehicle, as the motor says, "More! Give me more amperes!"
You yell a savage "Yes!" and tromp the pedal into the floorboard. And away
you leap!

You think I'm putting you on, don't you? But I'm not. That's just the way it
feels and happens, if you did everything right. But, momentarily, let's shove
the fantasy aside and get ourselves a step closer to the reality. I'm listing
3 parts to the mech-power assembly --- the drive motor, the gearbox, and the
transaxle.

MOTOR

If you've seen one motor, you've seen 'em all. That's because the wrappings
are almost identical for a given size, horse-power, and application. But inside that shell is what makes or breaks your EV, and where the differences
lie. I'm not going to teach you motor theory or motor principles in this
section --- there are probably a hundred books on the subject, I've listed
some of the best I've seen in References --- but I will try to let you know
what you're looking for, staring at, or about the connect up. If you can't
afford to outright buy, brand new or used, a motor of the exact parameters
your vehicle requires, you'd better visit the library and get some extra info
on motors; you'll need it when you're searching through heaps of them for the
right one. But, whether you've got the money or not, the more you know about
them, the more likely you'll be getting something that will work.

The motor's ratings --- horsepower, speed (rpm), torque, current draw, voltage,
operating temp, size, weight, shaft make, etc. --- will all come into the picture, but the type of motor you use will write the script. Is it an AC or a
DC motor? What kind of fields does it have? These are the two biggest questions. Let's look at the answers for AC or DC motors first.

AC versus DC MOTORS

Efficiency is one criterion that people never seem to fail to ask about. How efficient is it? As though, to most, the answer has any meaning. But, if you have to know, a good AC motor exceeds the efficiency of a good DC motor. Satisfied? You shouldn't be! In an EV, the power is coming from batteries and it's DC. If you put an AC motor in an EV, you're also going to have to install an inverter, to convert the DC to AC for use. But, the combined in-efficiency of the inverter and the AC motor will surpass the inefficiency of the DC motor. Not to mention the cost of the inverter required to handle that kind of current. Nor the weight of the two units compared with the one. Nor the fact that the AC motor circuits are trickier. Even the advantage of the AC motor in not having to have brushes replaced periodically doesn't make much of a dent in the case against the AC motor in today's EVs.

Well, that was easy, wasn't it? Shot that ole AC motor down in flames! But, there are still some things to think about in regard to the selection of the DC motor. The biggest thought: What kind of fields does the motor have? There are four types of DC motor (fields): series, shunt, compound wound, and permanent magnet. We'll look at characteristics peculiar to each, and then what works best, under what circumstances, in the EV. A lot of this in-formation may be new to you, but look at the drawings, and graphs, and study --- don't just read --- the list under each. Then, compare them with one another. By the time we get to the part where we figure what works best where, you'll probably know enough to select your own!

The Series Motor

The name is a 'series motor' but that really describes the way the field coils are connected: in series with the armature. Everything which flows through the armature (which is normally thought of as motor current) also passes through the field (see Fig. 2-1). If you opened up one of these motors, you would see that the field windings are large and few in number. Some other characteristics:

    1. Notwithstanding what occurs at saturation, there is a very large in-crease in torque for a given increase in current. The square rule almost applies; that is, double the current, and you get the quantity 'two' squared, or four times, the amount of torque. Because of inefficiencies, this usually ends up being somewhat less than the square.

    2. The initial inrush of current when the motor is started (referred to as 'breakaway') is usually twice what the motor normally draws, once at speed, for the same load. Hence, accepting the info given in #1, we can see that the motor, at breakaway, will provide almost four times the torque it normally produces during normal operation. As most motors have to start up 'under load', this is a desirable feature, assuring that the motor will not lug or stall, but quickly achieve operating speed.

    3. In view of this current surge during breakaway, the EV must employ slo-blo fuses or normal fuses which have a value at least twice the current requirement of the motor under its rated load. Otherwise, they'll blow on breakaway.

    4. As the load increases, the current will increase, but the speed will decrease (see Fig. 2-2). This makes the use of a series-field motor less de-sirable in a variable-load application.

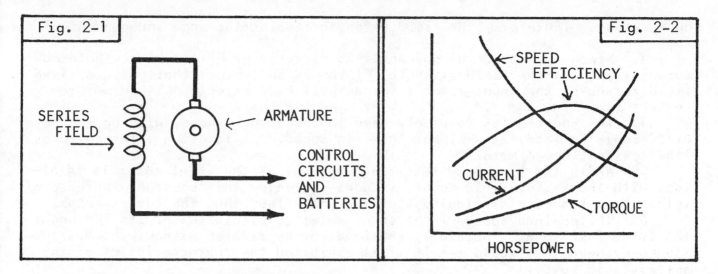

Fig. 2-1

SERIES FIELD

ARMATURE

CONTROL CIRCUITS AND BATTERIES

Fig. 2-2

SPEED
EFFICIENCY
CURRENT
TORQUE

HORSEPOWER

5. Because the CEMF (counter electromotive force) is absent during start-up, a means of current limitation for the armature is necessary until CEMF can be produced, or the motor may sustain damage.

6. The series motor depends entirely upon external loads for speed regulation. A suddenly-unloaded series motor will, therefore, overspeed and destroy itself; it should never be used in a situation where it might even momentarily be unloaded while under power.

7. Motor speed may be regulated by varying the amount of current that reaches the field and armature. See Controls section, Chapter 3, for further details.

8. The series motor's direction of rotation may be reversed by a simple shift of the field coil leads respective to the armature leads. Merely reversing the battery connections to the motor will **not** reverse the direction of the shaft's rotation.

9. In specific applications, the series motor may be designed to operate efficiently in both directions.   In most cases, it might be reversable, but may not operate as efficiently in that direction as it does with the other. An indicator of this might be where the brushes are mounted at some 'rake' or 'drag' (not 0° or 90°, depending on your point of reference); check this if in doubt. Likewise, if a blower is mounted on the motor, realize that it too will operate 'backward' if the motor is reversed. If you get one of these, make sure that the 'unintended' direction of rotation is attached so that it's your 'reverse' and therefore, used infrequently. For forward motion, then, you'll be running hot, straight, and normal.

The Shunt Motor

In the shunt motor, the field windings are paralleled with, or shunted across, the armature windings (see Fig. 2-3). They will draw their current separately from the batteries. Some characteristics of the shunt motor are:

1. The field current is usually designed not to exceed 5% of the armature's normal current requirement. Knowing this, you'll be able to check out, troubleshoot it, or figure the rheostat control values for a given motor (see section B of the Cubbyhole).

2. Because the resistance of the field coils is fixed (many turns of small size wire), the current through them, from a fixed source of power, will

be constant. Therefore, the field strength remains the same independent of the load.

3. Since the torque of any motor is directly proportional to the armature current and the field strength, it should be obvious that, with a fixed field strength, the shunt motor's torque will vary directly with armature current (see Fig. 2-4).

4. The shunt motor is widely used in industry because, with an increase or decrease in load, it will maintain its speed. It is often referred to as 'the constant speed motor'.

5. While the breakaway (starting) current of the shunt motor is identical with the series-field motor, it does not enjoy the 'squared' increase of torque, and has more difficulty starting under load than the series-motor.

6. The no-load speed of the shunt motor is within 10% of its RPM under the rated full load. Therefore, the load may be removed without the destructive overspeed that would result if it exhibited the characteristics of the series-field motor.

7. Breakaway current in the shunt motor must be limited (just like the series-field motor in the same circumstance). However, limiting the field current won't do; it must be a limiting of the armature current. This can be done with any of three common methods (see Control section, Chapter 3).

8. The rated speed of the shunt motor may be exceeded by as much as 25%, after the motor has reached its rated speed, by limiting the field current or limiting armature current. This is a nice 'emergency' speed feature but it may get you into trouble with the MB classification if you are just under the maximum speed limit on a level surface <u>without</u> its activation. If this is the case, install it afterward and hide it well!

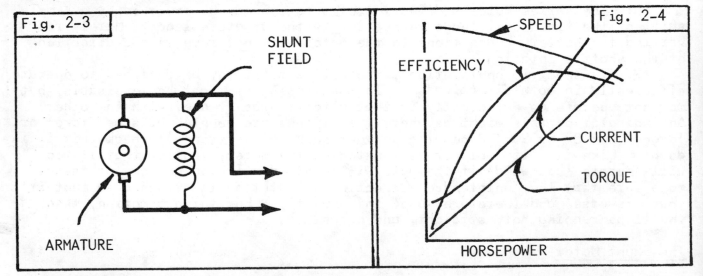

Fig. 2-3

SHUNT FIELD

ARMATURE

Fig. 2-4

SPEED

EFFICIENCY

CURRENT

TORQUE

HORSEPOWER

The Compound (Wound) Motor

Yep, you guessed it! The compound-wound motor derives its name from the existence of both series and parallel field coils within it (see Fig. 2-5). As you might also suspect, it enjoys the advantages of both the series motor and shunt motor without experiencing the bad points, but it's still a compromise situation. The series and parallel windings may be arranged differently, giving rise to the two different types of compound-wound motors: the Cumulative and the Differential. In the Cumulative, the current flow in each winding 'aids' the other and, in the Differential hookup, the currents oppose. Since the cumulative is the more prevalent and useful to the EV, we will discuss only this type of compound motor. Its characteristics are:

1. With the two field windings properly proportioned, the compound-wound motor can approach the series motor and shunt motor characteristics. To change it requires re-winding the motor.

2. The compound-wound motor has a very definite no-load speed (like the shunt motor) but its speed drops off more rapidly than the shunt motor with a current increase.

3. It requires less current than the shunt motor requires for a given increase in torque, but it does not reach the 'square' rule current found in the series motor.

4. If the field coil windings are 'brought out' of the motor case, so you can play around with them, you can install a bypass for the series coil. That way, when the motor has reached speed, after a nice, hefty 'series-motor' start, the series coil can be shorted out to achieve the desirable operating characteristics of the shunt motor alone.

5. By suitable reduction of the armature or field current, the compound-wound motor's speed may be increased, up to about 20%.

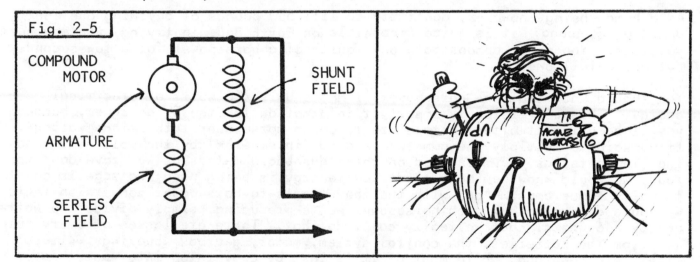

Fig. 2-5

COMPOUND MOTOR

SHUNT FIELD

ARMATURE

SERIES FIELD

The Permanent Magnet (PM) Motor

This motor is unlike the others in that it requires no field current; rather, its field flux is provided by permanent magnets. Hence the name. This greatly simplifies the construction of the PM motor and that means a lower cost motor. Some characteristics of this motor are:

1. A PM motor performs like a compound-wound motor which has the ratio of its fields wired for characteristics approaching those of a series motor.

2. The PM motor has a starting torque between the most common of the compound motors and that of a series motor.

3. PM motors render more 'drag' in a 'no-power' situation than other types of motors. That's because its fields are 'active' whether armature current is applied or not. This is considered a plus factor if regenerative braking is needed but a negative factor for normal coasting.

4. PM motors achieve higher efficiencies than the cost-equivalent series,

shunt, or compound motor. Part of this is attributed to a lack of need for field current, which is 'wasted' in other motors.

5. Since the field is constant in a PM motor, overspeed cannot be accomplished in the manner used for other motor types. Decreasing the load or increasing the voltage applied to the motor will increase the motor rpm beyond its rating.

DETERMINING MOTOR HORSEPOWER

Horsepower is an old-time term, but it's still functional --- so let's understand a few things about it. First, it describes the rate at which work is done. If you lift 550 pounds of weight straight up for a distance of one foot, and you do it in just one second, you've just demonstrated one horsepower. If it took you two seconds (or twice as long) to lift the same weight the same distance, you get an 'E' for effort, but you've only exerted one-half a horsepower. If you lifted the same weight two feet in two seconds, you're back to a horsepower. Try half that weight lifted two feet in one second and it's still a horsepower. One horsepower is equal to 550 foot-pounds per second and it involves mass, distance, and time.

As a human being, however, don't try to lift 550 pounds of anything one foot up in one second; it is quite impossible on Earth and, in trying, you may hurt yourself. You might demonstrate one-fourth of a horsepower for a few seconds, but not a full one.

You should know that one horsepower (1 HP) equals 746 watts of electrical energy. This conversion is important information for the EV designer, because you'll be using it often; motors are rated in horsepower rather than wattage. If we were to multiply the ammeter reading (in amperes) by the voltmeter reading (in volts) as they appeared on these dashboard meters as we drove down the road, we would know how much electrical energy is being used; wattage is equal to volts times amps. And, with the above watts-to-horsepower conversion factor, we could determine how much horsepower we're producing; simply divide the wattage by 746 watts. But we really can't do that. There are losses at every turn --- from the batteries, the control system, motor, gearbox, bearings, wires, tires, etc. --- and, while most of it is lost by conversion into waste heat, some of it is converted into vibration, and some into noise, and some into light (brush arcs). The inefficiencies of each system of the EV may be roughly determined, but they're normally expressed as a positive rather than a negative figure, i.e., a 93% efficiency rather than a 7% inefficiency. When we've got the efficiencies for each figured, we multiply them together and the resultant product expresses the entire system's efficiency. In reality, then, the actual horsepower available for the job (propelling the vehicle over hill, over dale, and along the dusty trail) will be less than half what the product of voltage and amperes divided by 746 will describe.

Figuring the required motor horsepower rating for your EV will keep you on tiptoes. If you believe the Detroit gang, you'll automatically select a motor horsepower rating which is the result of dividing the vehicle's total weight by 43 pounds per horsepower; that's what they've determined by long experience. I've got a far more involved way of coming up with the required horsepower, and in comparison, we disagree by at least a factor of twenty. Now, either I am a miser, or they're gluttonous. But then, too, they like to provide lots of acceleration, which I'm willing to sacrifice. And they have different priorities in terms of speed, range (for the fuel used), final vehicle weight, and torque. If you pick a horsepower rating less than what you need, the motor will commutate poorly, overheat, and have a much reduced service life. On the other hand, if you pick a motor which is overrated for the job, you're being extravagant, wasteful, and inefficient. It doesn't seem to bother some folks, but then, maybe you're different. If so, the next section will help you find the horsepower rating of the motor that your particular EV will need.

The Horsepower Formula for Electric Vehicles

Our selection of the motor's horsepower rating will be influenced by many factors --- some related to the components we use in its construction, and some related to how we like a vehicle to perform --- but most of these elements can be expressed in one formula:

$$\frac{(\mu)\ (W)\ (k)\ (v)}{1\ HP} = HP_m$$

where μ = the coefficient of friction
    w = total operating weight of the EV
    k = a constant (catchall)
    v = EV speed
  HP = motor horsepower

Pretty scary-looking, isn't it. Don't look too hard for the formula in any books, because I just made it up. No kidding! I do, however, remember how freaked I used to get when I saw a formula in a textbook, so I'm in full sympathy with your feelings right now --- but hang in there. By the time I get through explaining it, you'll see that I've just arranged for a very handy-dandy formula that you can plug things into, and, provided that you don't make any mistakes with your calculator (electronic, head, or pencil type), you'll quickly explore the many variables that represent your situation and EV design, and arrive at information-filled answers!

The Coefficient of Friction, or μ

By playing around with some physics stuff, anyone can come up with the expression μ, which represents the coefficient of rolling friction, and is expressed to the nearest one-thousandth (1/1000). It has no tag (inch, pound, etc.). By using it we take into account the interaction of many things --- a vehicle's speed, a tire's diameter, width, tread-type, and air pressure, and the kinds of surfaces over which we might drive our EV in getting from place to place. You don't have to do any computation to find values of μ because I've provided samples which have been obtained empirically (by close observations, not calculation --- see Fig. 2-6). If you use the chart, you will soon discover interrelationships which, if heeded, will help you limit the amount of horsepower your EV's motor will need to move you about. So that you don't miss any, I'll itemize.

1. The name of the game is to keep μ to a minimum.

			μ	μ	μ	Fig. 2-7
WHEEL	**TIRE PRESSURE (PSI)**	**WEIGHT**	**CONCRETE**	**GRASS**	**LOAM**	
4x18	20	500	.034	.058	.366	
4x30	36	1000	.018	.057	.322	
4x36	36	1000	.017	.050	.294	
5x16	32	1000	.031	.062	.388	
6x16	20	1000	.027	.060	.319	
7.5x16	20	1500	.023	.055	.280	

Fig. 2-6

TIRE DIAMETER · WHEEL DIAMETER

2. As the vehicle's speed increases, μ increases also. Not by much, true, but if reaching a particular speed in your EV is important to you, you'll want to include this in your final computations of motor horsepower. The increase of μ is about 5% for each 10 mph of vehicle speed.

3. To decrease μ, increase the tire diameter. The first bicycles had large tire diameters, and this is one of the two reasons why. Be careful, though; acceleration and hill-climbing will suffer if the motor and wheel rpm become too close to one another; you'll need some mechanical advantage for these instances. Oh, and don't confuse tire diameter with wheel diameter; one usually increases with the other, but they're not the same thing (see Fig. 2-7).

4. To decrease μ requires an evaluation of the tire width, air pressure, and the surface over which you ride; this should be evident after studying Fig. 2-6 for a few minutes, but here are the rules. For a hard surface, the minimum width and the highest (safe) tire pressure will give you the least rolling friction (minimum μ). But, drive those wheels (or the EV that's using them) into loose dirt and you'll come to a dead stop. That's because you've just achieved infinite μ. What you need for the soft stuff is a wide, soft tire (not soft like butter, but soft like partially-deflated). That way it has more surface area in contact with the ground and doesn't slice in and bog down. When you drive this kind of tire back up onto a hard surface, ugh --- it's got too much rolling resistance. Like trying to drive with a flat! Figure the terrain you'll expose your EV to, and that will dictate the width and air pressure for the minimum μ.

5. Tread type will affect μ, but here there's no general rule. Knobbies increase the rolling friction on hard surfaces but have some 'dig' for off-road use. Even those won't help you in sand. Take a look at its μ on the chart; if that doesn't convince you to stay off the beaches or out of the desert, nothing will. Stay with the smoother tires and good surfaces. Not too smooth, though; tires must have tread to be legal. As well, don't forget that you must have tread on your tires if you expect them to stop you when you hit the

brakes. Tires with too low a μ have a tendency to slide easier.
6. Road surface, as mentioned in #4 above, affects μ. The less packed it is, the larger the μ, and the more horsepower you'll need to get through (or over) it. But, if it's where you need or want to run your EV, get the right type of tire for the job. Or, otherwise expressed, pick your tire for the worse part of the road. A rough, hard road is just as bad as the loose stuff, sometimes; it consumes power in the 'up and down' movements (which your suspension system absorbs and dissipates as heat), as well as the propulsion necessary in the direction of your travel. These translate to a higher μ and the need for more motor horsepower so that, when all of these 'power robbers' have subtracted their percentage of the 'take', you've enough left over to get you (and your EV) where you want to go.

Some of these factors will point toward a particular type of tire and wheel to use and, once that's selected, you're ready to estimate the value of μ. I say 'estimate' because you may never really know what it will be, because of these and still other variables. But, whatever the value is, stick with it. Later on, we will put a fudge factor into the formula, which safeguards you from making too conservative an estimate on the required motor horsepower.

Vehicle Weight

This is 'W' in the formula, and it's the vehicle's operating weight --- bodies, batteries, box, baggage, and booty, remember? In pounds. This is the other part of what determines exactly how much rolling resistance (Fr, or friction, rolling) the vehicle has. You see, the coefficient of rolling friction (μ) is just a number, determined by all those previously-discussed factors. Note, however, that weight is not among them. It has nothing to do with the coefficient of friction, and yet it does greatly affect the rolling resistance of the EV. By multiplying the two together --- weight and μ --- we now have a value which may be thought of a 'a resisting force' to motion. Do not confuse this with the force which resists initial movement of the EV; that's a product of the weight and the μ_s, or coefficient of static friction. We won't be dealing with this, but I might add that its value is several times that of F_r. Once the EV is in motion, μ_s is replaced by μ, which will remain there for as long as the vehicle is in motion. This is what attempts to bring the vehicle to rest, and will, if you disconnect battery power.

Since there's a direct relationship between weight and μ, an increase in either is going to increase the rolling resistance of the vehicle. This may be referred to as the draft, which usually describes the effort of a pulling action. You know, like draft horses. Or, have yourself a draft. Hmmmm. It's rated in pounds. Some portion of the horsepower the motor produces will always be 'neutralizing' this force. If we surpass it, we have acceleration. If we equal it, we have a constant speed. If we fail to match it, we're decelerating, or we never got started.

The Constant 'k'

Oh yes, you must have seen this guy before! In just about every formula there is a 'k'. They call it a constant, but I don't understand that --- because, with different values of the other factors, it can change. So, call it what you like. Catch-all. Fudge factor. What it does is put a whole lot of 'real world realism' into a theoretical formula. With 'k', you don't need a formula that's a mile long to take care of every other thing that will make the formula, without it, just so much nonsense. In other words, it gets the designer off the hook, because it describes air resistance, winds, bearing and gear losses, tire distortion losses, heat, noise, vibration, surface irregularities, changes in the F_r as speed changes, changes in motor efficiency as it comes to rated RPM, etc. etc. etc.

Normally, 'k' is expressed as an efficiency, like .80 for 80% efficiency. But, if we put it on top of the line, along with W, μ, and 'v', we'd run into trouble because this would muck up our answers, giving us instead something that looks like pre-orbital logistics for Venus. So, either we express it as an efficiency and place it under the line, or we invert it, and place it above the line. Aaahhh! Pull away those cobwebs. If we determined that our efficiency was indeed 80%, our value of 'k', if placed above the line, must be 1/.80, so we'll divide 1 by point-eight-zero (.80). And we get what? 1.25, of course! It's your choice. If you want to express 'k' as an efficiency, it's gotta be below the line. I like to keep things simple, so I put 'k' above the line. If you want to, then use the conversion of efficiency to one-over-efficiency (1/efficiency), or 'k' (see Fig. 2-8). If you have factors between the values I've provided, interpolate!

Fig. 2-8	% efficiency	k	% efficiency	k	% efficiency	k
	100	1.00	55	1.82	10	10.00
	95	1.05	50	2.00	5	20.00
	90	1.11	45	2.22	0	BINGO
Table of percentage of efficiency conversion to 'k'	85	1.18	40	2.5	Values of 'k' are the inverse of percent of efficiency, or unit 1 divided by efficiency	
	80	1.25	35	2.86		
	75	1.33	30	3.33		
	70	1.43	25	4.00		
	65	1.54	20	5.00		
	60	1.67	15	6.67		

Efficiencies multiply; they don't add. Therefore, if you have three things which check out to be, singularly, 40%, 85%, and 65% efficient, multiply them together to determine total efficiency. This would be 22.1%! If you added them together and divided by three to get their average, you'd wind up with 63.3% for an answer, and that's very misleading! A quick check for any such calculation is the expression: the efficiency of any one system cannot surpass the efficiency of any one part. Since the lowest efficiency we listed was 40%, we know that our combined-efficiencies answer could not be more than that figure.

The value of 'k' may be very difficult to come up with. In that case, guestimate (an exquisite blend of guessing and estimating) it. This is where you get generous with the possibility of high losses. It's sometimes said to get 'k' as close as you can to the value you think it is, and then figure two to four times that amount. There's a contradiction here, but I've done it that way,

Fig. 2-9	MPH	FT/SEC	MPH	FT/SEC	MPH	FT/SEC
	1	1.5	18	26.4	40	58.7
	2	2.9	20	29.3	42	61.6
	3	4.4	22	32.3	44	64.5
Table for conver-	4	5.9	24	35.2	46	67.5
sion of _miles per_	5	7.3	26	38.1	48	70.4
hour to _feet per_	6	8.8	28	41.1	50	73.3
second and vice-	8	11.7	30	44.0		
versa.	10	14.7	32	46.9	x ft/sec = 1.467 MPH		
	12	17.6	34	49.9	x MPH = .682 ft/sec.		
	14	20.5	36	52.8		
	16	23.5	38	55.7		

and it's worked. Try it! At least, this should tell you that to ignore one factor and take painstaking efforts with another is not productive.

Vehicle Speed

The speed of the electric vehicle is represented in the formula by 'v'. I'm hoping that, by putting it in the small letter, I won't offend too many physics folks; normally, 'v' represents velocity, which is not only speed, but speed in a given direction. Anyway, this is the 'rate' in the definition of horse-power. Once we've got the draft (EV weight times the coefficient of friction) calculated, that force times the speed of the EV becomes the expression of the rate at which work is done. More speed (a faster rate) with the same load means more horsepower, right? Right!

Since it's not very meaningful to multiply hours by seconds and feet by miles, we have to convert them as necessary. Since we'll need to deal with seconds and feet (mine are already propped up just beyond the typewriter), we'll con-vert miles per hour into feet per second (ft./sec. --- see Fig. 2-9) for values from 0 to 50 miles per hour.

Divide by Horsepower

Okay, before we get back to the formula, there's one more thing to mention. Or one more question to answer. Like, why is there a one-horsepower (1 HP) under the line on the left side of that equation? The answer is simple. We want our final answer to give us the required motor horsepower for the given information. But, we're going to come out with something, after all that multiplying and dividing, which is going to be expressed in foot-pounds per second. So ... by dividing by the equivalent of one horsepower's worth of 'foot-pounds per second', we will get the number (or fraction) of horsepower required. Since one horsepower is equal to 550 ft-lbs/sec, that's what we want to divide into the rest of the muck.

Meanwhile, Back at the Formula ...

So, our formula looks like this now:

(1) $HP_m = \dfrac{(\mu)\ (Weight)\ (k)\ (speed)}{550\ ft\text{-}lbs/sec} = HP_m$

Looks a little less threatening, don't you think? Let's really take the stuffing out of it altogether. How about we work a problem; just you and I. Let's say that we have 4 x 30 tires (4 inches wide and 30 inches in diameter) and we drive on level concrete (that gives us, from Fig 2-6, a μ of .018, yes?) in an EV that weighs 1000 pounds (dry) at a speed of 30 mph. What's the required motor horsepower?

First look at the chart, and convert that 30mph into feet per second. It's 44, isn't it? And we consider ourselves to have a 75% efficient system, or 'k' value (see Fig. 2-8) of 1.333. So:

(2) $HP_m = \dfrac{(.018)\ (1000\,lbs)\ (1.333)\ (44\ ft/sec)}{550\ ft\text{-}lbs/sec}$

Do your calculations on fingers, calculator, abacus, with a pencil, in your head, etc.

This is what I've got:

(3) $HP_m = \dfrac{1055.736\ lbs\text{-}ft/sec}{550\ ft\text{-}lbs/sec}$

or $HP_m = 1.919952$

Okay, your answer may not have come out that exact, but you won't find a motor that's got a rated horsepower of 1.919952 imprinted on its ID tag, so we'll do some realistic rounding-off, and arrive at about 2HP. Isn't that neat!

The driver of this EV was putting about on the golf course when, suddenly, it went up over a little rise, and dropped into a sand trap. Since the nearest thing to this in our chart (see Fig. 2-6) is loam, we find that the coefficient is about .322 now. How much horsepower will it take to get us out of this stuff?

There's two ways to calculate this. One, since the coefficient is larger, we automatically know that the rolling resistance is greater; hence, the EV will need more horsepower. Since we knew the coefficient before and we know it now, it's only a matter of dividing the one for loam by the one for concrete and multiplying that factor times the existant horsepower requirement. So that you can see that this is the same as merely inserting the new value in the formula and running it out that way, I'll do it the second way first.

(4) $HP_m = \dfrac{(.322)\ (1000\ lbs)\ (1.333)\ (44\ ft/sec)}{550\ ft\text{-}lbs/sec}$

or $HP_m = 34.33808$

If we take the ratio of the coefficients, I get:

(5) HP_m= 1.919952 × .322/.018

or HP_m= 34.3287

which is pretty close to the answer for #4 above. If you know which way each factor will 'throw' the answer, there's a couple of tricks you can use to find the new answer without running down the battery in your calculator!

Whoops! Don't forget about . . . Hill Climbing!

Don't go out and buy a motor yet! To keep that formula clean and easy to work with, I left out a rather important factor --- hill climbing. If you will notice, each example uses the word 'level' somewhere in its description of the terrain. A small word, but a great influence on performance. If you travel perfectly level in your EV, you are operating perpedicular to gravity, and it does not show its presence, other than keeping you in contact with the road. But, just as you know that when you go downhill, your EV will go faster, you also know that the vehicle will tend to slow down as it begins to travel uphill. Why? In one instance, gravity assists propulsion and, in the other, resists it. If you are accustomed to driving or riding around in a big car, you may have never really noticed the effect of gravity, other than the necessity to press down a little more than usual on the gas pedal when the car started to climb a hill. But, if your past experience in climbing hills is taken from the front seat of an old VW bus, you have an entirely different view of uphill grades; you've crawled along and had the chance to really study a lot of scenery. The differences are easily explained in saying that, with the first vehicle, there's a conspicuous 'excess' of horsepower available and, with the latter, a damnable 'absence' of it.

I've run out the calculations (see Fig. 2-10) for the required horsepower to take a half-ton (1000-1b) EV up varying grades at varying speeds. Grade 12 is about the steepest that most road departments allow; beyond that point, they're unable to keep some vehicles on the road (like snow-removing equipment, where applicable). Unless you live at the top of a pass, or at the bottom of a pit, you will not need to concern yourself with values not represented on the chart. Also note that the same vehicle has only half the horsepower requirement if it proceeds up the grade at one-half the speed. By the way, these values are shy the amount of horsepower needed to get the vehicle to those speeds on level ground. So, only after you've calculated the amount of horsepower needed on level ground, are you ready to add the amount of horsepower needed to propel that vehicle up those grades at varying speeds. If your vehicle's weight exceeds 1000 pounds, figure a conversion factor and multiply it times the appropriate values. If your vehicle weighed 2000 lbs, you'd double those figures. If you've kept vehicle weight to 750 pounds, multiply the figures by .75, or three-quarters. In any case, divide your EV's weight (or estimated weight) by 1000 pounds, and that gives you the factor. Okay?

The key to hill-climbing is in the gears that make up the ratio of rpm of the motor to the wheels. Theoretically, any horsepower'ed vehicle can make the grade; it's all a question of whether there's a low enough gear to shift into,

Figure 2-10		\multicolumn{10}{c}{MILES PER HOUR}									
Degree of Rise	% of Grade	1	3	5	10	15	20	25	30	35	40	45
		\multicolumn{12}{c}{REQUIRED HORSEPOWER}										
0 34'	1	.03	.08	.13	.27	.40	.53	.67	.80	.93	1.07	1.20
1		.05	.14	.23	.47	.70	.93	1.17	1.40	1.63	1.87	2.10
1 9'	2	.05	.16	.27	.53	.80	1.07	1.33	1.60	1.87	2.13	2.40
1 43'	3	.08	.24	.40	.80	1.20	1.60	2.00	2.40	2.80	3.20	3.60
2		.09	.28	.47	.93	1.40	1.87	2.33	2.80	3.27	3.73	4.20
2 17'	4	.11	.32	.53	1.07	1.60	2.13	2.66	3.20	3.73	4.27	4.80
2 52'	5	.13	.40	.67	1.33	2.00	2.67	3.33	4.00	4.67	5.33	6.00
3		.14	.42	.70	1.40	2.10	2.80	3.50	4.20	4.90	5.60	6.30
3 26'	6	.16	.48	.80	1.60	2.40	3.20	4.00	4.80	5.60	6.40	7.20
4	7	.19	.56	.93	1.87	2.80	3.73	4.67	5.60	6.53	7.47	8.90
4 34'	8	.21	.64	1.07	2.13	3.20	4.27	5.33	6.40	7.47	8.53	9.60
5		.23	.70	1.17	2.33	3.50	4.67	5.83	7.00	8.17	9.33	10.50
5 8'	9	.24	.72	1.20	2.40	3.60	4.80	6.00	7.20	8.40	9.60	10.80
5 42'	10	.26	.80	1.33	2.67	4.00	5.33	6.67	8.00	9.33	10.67	12.00
6		.28	.84	1.40	2.80	4.20	5.60	7.00	8.40	9.80	11.20	12.60
6 17'	11	.29	.88	1.47	2.93	4.40	5.87	7.33	8.80	10.27	11.73	13.20
6 50'	12	.32	.96	1.60	3.20	4.80	6.40	8.00	9.60	11.20	12.80	14.40
7		.32	.97	1.62	3.23	4.86	6.47	8.08	9.70	11.32	12.93	14.50
7 24'	13	.35	1.0	1.73	3.47	5.20	6.93	8.67	10.40	12.13	13.87	15.60
8	14	.37	1.1	1.85	3.70	5.50	7.40	9.25	11.10	12.95	14.80	16.60
8 31'	15	.40	1.2	2.00	4.00	6.00	8.00	10.00	12.00	14.00	16.00	18.00
9		.42	1.3	2.08	4.17	6.20	8.33	10.42	12.50	14.58	16.67	18.70
10		.46	1.4	2.32	4.63	6.90	9.27	11.58	13.90	16.22	18.53	20.80
11		.51	1.5	2.53	5.07	7.60	10.13	12.67	15.20	17.73	20.27	22.80
12	21	.55	1.7	2.77	5.53	8.30	11.07	13.83	16.60	19.37	22.13	24.90
13		.60	1.8	3.00	6.00	9.00	12.00	15.00	18.00	21.00	24.00	27.00
14		.64	1.9	3.22	6.43	9.60	12.87	16.08	19.30	22.52	25.73	28.90
15		.69	2.1	3.45	6.90	10.30	13.80	17.25	20.70	24.15	27.60	31.00
20	35	.91	2.7	4.57	9.13	13.70	18.27	22.83	27.40	31.97	36.53	41.10
25		1.13	3.4	5.63	11.27	16.90	22.53	28.17	33.80	39.43	45.07	50.70
30		1.33	4.0	6.67	13.33	20.00	26.67	33.33	40.00	46.67	53.33	60.00

NOTES: (1) HP values computed for a 1000 pound vehicle. (2) HP figures for hillclimbing ONLY. ADD values to computations of HP for same vehicle/same speed on level ground. (3) % of grade = 'X' feet of rise/100 level feet.

and how long your attention span is, as you rack up the hours going up the 'pass'. But more on that in the Gearbox section (this chapter).

MOTOR VOLTAGE AND CURRENT RATINGS

The proper voltage and current ratings must accompany the horsepower rating of your EV's motor. It's going to start getting tough to find a motor which has the right ratings all the way down the line but, with other decisions made, you'll not have much leeway here. The voltage of the main battery bank should be high (to keep heat losses in the wires to a minimum) but within the range of available motor voltages. However, for battery banks with voltages ranging from 12 to 48 volts (for instance), we'll need motors rated between 6 and 36 volts, respectively. How did I arrive at that figure? Well, I guessed. But I'll bet that I'm close. Let's see what I'm doing.

If you take a medium electrical load, say the headlights in your car, and turn them on, what happens? They go on. What else? If you've got a voltmeter connected across the battery, you will notice that the voltage of the battery (its potential) drops to a lower value. Maybe half a volt lower. Now, hit the dimmer switch and get those high beams on. This increases the load, maybe doubling it. Note the voltmeter reading. Yep, it's dropped down even further. Leave 'em on for an hour or so and then look at the reading again. Ah, yes! It's dropped even further. Six hours later, it may not even show a reading! Sorry, we've discharged your battery. A pittance compared to the knowledge that you've gained.

The same things happen in an EV. When you're underway, you're pulling the rated current from the batteries. For a 24 volt motor and a 36 volt battery bank, and a 1.5 HP motor, this will be around 40 amperes. That kind of current 'draw' is going to pull down the pack voltage quite a bit. Almost to the motor's voltage rating, but not quite. Almost any motor will operate quite well if the voltage is within plus-or-minus 10% of its rated voltage. Beyond that, it will heat. But, a compromise is needed at the higher end. Once the batteries have been discharging for a while, the voltage will drop lower. And still lower, yet. And, since the idea is to keep the voltage high enough so that it stays away from the lower limit of the motor's voltage rating, we might start out with a little bit higher voltage. As the voltage will fluctuate with speed and load, it's not hard to understand the preference of the compound or series motor over the shunt motor in EVs; shunt motors have a propensity for overheating with fluctuating voltages.

A word of caution is in order. With a battery pack voltage higher than that of the motor's rating, it becomes necessary to protect the armature from overcurrent during breakaway, or when starting the motor from a standstill, under load. While this subject is extensively covered in the Control section of the next chapter, it means that we must always stay 'soft' on the accelerator pedal when starting the EV. It has the additional advantage of nursing the batteries to go that extra mile, but even if it didn't, we'd still need to do it to protect the motor.

The current rating of a motor is usually typed on the motor's ID label. If it isn't, note the motor current draw when you test the motor, preferably under a load. This will say a lot about the ratings to look for in batteries (their design discharge rate) and values of components to use in the control system. If you've looked over those sections, noted the readings, and found them to be an impossible match, reject that motor and keep looking.

MOTOR RPM

The range of RPM in the motor will be important, particularly if you're going to use a fixed gear ratio. But, whatever the application, you must operate the motor at, or near, its rated speed. This is marked on the motor's tag; if it's not, and you can't just look it up in a manufacturer's catalogue, you're in trouble. You need to know that rating! It describes not only the normal, design rating rpm, but as well, the rpm at which the rated horsepower is achieved. At half that speed, you might have three-fourths of the horsepower rating available, or only one-third. How much you have depends on the type of motor it is, and what it was designed to do. And, just as in the circumstance of under- or over-horsepower and its effect, the speed of the motor will determine its efficiency, tendency to overheat, and torque characteristics.

A series motor won't have as much difficulty with this, because of its high torque antics, but the compound and shunt motors will operate poorly at speeds significantly under rated speed. Don't get too far before you find out what it is.

Provided that you can supply the electrical power to the motor, it will not be difficult to determine what the motor's speed should be to get the vehicle to a given MPH. Just as the horsepower figures are obtained, so are the rpm. See the Gearbox section, this chapter.

OTHER MOTOR FACTORS

There are some things you'll want to include on your checklist when you go shopping or scrounging for motors, but you won't find them written on a metal tag affixed to the motor. And some of these factors will not be evident by just looking at the motor, or even by stripping it down. And, because a dealer won't always let you test the motor out before you buy it, you have to guess. So, make it a good guess. Learn the indicators, and look for clues. Keep your eyes open, listen to what's being said (and what isn't), and be skeptical.

While you're looking, there are plenty of things which affect a motor's usabili to check for. To whit: cooling provisions, motor weight, mate-up hardware, mountings, electrical connections, types of bearings, lubrication ports, shaft type, and of course, cost. Now for some detail.

Cooling Needs

A motor which is 75-85% efficient is also 15-25% inefficient. And something must happen with that inefficiency; it's got to go somewhere, disguised as something. Some is vibration, some light, some noise (audio vibration), but most is heat. In the summertime, you'll want to just dump excess heat into the atmosphere. In the wintertime, you'll be trying like crazy to get some of it into the cab. But, either way, you want to get it away from the motor. Heat melts insulation, expands and contracts parts beyond tolerance, and thins the lubricant in the bearings (I don't give a hang if they are 'sealed for life'). A well-designed, efficient motor generates little heat, and usually has no problem in dissipating it. But even a good motor in an EV is going to be running inefficiently at times (starting, for instance) and it may not, in itself, be able to rid itself of its own heat. And that's not saying what the score is with the rest of the motors that most everyone will have in their EV. So, give some attention to cooling that motor.

The easiest way that cooling is accomplished is to leave the motor open to air; then, when you're moving along, it gets a nice breeze. Or, if it's in a cubbyhole and not getting natural circulation, install a blower to pull or push air over its surfaces. The more CFM (cubic feet per minute of air), the better. But remember that when you need the cooling most is when the motor is operating least efficiently and that is usually at low speeds (starting and maneuvering). And what if you stop? What happens to your cooling system then? The best EV has the best motor, or a well-cooled Brand X.

I've seen a couple of neat innovations along this line. The first was an arrangement by a fellow in Palmdale, California. He bead-blasted the outer shell of the motor housing (which removed all the paint and primer), drilled and tapped some holes, and with a liberal application of transistor-mounting compound, bolted on some nice aluminum fins all around the circumference of the motor. Exit the heat problem. Another fellow has a less strenuous arrangement. He wrapped his motor in a cloth, arranged a gallon or so of water above the motor, connected a small tube to the bottle and buried it in the cloth, and rigged up a pull string to loosen the clamp on the hose. When he needed to cool the motor, he pulled on the string and water flowed down into the cloth. The air striking the cloth evaporated the water. That process absorbs heat, thereby cooling the motor. It worked well enough, but heaven help him if he fails to refill the water jug; with a undampened cloth wrapped around the motor, it'll broil in its own heat!

Just mounting a fan in front of the motor is not going to increase its cooling by much; it's highly suggested that you enclose the motor itself in a shroud so that the same blower or fan assures a rapid air movement directly above the motor's housing surface. If you live in cold country, you might go the one step further and arrange for re-routing the heat into the cab during the wintertime. But ... don't get fancy, just effective.

Motor Weight

If you get some kind of motor that's a reject from a World War II troopship, the EV may get a case of the 'squats'. I do agree that some of the light steel or aluminum motors are cheapos, but surely something exists in between, so keep looking. If the motor housing looks molded, it's been poured, and it's all right for a stationary situation (helping to keep the building from blowing away in a strong gale) but it has no place in your EV. If you can't carry it and the gearbox over and set it on its mounts, it's too heavy (ignore this if you're scrawny or over 60). Of course, I'm referring to aspiring members of the HTC (Half-Ton Club) class of EVs; a 10- to 50-horsepower motor is going to take a hydraulic lift to get into your EV.

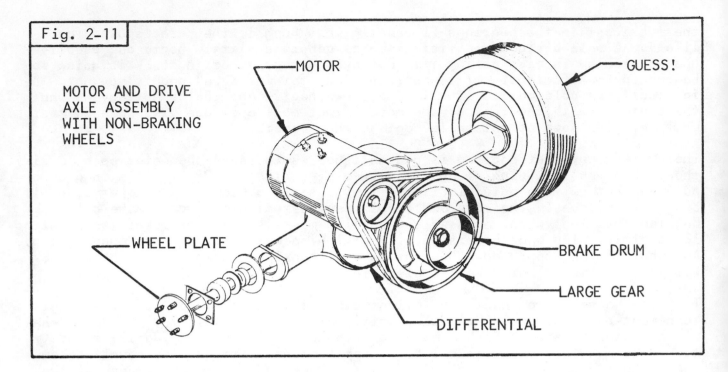

Fig. 2-11

MOTOR AND DRIVE
AXLE ASSEMBLY
WITH NON-BRAKING
WHEELS

MOTOR

GUESS!

WHEEL PLATE

BRAKE DRUM

LARGE GEAR

DIFFERENTIAL

Motor Mate-Up

Somewhere along the line, you're going to have to connect the motor to the gear-box, and connect the gearbox to the drive axle, and the axle to the wheels, etc. So, consider these connections when you get the motor. What kind and size of shaft is coming out of it? At one or both ends? (It's usually just one). Is it splined, or does it have a keyway, or space for a key? How long is the shaft? If a gear or pulley is attached to it, will this do or will you need to replace it?

The tendency, when coming up against these particulars while looking at a motor, is to ignore them altogether or dismiss the problem, putting it off to deal with later. Fight this urge. Some of those adaptors are a real bear to find. You might even need to have one machined. Or, worse yet, have the motor shaft mach-ined to accept a standardized fitting, coupling, gear or pulley. If you really must have that motor, then try to get something to fit it right then. In many instances, a surplus place will have the other part or end of it somewhere. Don't just accept someone's word that the other part is commonplace; you can always ask to make it a condition of the sale, if it's so readily-available. Then watch, and see if someone tries to wiggle out of that deal!

Study the info in the drivetrain section --- the kind of drivetrain you'll use and any relevant decisions to the selection --- before you go after the motor. That way, you'll have a smidget of an idea of what you're looking for.

Mountings

Motors are designed to operate in different positions. Most are designed for horizontal operation; this is simple to do, because ball bearings will handle most of the load and we don't have to get into the expensive, tapered roller bearings needed for end thrust vertically-mounted motors. And, I suppose, there are some motors which will vary in tilt between the two, but they will also have to handle end thrust in varying amounts, so they'll incorporate the appropriate bearings. All of this doesn't matter, except to tell you that you should get one that's designed to operate in the position in which you wish to mount your EV's motor. A vertically-designed motor can be operated successfully horizontally, but it's a no-no to operate a horizontally-designed motor vertically. As well, it's important to know which way the vertically-mounted motor is suppose to face (drive shaft end). It's probably safe to assume that it's UP --- but, with the cost of that motor, why guess? Open the critter up and see for yourself!

You might get an appropriate gearmotor (gearbox and motor) for your EV, but if not, and you're building the drive train, think about shock-mounting the motor. If you're messing around with lots of torque, the motor is going to want to spin and, if hooked solidly to the frame, is going to want to make the framework flip in a direction opposing the rotation --- in the same manner a gun will recoil when fired.

Bearings

With a good motor, bearings won't be a problem. But, whether you've determined the original, designed mounting position (vertical or horizontal) or not, you should check the bearing type. Is it a sealed bearing? Or is there a lube (zerk-type) fitting? What supports the motor shaft --- bushings or bearings? Check both ends, as they sometimes use one of each in the same motor. If it's a bushing'ed motor, I wouldn't use it. Not unless I could find out if it will take the punishment the EV will impose. If it's got bearings, what are they? Ball, roller, needle, or tapered bearings? These aren't different brand names; they're different types of bearings, designed to do different things. If the motor is mounted horizontally, it will mostly need a bearing capable of handling large radial loads; that calls for a roller or ball bearing. If the motor is mounted vertically, or at any angle from the horizontal, it means that it must be able to withstand some end-thrust as well; this means a tapered roller bearing. Each type of bearing can take the other type of load to some extent, but it's usually less than 10% of the rating of the type of load it's designed for. If this sounds familiar, fine; if not, get some additional reading material or talk to motor manufacturers.

Electrical Connections

A few motors have a plate which screws over a small recess in the motor housing, where external wires may be connected to the motor's windings. And, if you're lucky, when you remove this metal plate, there will be a wiring schematic shown on its reverse side. Or somewhere else on the motor. Unfortunately, most don't have it; you're left with some wires dangling out of a hole, or half a dozen vacant threaded connecting points for external wires. If that's the case, and you haven't the slighest inkling of how to proceed, trundle that motor and yourself down to the nearest generator or motor repair/rewinding shop, and have them tell you whatever they can. Don't settle for just "It's a shunt motor, kid!" Have them render an opinion as to the type of windings, probable speed, etc. If it's a compound motor, get an estimation of whether the ratio of the windings approaches the characteristics of the shunt or the series motor. A sharp motor man can tell you a lot --- make, manufacturer, application, rpm, types of fields, voltage, and current ratings, etc. --- so it pays to take the time and find an 'egg-spurt'. Once you do, listen to what he has to say, writing every bit of it down right then, or immediately after. It's truly amazing how fast things you've never heard before will slip away, beyond mental recovery.

COST

This is where it all comes together. Can you afford it? After all the work of getting each one of the factors aligned and compatible with every other --- the right rpm, horsepower, current and voltage ratings, weight, etc. --- now you have to deal with money. Americans have a habit of asking the price long before anything else, so maybe you knew it all along, but now it comes down to the wire. Can you afford it?

If it's got all the right ratings --- you've predetermined what you need and it has a name plate that gives everything but the rank and date of birth --- buy it. Scrape the dough together, and buy it. Why? Because that'd be one of the most unusual situations I've come across, if it happened to me. Most of us will end up with something where we have to guess at half of what we've got on the counter in front of us, trusting luck and intuition and what little we do know to carry us through. And we know that we will have to make a special mounting bracket, and it's longer than what we wanted, so we have to chop and fit, or we have to ignore that its casting is a little thicker (and, consequently, heavier) than what the EV can afford. And, knowing that we've got to make all of those compromises doesn't help very much when the guy is still asking too much. Nope, I've come to a frame of mind that when ('if' would be a better word) I find something that is right out of the mental picture I've conjured up, I'll pay the price. That doesn't mean that I'll always take what they ask first time, just that I won't haggle it down to the bone because I don't want to pay more than I have to. Maintain the pride, by all means, but don't get disrespectful of your luck if you've actually found that perfect motor.

If the motor is being salvaged from a metal heap and the guy won't let you take it somewhere to have it checked out, try offering a deposit that's more than what he's asking. If he accepts, get a receipt and make sure it's plainly written that you will receive the full amount back after you bring it back, and before you start haggling over the price. If it's still No, take some notes, look it over with the hawk's eye, and leave. This serves two purposes. First, it gives you a chance to check out what you do know with someone in the know. Or to check out some manual. If your notes are good, you may find everything you need to find out. Second, it lets the owner of the junk heap know that you can and will walk away if the thing isn't right. Whatever you do, don't suddenly get paranoid, thinking that now that you've discovered what appears to be an excellent EV motor, that before you make it back, swarms of EV motor-hunters will have stripped the place clean. Resist and beat this urge to 'buy now, or lose it forever'.

With some caution, you can learn a lot about the motor you've found and are contemplating buying. But the odds have it you'll go into the sale partially blind. Try for a money-back if it doesn't work, even if you have to forfeit part or as much as half your money. 'Tis better to have half your money than

none of it and a motor that's only good as a boat anchor. Take your best shot.
Good luck!

GEARBOX

You've probably heard the term gearbox before. Maybe it was called a transmission? Sometimes the closest some folks come to hearing it is, 'put the
vehicle in reverse, or maybe, first gear". Same-same. It's not likely that
many folks could point to one; in most cars, it's very well hidden. It's at
the 'other end' of the stick shift. If we're determined to glimpse this mys-
tery, we squiggle under the car and only find it shrouded in oil and dirt.
If you've seen the inside of one, particularly if it's an automatic, it's a
nightmare of cogs and assorted shapes and sizes of metal. However simple or
complex, our EV will need one. So, let's understand what it is, why it's
needed, and how it does all the many things we may require of it.

GEARBOX FUNCTIONS

In the pragmatic world, 'what' something is is usually defined by 'why' it is.
Or, if we knew the 'why', it automatically flows into 'what'. Before I get as
confused as you may be, let's see why we need something between the motor and
the wheels.

That the motor has a design (rated) rpm has been discussed. Also, it's been
mentioned that this is the speed at which it's designed to deliver its rated
horsepower and, at speeds below this rating, it only delivers some portion of
its rated horsepower. So, if I add in the obvious fact that the electric
vehicle will vary in its speed (miles per hour) from zero to its designed maximum, it should be further obvious that we have a mismatch. That is, we have
only one rpm, or a small range of rpm in the motor where we have power, and
we have a substantially larger range of vehicle speed and wheel rpm requiring
that power. Let's call this Problem One.

Our second problem originates in the variations of load that we will experience
at the wheels. It's the difference between starting the EV downhill, starting
it on the level, or starting it on upslope. Or, it's the difference between
the rolling resistance and the static resistance mentioned in the section on
factors influencing μ , the coefficient of friction. Sure, the static resistance only exists until we get moving, but if you've barely got the power in
the first place to start, you might end up 'push-starting' the EV to overcome
this initial resistance, which is multiples of the value of rolling resistance.
Or, the variation in load may be attributed to having to buck a strong headwind,
or hauling a heavier-than-normal load in the EV (relatives riding along, thrill-
ed by the idea that one of the family has an EV). Or it may be a difference
in terrain; today you're driving out to the farm over a freshly-graveled dirt
road. We'll call load variations Problem Two.

Performance is Problem Three. While nursing the batteries is going to give us
the most out of their charge, sometimes we need a little Umphh as we come off

the line. Heck, sometimes we <u>want</u> it, whether there's a need or not! Or we expect it of anything we drive now, because we had it with this gas-powered automobile. If we rig the vehicle with one 'speed' and that's something where we'd be in third gear, it's pretty obvious that we're not going to spin any wheels coming off the line in third gear.

Our fourth problem comes when we want to change the size of tires that we have on our vehicle, although that may not be immediately evident as a problem (but we'll call it Problem Four). Or maybe we need some way to disconnect the motor from the wheels; it can be performed with a clutch but a 'neutral' position is better (this is Problem Five). And then, what about ...

Enter the Gearbox. With one rather primitive device, we deftly sweep away all of these problems. How? Funny you should ask; that's what the next section is about!

INSIDE THE GEARBOX

We're still answering 'what' the gearbox does by looking into it, and seeing 'how' it does it. Basically, the gearbox is a box full of gears. At first glance, it looks like they were just thrown in there, but if we watch someone move the shift levers (that's the stickshift on the floor or the lever on the steering column), we see metal knobbies sliding to and fro, up and down, meshing with other knobbies; these are the gears.

What else do we notice? Not much ... until someone turns the 'input' shaft; this is the thing which normally hooks to, and is turned by, the motor (engine). Now the gears rotate, at least two at a time and maybe more, depending on how we move the shift levers. And we'd notice in looking at this imaginary gearbox, that another shaft, which protrudes from the gearbox and looks very similar to the 'input' shaft, also rotates; this is the 'output' shaft. If it were in a vehicle at the time you looked at it, you'd see it connected to the wheels through another 'black box'; that's the transaxle, or differential; we'll talk about it in the next section.

If you were very observant, the next thing that you should notice is that the output shaft doesn't always turn at the same rate as the input shaft. That is, if you noticed some mark on one and a mark on the other and rotated one a full revolution, you'd see that the other either rotated through part of the revolution or it rotated several times. And, if you played some more with the shift levers, you could get it to increase or decrease the number of times one shaft rotated compared with the other. And, if you took stock of which shaft was doing how many revolutions compared to the other, then the 'input' shaft always (or almost always) turned more revolutions for each revolution of the output shaft.

At this point, what do we know? Three things. One, if we use speed and shaft revolutions as interchangable terms --- one shaft turns at a faster speed (number of revolutions) than the other --- we can say that, in the gearbox, speed changes (from input to output). Two, the input speed is greater than the output speed. Or, conversely, we get a slower speed out of the gearbox than whatever we put in. Three, we can vary the amount of speed change by changing the positions of the shift levers. In fact, there's one position where the output shaft <u>reverses</u> its direction of rotation (this is reverse gear) and another where we might actually get the same or more speed out of the output shaft than the input (this is overdrive).

Now you may be wondering how that solves any of the five problems we've uncovered. Actually, we're doing okay because we just eliminated our first problem. I'm sure that you noticed that there was one position in the gearbox where you turned the input shaft but the output shaft didn't turn; that's neutral. Problem 5 solved, and four to go.

GEAR RATIOS

For the solution to these other problems, we must look at some fundamentals of gears themselves. Maybe you've never had the opportunity to see gears before, but I'm sure you've seen the chain-and-sprocket on a bicycle before, right? Well, the sprocket is a rather general kind of gear. Or maybe you've seen the pulley and V-belt as you stared at a car's engine and that's something which connects the alternator to the crankshaft. A gear is kin to the pulley and sprocket but it's different because you won't see it with either one of these. In fact, they don't combine with each other, but stick with their own kind: a gear with a gear, a pulley with a pulley, and a sprocket with a sprocket. Here's another observation you should make. In the gearbox, we saw a whole bunch of gears but, in no application do we see less than two of each --- sprocket, gear, or pulley. Takes two to tangle!

Something should be disturbing you at this point. Maybe, several somethings, but I'm referring to the input versus the output shaft speeds in the gearbox. If there are only gears in there, how do we get less speed on a shaft? Maybe you should take a closer look at the bicycle. Well, isn't that interesting --- the sprockets are of different size (diameter)! A big one on the front and a little one on the back. Now, get a friend to lift up the rear end of the bicycle while you turn the pedal. Go ahead, turn it one revolution. What do you see? The bicycle wheel went around several revolutions. Using some chalk and noting start and finish, and the percentage of a full revolution if it's not a whole number, the number you come up with is the gear ratio. Yeah, no kidding! If you were to count the number of teeth on each of the sprockets and divide the larger by the smaller, you'll also come up with the same ratio. And, if you measure the diameter of the one sprocket and the diameter of the other (in inches, with a ruler), you will again come up with that magic number. If you don't believe me, try it!

The ratio, then, is an expression of comparison, defining the difference between the number of teeth, the diameter of the sprockets/gears/pulleys, or their rpm when one is rotated. A ratio of speeds. Note that the chain that connects the sprockets together is traveling at a certain speed. From this we can agree that the circumferential speed or velocity of the two sprockets is identical; if it were not, the chain must be slipping on one or the other So say the physics boys, if all of this is true and we have different gear ratios, we must conserve angular momentum. Or, interpreted, we can't lose speed without gaining something. The something we gain is torque. The high speed shaft has torque, too, but the lower speed shaft has more torque; if you want to know how much more torque, you multiply the higher speed shaft's torque by the 'ratio'.

Torque is a word that gets abused a lot, and I'll continue the trend here for convenience. Loosely speaking, we can take horsepower and we can make speed or we can make torque, but not a lot of both at the same time. To understand why it might be important to have more torque than speed, let us once again look at the unit of horsepower:

(6)   1HP=550 ft-lbs/sec.

Let's rearrange the formula to illustrate a relationship; now we have

(7)   1HP=550 x **pounds** x ft/sec.

which is the same as #6 above, but spread out and broken up. The familiar-looking 'ft/sec' is speed; a converted MPH. The 550 is just a number, which we'll leave isolated for our purposes. And we have pounds. This may be thought of as the magnitude of the force required to push the EV. As well, for the following illustrations, we'll consider that it wraps up the vehicle weight, μ, and 'k' into one, finished expression.

In equation #3, we worked out a problem to find the required horsepower for a 1000 pound EV traveling on a flat surface with a μ of .018 and a speed of 30mph, figuring a 75% overall efficiency in the system. The data was converted to its necessary form for use in the formula and we come up with:

$$(3) \quad HP_m = \frac{(.018)\ (1000lbs)\ (1.333)\ (44\ ft/sec)}{550\ ft\text{-}lbs/sec}$$

Right? Let's find the 'pounds' part that we referred to in equation #7.

(8)   Pounds=(w) (μ) (k)

   or   =(1000lbs) (.018) (1.333)

           =23.994 pounds, or 24 lbs.

Now, if we multiplied this pounds times the speed, 44 ft-sec, we'd still get a required horsepower of 1.91952, so there's been no hocus-pocus. But now we have a figure that represents the true force required to move this EV.

HILL-CLIMBING AGAIN!

So, let's now say that the owner of the EV in this discussion is trying to visit his or her ladyfriend or manfriend, and that person lives up a small hill. Uh-oh! Remembering the hill-climbing chart (angle versus speed and horsepower), you've quickly checked with the nearby road department. So, they look it up in their charts and tell you that it's a 4% grade. Now, a look at our chart (see Fig.2-10). A 4% grade is 2°17' and our vehicle, like the one the chart describes, weighs 1000lbs (how convenient!). And since we're traveling at 30 mph, let's see how much more horsepower it is going to require to take us up this slope. 3.2HP? Mercy, you're gonna have to get another ladyfriend/manfriend! You can't make that!

True, you can't. At least, not at 30 mph. Try it at 15 mph. Looking at the same slope under 15 mph, we get 1.6 HP required. But, check out footnote #3: Horsepower figures obtained from our chart must be added to the HP figures determined for EV travel over a level surface. So, the chart horsepower fights gravity, not rolling friction. Problem is that we haven't computed the necessary, level-travel horsepower for our vehicle at 15 mph. Would you care to venture a guess at what it will be, compared to the horsepower required at 30 mph? Would you believe one-half as much? Let's see.

$$(9) \quad HP_m = \frac{(.018) \ (1000 lbs) \ (1.333) \ (15 \ mph)}{550 \ ft\text{-}lbs/sec}$$

$$= \frac{(24 \ lbs) \ (22 \ ft/sec)}{550 \ ft\text{-}lbs/sec}$$

$$= .96$$

$$= .96$$

Or, little less than 1 HP. Now, adding this to the value of horsepower required to climb a 4% grade at 15 mph, we have:

$$(10) \quad HP_m = .96 + 1.6$$

$$= 2.56$$

That's at least half a horspower (.64 HP to be exact) more than what our EV's motor is. Can't do it at 15 mph. Hope you're not already late! Since we're so close now, let's compute it for 10 mph. A check at the chart reveals 1.07 HP required at 4% grade and 10 mph. Since speed and horsepower are in direct proportion, the required (flat-surface) horsepower at 10 mph is two-thirds that required at 15 mph, which we found in #9 above to be .96 HP. Two-thirds of .96 is .64 horsepower. What's the total horsepower requirement? It is:

$$(11) \quad HP_m = 1.07 + .64$$

$$= 1.71$$

Hurray, your 2 HP motor can handle that.

Work with this type of problem and all its variables until you can interchange and short-cut the formulas. To keep you out of trouble, here are a few 'mention-ables':

1. When using the incline/speed/horsepower chart (see Fig.2-10), don't forget to compute a 'conversion factor' for your EV's weight. Since the chart's assumed vehicle weight is 1000 lbs., simply divide your EV's weight by that amount. If your EV weighs less than 1000 lbs., you will come out with a factor of less than one, and all of the chart's figures will be lowered when multiplied by the 'factor'.

2. The chart does not contain increased rolling resistance figures or air-resistance effect for higher vehicle speeds. These must be computed separately.

3. My examples thus far (equations #3 through #9) have used conservative fig-ures. That is, overall efficiency of the system is estimated higher than it will likely be; a 75% efficiency is actually quite good. As well, a μ of .018 is quite good; road surfaces and tire parameters will seldom permit this kind of performance. If you have to determine the motor horsepower at an early stage in the game, figure low on efficiency (not higher than 50%) and high on μ (.050 or higher) so you'll be sure to have sufficient power for your EV's needs.

Here are some problems to work. I've worked them out, and provided answers, in the Cubbyhole, section C.

1. George has a 1600-lb EV which he takes for a summer day's drive. He's got 6 x 16 tires, and he's driving on concrete with a 15 HP motor under the hood. Figuring that his EV is only 25% efficient and he weighs 180 pounds himself, can George get up to 35 mph on this level road?

2. In the continuing saga of George Windy, we find him taking a pit stop at the bottom of BreaksEasy Pass, contemplating the climb. The sign says its a 9% grade. At what speed can George climb this hill?

3. Yep, it's Windy again! Ole George has taken a wrong turn somewhere and is confronted by one mile of loamy field if he wants to get across to the highway without a lot of backtracking. He lets some air out of the tires to decrease the μ by 25%. How fast can he traverse this field?

4. George arrives at his sweetheart's place, but finds his beloved Mertha Tired in a tizzle---she needs something from the store 5 miles away but it's going to close in 13 minutes unless the EV will get them there in time. She moves her ponderous 350-lbs into the EV. Can Windy and Tired make it?

FINDING GEAR RATIOS

The last section has shown that a low-horsepower-motor'ed EV can make it up the hill; it's just at a lower speed than the higher-power motor. The last section sets the stage for this one. We don't have to have an awful lot of horsepower in the EV's motor to climb hills, provided that we aren't in a big hurry. But it's not just a matter of going slower. Obviously, the EV will be moving slow. But, that can't apply to the EV's motor, or it's going to burn up, or jerk us to a stop in short order. That's because at rpm sig-nificantly lower than the rated motor rpm, it can't deliver its rated horse-power. We've got to have a way of keeping the motor rpm up there, but allow the EV to go slower. And we've come full circle --- back to gears again!

By increasing the gear ratio, we do two things. We allow for a greater dif-ference in the speed of the motor and the speed of the wheels (which is dir-ectly proportional to the EV's speed). This allows us to maintain the rated motor speed and, therefore, the rated horsepower. As well, in decreasing the speed in the gears, we increase the torque. This is almost the same as keeping the motor in the proper rpm range but it's also an indicator that we make the best use possible of the horsepower that the motor can deliver. In other words, when we get the proper gear ratio, we have every bit of the horsepower available. Let's re-hash that horsepower formula again. First,

FIG. 2-12

A COMPLETE DRIVETRAIN —
MOTOR, TRANSMISSION,
AND TRANSAXLE

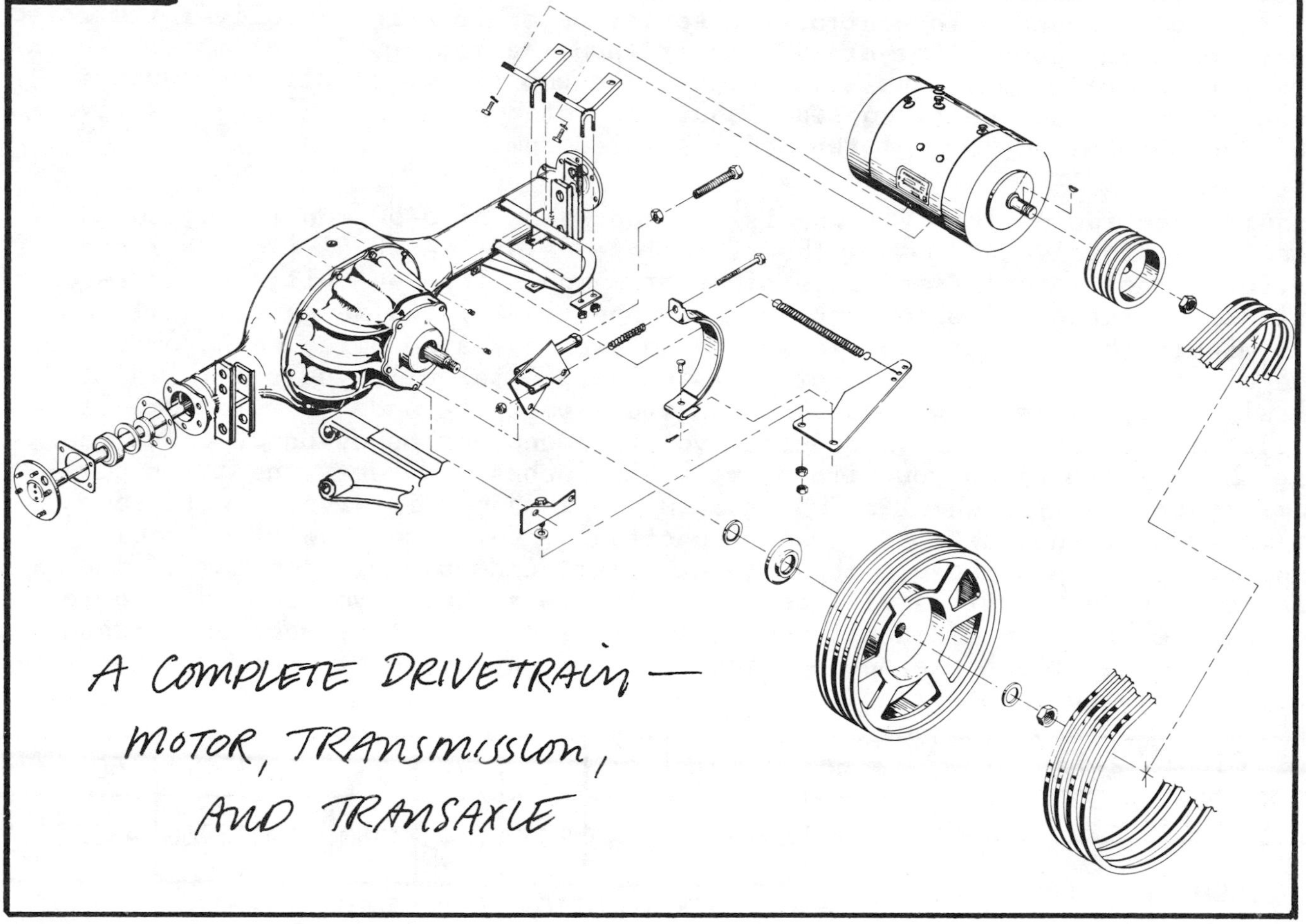

let's redo one of particular importance:

(7)   1 HP=550 x pounds x ft/sec

We could re-state this one as 10 pounds at 55 ft/sec (37.5 mph), or 55 pounds at 10 ft/sec (6.8 mph), and it still equals one horsepower. But what is the essential difference? Well, the 10 pounds at 55 ft/sec might describe a vehicle on a level surface, whereas the 55 pounds at 10 ft/sec might describe the <u>same</u> vehicle climbing a slope. We have a difference of 5.5 times the force required between the level ground and the slope, and 5.5 times the difference in speed. But, the horsepower formula doesn't only deal with the required horsepower; it's also dealing with the available horsepower. And that means that, at the lesser speed (or rate of delivery), it's got more force that it can deliver. That's what we refer to as torque. And the gear ratio supplies us with it.

Now let's find what gear ratios we need between the motor and the vehicle. First, we should have a slim idea of what narrow range of rpm of the motor gives us the rated horsepower. Second, we need to figure at what rpm the wheels turn at various road speeds. And third, we need to determine the diameter of the wheel.

The first answer is the toughest to find because it depends on what motor you get. A shunt motor has very poor delivery of its horsepower much beyond 25% of its rated speed. In contrast, a series motor is able to deliver its rated horsepower to speeds that are 50% lower than the rating, if not more. Adjust for your motor's characteristics; for our examples, we'll allow a maximum range of 50%. So, we'll consider that the rated horsepower is only delivered in the range of 50-100% of the motor's rated rpm.

Finding the rpm of the EV's wheels at roadspeeds of 5-50 mph is not too difficult; it involves figuring the circumference of the wheel (in feet) and dividing that into ft/sec conversions from mph. Then we multiply the revolutions per second times 60 seconds (for one minute) and we get revolutions per minute (RPM). But, before we can go even one step here, we have to know the diameter of the wheels that we're using. After all, you can't find the wheel's circumference without knowing the diameter! And, just to make it easier on you and me, I've provided you with another handy-dandy chart (see Fig. 2-13) which gives you tire diameter in inches and feet, the tires circumference, and the wheel's RPM at 5-50 MPH in 5 mph intervals, with some ft/min conversions as well. When you actually get some wheels for your EV, make sure that you measure the tire diameter, and not the diameter of the rim, or your gear ratios will be off. With this chart, you should be able to compute the size of wheels you will need for the motor, gearbox, transaxle, and your desired vehicle speed. You can find any one of the others, knowing the rest of the information.

Figure 2-13 TIRE DIAMETER		Tire Circumference in feet	5	10	15	20	25	30	35	40	45	50	MPH
			440	880	1320	1760	2200	2640	3080	3520	3960	4400	ft/min
in INCHES	in FEET		TIRE REVOLUTIONS PER MINUTE (RPM)										Tire revolutions per minute (RPM)
6	.5	1.57	280	560	840	1120	1400	1681	1961	2241	2521	2800	
8	.667	2.09	210	420	630	840	1050	1260	1470	1680	1890	2100	
10	.833	2.62	168	336	504	673	841	1009	1177	1345	1513	1682	
12	1	3.14	140	280	420	560	700	840	980	1120	1260	1400	
14	1.167	3.67	120	240	360	480	600	720	840	960	1080	1200	
16	1.33	4.18	105	210	315	420	525	630	735	840	945	1050	
18	1.5	4.71	93	187	278	374	467	560	654	747	840	934	
20	1.667	5.24	84	168	252	336	420	504	588	672	756	840	
22	1.833	5.76	76	153	229	306	382	459	535	611	688	764	
24	2	6.28	70	140	210	280	350	420	490	560	630	700	
26	2.167	6.81	65	129	194	259	323	388	452	517	582	646	
28	2.333	7.33	60	120	180	240	300	360	420	480	540	600	
30	2.5	7.86	56	112	168	224	280	336	392	448	504	448	

Just so that you will be familiar with the proper use of this chart, let's consider an example. Say that you get a motor that has a rated speed of 1800 RPM. Since we are only considering the range of 50-100% of this RPM for proper transfer of the motor's horsepower, we must keep the motor's RPM between 900-1800 rpm. Let's further suppose that we have wheels which are 18 inches in diameter. And, considering the vehicle's weight, efficiency, μ, and motor horsepower, the vehicle can attain a speed of 35 mph under the best of conditions --- a hard, level road. What gear ratios might we want to use?

In Fig. 2-13, we find that at 35 mph, an 18-inch tire is turning at 654 rpm. And, seeing as how that's tops for the motor, its turning must be at its rated speed --- 1800 rpm. What's the ratio of the gears? Divide 1800 rpm by 654 rpm. My calculator (even on a low battery) says it's a 2.75 ratio. All right, how slow can the vehicle go before it reaches the low end of the acceptable motor rpm (900 rpm)? That's not so tough, either. We divide 900 RPM by the 2.75 gear ratio and my Heathkit unit puts it at 327 rpm. Okay, look at the chart (Fig.2-13), along the horizontal line to the right of the 18" tire markings. Well, we don't find a MPH listing for 327 RPM, but we can see that it's between 278 rpm (15 mph) and 338 rpm (20 mph). It's not hard to figure the exact MPH because the RPM and MPH are directly proportional. Therefore:

$$(12) \quad \frac{278RPM}{327RPM} = \frac{15mph}{Xmph} \quad \text{or} \quad Xmph = (15 \text{ mph}) \frac{327rpm}{278rpm}$$
$$= (25mph) \ (1.176)$$
$$= 17.6 \text{ mph}$$

What we've got is this: if we have a gear ratio of 2.75 between the motor and our 18" wheels, we will have the full motor horsepower available at the wheels between the speeds of 17.6 mph and 35 mph. Note that this is a 17.4 mph difference in speed.

All right, what's our next gear ratio? Since we can't go lower than 900 RPM on the motor and 17.6 mph for the EV without lugging the motor, let's make that our 'shiftdown' point. It's a shift down in gears, but it's a shift up in the gear ratio. If we don't allow an overlap in the gears (and no gap, either), our next gear ratio is easily computed. Let's now make the low end of the 2.75 ratio (900 motor rpm and 327 wheel rpm) the high end of our next gear. So, we divide 1800 rpm by 327 rpm; that gets us a 5.50 ratio. Let's find its lower rpm. That would be 900 (motor) rpm divided by 5.50, or 164 (wheel) rpm. Again looking at our chart, we don't find a listing for 164 rpm; rather, we see that it's between 93 rpm (5 mph) and 187 rpm (10 mph). Again, we can easily find the exact speed (in mph) for the lower end of this gear ratio. You do it on your scratch paper and I'll whiz it out on my calculator, and we'll save book-space for other things, okay? I ended up with 8.8 mph.

We'll need to start the EV from a dead stop and, if we want to run the quarter mile in less than a quarter-hour, we'd best use one more ratio. With no overlap and no gap in the gears, this means that our 8.8 mph speed is the shiftdown point (or shift up point, depending on whether you're decelerating or accelerating). Or, it's the low rpm (wheels at 164 rpm and motor at 900 rpm) for 'second' gear and the high rpm-end of the 'first' gear. This means we divide 1800 rpm by 164 rpm; the gear ratio for 'first' gear in our EV may be

11.0 (a rounded-off 10.97). And, what is its lower end? That'd be 900 (motor) rpm divided by 11, or 82 (wheel) rpm. Or 4.4 mph, by my calculations.

Author's Note: These gear ratios represent the total calculated ratio of motor to wheel RPM. While the gearbox might be called upon to affect this entire reduction, this may not be the case if a transaxle (see next section) is used. That is, you may need to divvy the total ratio between the gearbox and transaxle. It would not be difficult, then, to find a gearbox with a 2.5:1 ratio and a transaxle with a 4:1 reduction, but it might be very difficult to find either with a 10:1 ratio, which is the product if this gearbox is mated with this transaxle. End of note.

You might want to stick in another gear (higher ratio) to take care of the 0-4mph range; it'd be like the 'granny' on the old trucks. Or, if you 'gap' the gears, the lowest gear (highest ratio) will be about right. A 'gap' is the opposite of 'overlap'. If you allow a 'gap' in the gear ratios, this means that when you shift up (to a higher gear), you will not have quite as much horsepower available to you. So, you don't get the acceleration at the low end of a particular gear's range. But, it might save having to go to a four-speed tranny (hip talk for 'transmission', which is establishment talk for what truckers, before CB, used to call a gearbox). Or, it might save sacrificing at the top end of the gears (highest speed). Whatever happens, do not sacrifice at the low end of first gear. If you ever have to start under load, you'll find it well-nigh impossible.

THE FIXED-GEAR vs THE GEARBOX'ED EV

If you wish to design an EV with a speed of more than 30 mph on the level, you will need at least a three-speed gearbox. If you want it to go more than 15 mph, you'll need two gears. A PASEV under 15 mph and a UTLEV under 10 mph top speed can qualify for a 'fixed' gear ratio, which means you have one, unchangeable ratio of gears, pulleys, or sprockets. This arrangement is several magnitudes simpler in design and construction; hence, it lends itself to home manufacture. I recommend that you buy (not build) the gearbox for any EV because, if it's to last you any length of time, it's got to be well engineered, lubricated, balanced, heat-resistant, and durable. 'Homebuilt' has a bad connotation to most people for two reasons. One, manufacturers don't like the competition, so they equate 'homebuilt' with 'patchwork'. Second, most homebuilders remember the first stuff they built. Without getting too sentimental about it: it stank. That's because the knowledge that 'anything worth doing is worth doing right' doesn't come from thinking about it, but from experience. And all those years of _inexperience_. At any rate, if you're homebuilding it, it stands a good chance of adding to the already rotten reputation of 'homebrew' unless you really engineer it, and build in quality.

Simple Single-Wheel Drives

The simplest single-wheel drive I've seen is: Affix a small rubber or metal gear-like thing to your motor's shaft and press it against the rim of your drive wheel (see Fig. 2-16). A lot of the MOPEDs (_motor_-assisted _pedal_ bicycles) use this technique. There's a limit to the amount of torque that can be applied to the wheel before the drive starts slipping or ripping up the

tire's rubber. As well, it can get pretty messy through mud, snow, or rain.
But it's done by others, and you can join the crowd. This method is recommended for only Class 5 or 6 PASEV.

A Jack-Shaft, Single-Wheel Drive

If you are running anything but meshed gears, you must observe some proper
'distancing' between the shafts holding the separate pulleys, gears (for
gearbelts), or sprockets (see Fig.2-14). Since we may not have that much
room allotted for the motor and transmission, you might want to use a 'jackshaft'. This is an intermediate shaft between the drive shaft and the axle
(see Fig.2-17), and it allows you to increase the overall gear ratio in two
steps rather than one step requiring the use of a large, unwieldy gear. It's
usually mounted in bearings or bushings at either end of its shaft which are,
in turn, mounted to the EV framework. If you are using a suspension, but not
using a driveshaft which can flex to account for suspension movement, then it
must be mounted to part of the axle, as must the motor.

SHAFT TORQUE

Once you've coupled a drive shaft to another (driven) shaft by gears, belts,
or chain, it will have speed and torque. How much depends on the gear ratio
between the shafts. If it's one-to-one, the speed and torque will be identical
with the drive shaft. If the ratio is two-to-one, the second shaft will have
one-half the speed of the drive shaft, but twice its torque. And vice versa
for one-to-two ratio. We can drive still another shaft off this driven shaft
to get a larger overall gear ratio, as desired or required. But, when you get
down to the axle of the vehicle, watch out! A small blunder there can effectively cut the benefit of your overall gear ratio in half!

To illustrate this point, imagine a driven shaft (Y) which has a gear that's
twice the size (diameter) of the gear (X) on the driveshaft (see Fig. 2-15).
As well, I've attached a wheel to the driven shaft which has the same diameter

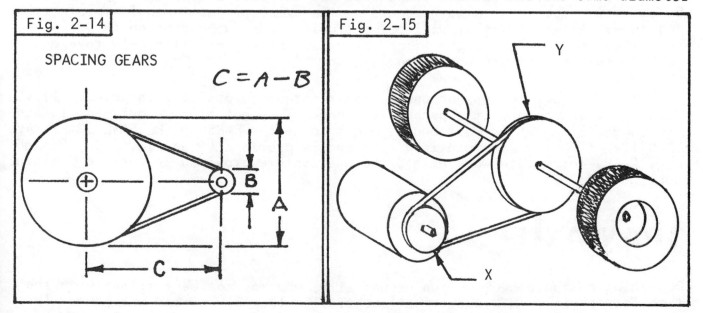

Fig. 2-14

SPACING GEARS

$$C = A - B$$

Fig. 2-15

as the gear; that's the rear wheel in an EV, okay? All right, what's the gear ratio between the drive shaft and the driven shaft (axle)? Well, if Y is twice the size of X, then the ratio must be 2:1. That's speed, of course; the torque on the driven shaft is twice that of the driveshaft. We get into this EV and, noting the marvelous acceleration, we drive merrily away.

A week later, this EV owner gets this book and, in the section on the coefficient of rolling friction (Determining Motor Horsepower, Chapter 2), he reads that increasing the tire (and wheel) diameter will help decrease the rolling friction. Well, that's easy enough. Out he goes, buying a set of wheels/tires that have twice the diameter, and he exhanges them with the ones already on the EV. He hops in, accelerates, and ... whoa! What's happened? There's not nearly the acceleration! This is suppose to be more efficient! What gives?

By putting a wheel on the axle with a gear that's half the size, you won't have nearly the force available to accelerate your EV. While the _torque_ remains the same for anything that's tied to the same shaft, you're further away from the 'action'. Since torque is equal to force times a distance, if you _increase_ the distance from the center of the axle, you _decrease_ the force that the wheel's rim is able to exert against the rolling resistance. What works _for_ you in a torque wrench works _against_ you in this setup. The tire is traveling faster --- twice as fast for twice the diameter --- but that will only help you on the EV's high end, since it equates to more speed.

If you want to use those large diameter wheels _and_ still get more torque than this situation allows, there's a number of things you can do. First, if you're using gears/gearbelts, sprockets/chain, or pulleys/V-belts, increase the size of the gear, sprocket, or pulley that you have on the axle or decrease the size of the axle's counterpart on the driveshaft; with a larger axle gear, you'll not only have a larger gear ratio, but the torque will be larger because the forces will be used at almost the same distance from the center as the 'drive' is applied. If you have a gearbox/transaxle in use, and they're enclosed, you're stuck; use smaller tires or get a ratio change in the gearbox, transaxle, or both. You can compensate for the loss if you can't prevent it. Be careful, though, with large gears on the axle; you must provide protection for them. After all, they will be protruding down; depending on the size you use, they may only clear the ground by a few inches, and it'd only take one rock to put your tranny out of commission.

Work out any gear ratios and on-the-shaft torque comparisons on paper. If you trust your intuition, it's generally wrong. They get hairy sometimes, so don't try to do them just in your head. Don't forget: GEARS ON THE SAME SHAFT HAVE IDENTICAL TORQUE. I've provided some sample problems (see Fig. 2-16 through Fig. 2-19) for you to work with; the answers are provided in section D of the Cubbyhole.

TRANSAXLE

Depending on the crowd you run around with, you may not be familiar with the term 'transaxle'. How about 'differential'? They're one and the same. This goody goes between the wheels and the gearbox. Sometimes it's connected internally to the gearbox, and sometimes they're connected together by a driveshaft (or propeller shaft, having no relation to wind-electric machines, incidentally). It performs many functions. First, it translates the rotary motion in one plane to a rotary motion in another. Second, it provides a gear ratio which, when combined with the ratio of gears in the gearbox, forms the total ratio of motor-to-wheel rpm. Third, it provides a differential rotation between the two wheels it drives.

When a vehicle turns, each wheel is at a certain distance (radius) from an imaginary center. To cover the same arc (number of degrees), the wheel that is farthest out has to follow a longer path. If the two wheels are 'locked' together and forced to turn at the same rate, something has got to give. So, either the inner wheel breaks traction and spins faster or the outer wheel breaks traction and spins slower. If the vehicle is traveling on a dirt road, this effect is not that noticeable. If it's on a hard surface, one wheel will continually slide (whenever the vehicle turns) and, in the abrasion of rubber on concrete, there's no guessing which one loses --- the rubber. So the tire wears a lot faster. If you are really powering through the turn, the wheel will break and make traction and the result is an irritating 'chatter'. Not so much the noise kind, but the teeth kind. Very jarring.

With a differential installed between the two wheels, the two wheel axles are not connected to each other. Rather, they are internally connected to another set of gears in the transaxle. When the vehicle makes a turn, the wheels can still get power, but at differential amounts. And, therefore, different speeds. If you are fascinated by this concept, check out a good book on it and see how it's all done. If you want to see if your vehicle has the true differential action, you could jack up one side, get one rear wheel clear of the ground, set the emergency brake tightly, and put the tranny in gear or drive. You'll see the clear wheel turn at twice the normal speed, and the other wheel will be stationary.

Differential action has its drawbacks, as many motorists have found out. Say you park your vehicle on an upslope and the left wheel is on ice. Now try to start. The wheel on firm ground gets no power, while the one on ice gets it all, spinning like crazy. So, one robs the other in a bad situation. Some vehicles come with the ability to 'lock' into positraction, which connects the axles together for situations like the ice under one wheel, or where differential pulling is a handicap.

If your EV needs a transaxle, get one. Again, as with the gearbox or other complex mechanisms that may form part of your EV, just get one ready-made. Auto wrecking yards are a good source for 'rear ends', as they're also called. Obviously, you don't want the first thing you see (unless you have extraordinary good luck at such things). You will need to determine the ratio. You can play around with the rear end or the transmission for the appropriate gear ratios, but once you've got both of them, that's that. Know the approximate ratio you need; anyone in auto wrecking should be able to quote you the gear ratio of a rear-end to within 10%. You'll rarely find one that's an even number 3.5 or 4.11 are more common.

Other things to check, too. Width of the whole assembly. Weight (get real

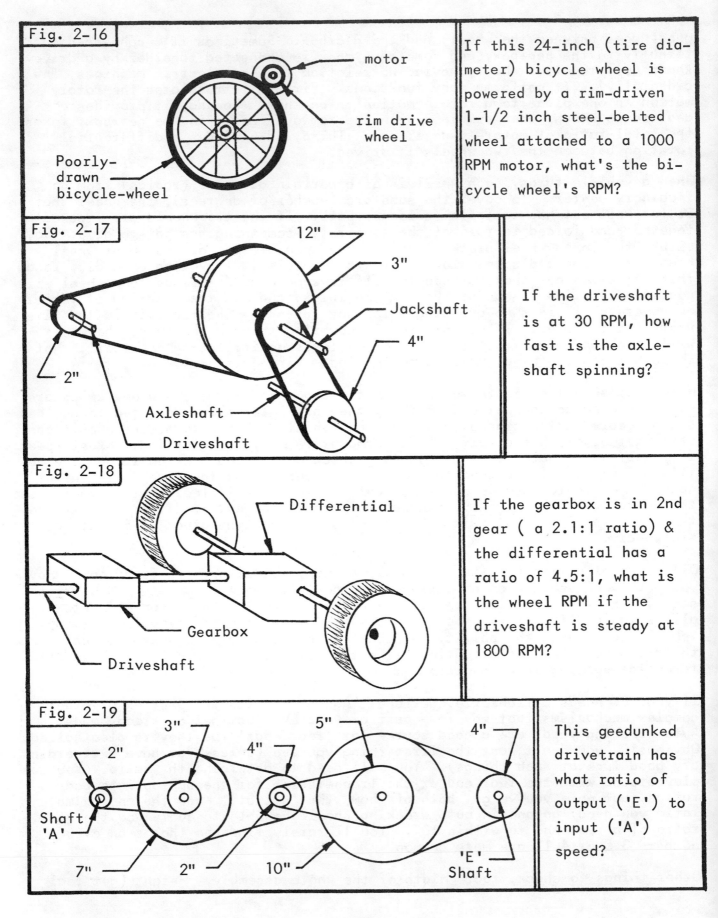

Fig. 2-16

motor

rim drive wheel

Poorly-drawn bicycle-wheel

If this 24-inch (tire diameter) bicycle wheel is powered by a rim-driven 1-1/2 inch steel-belted wheel attached to a 1000 RPM motor, what's the bicycle wheel's RPM?

Fig. 2-17

12"

3"

Jackshaft

4"

2"

Axleshaft

Driveshaft

If the driveshaft is at 30 RPM, how fast is the axle-shaft spinning?

Fig. 2-18

Differential

Gearbox

Driveshaft

If the gearbox is in 2nd gear (a 2.1:1 ratio) & the differential has a ratio of 4.5:1, what is the wheel RPM if the driveshaft is steady at 1800 RPM?

Fig. 2-19

3"

2"

5"

4"

4"

Shaft 'A'

7"

2"

10"

'E' Shaft

This geedunked drivetrain has what ratio of output ('E') to input ('A') speed?

particular about this item). Drum and wheel size and type of brake connections (mechanical, hydraulic, etc.). Most rear ends have the wheel, drums, and brakes all together; you can eliminate a lot of work at this stage if you look hard and be picky. On the other hand, you might end up with something that was someones else's headache, and it's now yours. Anything you build around a mistake is an accomplice to the fact and becomes a mistake, too. Bone up on rear ends (that truly was unintentional, folks) and know what you're getting.

A high-speed PASEV will need a differential if it's got a twin-wheel rear drive. A single-wheel rear drive PASEV won't need one because it doesn't have two wheels to differentiate between. A slow-speed PASEV might not need one. A high-speed UTLEV with twin-wheel drive might need one, but positraction is nicer than a differential action when you're hauling around the loads. A low-speed UTLEV does not require a differential.

There are a few ways to get around using a differential, if your situation permits. One, put the power on only <u>one</u> of the rear wheels, and let the other freewheel. If you're climbing and turning at the same time, you might have problems with this; it is, nevertheless, a possibility. Second, drive each wheel with a separate motor. Two motors for two wheels. You can then electrically control any tendency for positraction, if it exists. The third possibility for ridding yourself of the differential is to use a single wheel, rear-drive, as aforementioned.

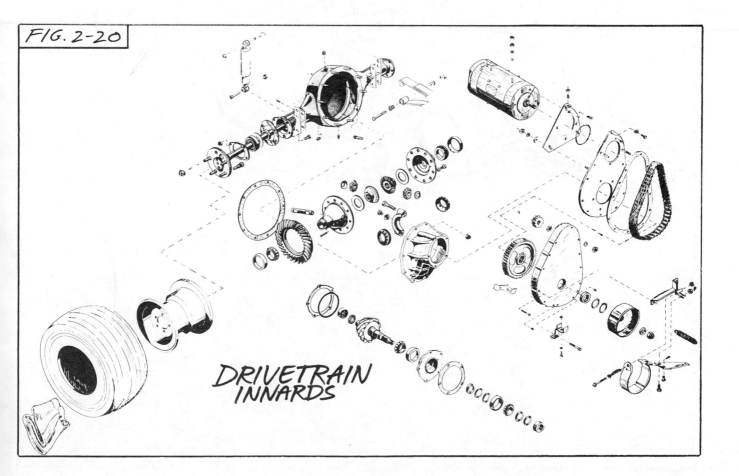

FIG. 2-20

DRIVETRAIN INNARDS

3 ELECTRICAL POWER

With little exception, the information found in Chapter 2, Mechanical Power, would describe almost any type of motor vehicle. With this chapter, we will explore the first basic departure from the world of gasoline-powered engines; here, there are few similarities to the 'modern' car. This is not to say that we are dealing with a different type of electricity. In the regular motor vehicle, electricity is used to start the engine and to run the vehicle's equipment; only a small portion is used to 'control' the engine itself. In the EV, however, the electricity is the source of power; while its primary purpose is for propulsion, it must also operate support equipment.

There is a certain mystique about electricity (in general) and its application to electric vehicles (in particular) which makes it a clumsy tool at best, or an insurmountable obstacle at least, when we fantasize about an EV. It is the purpose of this chapter to 'explore' this realm and 'expose' the beast to understanding. The five sections --- Batteries, Control, Monitor, Equipment, and Charging --- represent a major assault and, I hope, a successful de-clawing!

batteries

Battery selection is very important in the EV, but it's actually quite a way down the list when it comes to design priorities; that's because the choice is affected by other things in preliminary designwork --- torque requirements, speed and range, vehicle weight and size, etc. --- and only when you've firmed up decisions on these will you be ready to 'think' batteries. Which is odd, because in a manner of speaking, the type, size, and number of batteries that you will eventually install in the EV will greatly affect those other parameters. Before we get into a "which came first ... " situation, let's consider some factors which have little to do with an EV, but a whole lot to do with batteries.

If you had a wind-electric system, the kind of batteries you'd get for it would be very similar to the ones used in EVs. In the stationary setup, such a battery would last --- with proper operation, maintenance, and care --- for as long as 15 years. The same battery, in an EV, would be lucky to last four years, and the figure is probably a lot closer to two years for a normal service life. That's the average, which means that some last a lot longer. At best, it'll be shorter than what the stationary setup will provide as a service life, but there are many things that can stretch out the time, provided that you know 'em and abide by them. Let's get you informed!

RATINGS

There are four major ratings to consider for your EV's batteries --- capacity, rate of discharge, deep-cycle, and voltage. Plunge ahead!

Capacity

Capacity describes a battery's storage capability. This is not rated in KWH (kilowatt-hours). The first thing you should understand is that batteries do not store electricity. Rather, the electricity that goes through a battery during charging causes a chemical reaction. Then, when you put a 'load' across the battery, this causes the chemical reaction to reverse, releasing electricity. Temperature, the rate of discharge, and other factors will determine how much electrical energy you can expect to 'get' out of a battery. So that manufacturers can have some common ground in describing a battery's capacity, they've developed a rating system called the ampere-hour, or amp-hour, or AH (if you've got to write it a dozen times). The number preceding the AH is the capacity of the battery; 60 ampere hours or 205 AH are examples.

Rate of Discharge

The AH rating is, by itself, useless. A battery which is designed to deliver 3 amperes for 20 hours won't necessarily deliver 20 amperes for 3 hours, and certainly not 60 amperes for one hour or 120 amperes for 1/2 hour. But, if you multiply the amperes by the hours for each of these, you'll get 60 AH (this is similar to multiplying apples by oranges which, if you remember in grade school, was supposed to be a no-no). So, manufacturers will not only specify the AH rating, but also indicate the 'design discharge rate' in hours. Automotive batteries, for instance, are given a 20 hour rate. To determine the amperage, you need only divide the AH rating by 20, and you'll know the rate of discharge. So, the manufacturer will guantantee that a 60 AH automotive battery will deliver 3 amps for 20 hours. In reality, the battery is really designed to deliver a gargantuan amount of power, like 300-500 amps, for a few minutes. That's because, in a car, the battery has one real purpose: to start the engine. And it won't do that at the rate of 3 amps in 20 hours.

I've already indicated that a battery won't deliver varied amounts of current at different rates than the specified one, but understand that the general rule is: the higher the discharge rate (relative to the rated discharge), the less AH worth of capacity the battery will deliver. This is because of increased losses due to internal resistance, etc. But, if the discharge rate is less (or the hours longer) than the specified rating, you can expect to get more AH of energy than the specified amount. This should indicate that an AH rating does not define the true capacity of the battery --- just what it will deliver at a particular rate of use.

The battery you want to get for your EV will have a high rating --- probably above 220AH --- but you should get it at a discharge rate of 6 to 8 hours, perferably the former. The motor likes current, so you have to get a battery that will deliver current without sacrificing some of its capacity in heat losses.

Deep-Cycle

There is only one 'type' of battery to get for your EV, and that's the 'deep-cycle' variety. The name defines the battery's unique design: an ability to withstand discharge to a very low value, say 15-20% of its capacity, repeatedly, without damage or destruction. Do that to a car battery, and you're going to be in the market for a new battery. Deep-cycle batteries, however, will do it as many as 2000 cycles (each cycle is composed of a charge and discharge). In a wind-electric system, that is. Put it in an EV and maybe you'll get 400 cycles; the number is lower because there will be higher, more frequent, peak loads in a mobile setup.

One of the characteristics of the deep-cycle battery is thick plates. Those of an automotive battery are paper-thin nowadays, for lots of surface area. But, a thick-plated battery is not necessarily designed to deep-cycle. Don't be misled by a dealer that offers a 'Heavy-duty' battery, or a 'Super Heavy Duty' battery, or even a 'Son of King Kong' battery. Deep-cycle is what you ask for; take nothing else. It won't be easy to find. As wind-electric systems and EVs proliferate, the battery market will expand and we'll get the full spectrum --- el cheapos to quality -- and, this being America, they'll all sell for the same price, just to confuse you. As well, advertising is always a bit less-than-accurate in its phraseology, whether intentionally, or through ignorance. Be persistent, skeptical, and move slowly. The time to replace your batteries comes all too soon. Don't rush it by getting anything less than what you need.

Voltage

Batteries consist of two or more cells, each being approximately 2.2 volts. Thus, a six-volt battery has three cells and a twelve-volt battery has 6 cells. It's always easy to tell 6V from 12V batteries because there's one fill cap per cell. There are other batteries which have more than 12 volts, but the standard deep-cycle battery of 200 AH (or more) capacity weighs so much (all that lead), that the kind you're likely to come up with will be a 6-volter. By the time you get into the ratings around 350 AH or higher, you'll wish that they supplied them in 3-volts (nope, that's like a $3 bill) or 2-volt packages, making it easier to move 'em around! Don't schedule any visits to your local chiropractor, though; it will be our sincere desire to keep even the battery weight down to where you can handle the 6 volt batteries that make up the pack. The final battery pack voltage should be as high as possible. The deciding factor may be what you find for a motor, but if you're still looking, try to get one with a voltage rating that's fairly high. Yes, with a lower voltage, you will not need as many batteries (see The Battery Pack, this section). But ... a few things work for you with a higher voltage system. First, you will have more batteries --- but they will have smaller AH ratings, which will mean less cost and only a little more weight. Second, your line losses will be smaller. Okay, so what are line losses? Frequently expressed as I^2R (pronounced Eye Squared Are), this is a representation of the heat losses experienced in the wires before the energy gets 'used' by the load. Since the power (watts) delivered is the product of voltage (E) and current (I), if you operate at a smaller voltage, you will need to supply more current to deliver the same amount of power. But the heat losses in the wires are a function of the wire's resistance and the current. If you halve the voltage, and double the current, you get the same power. But, when you double the current, you've got <u>four</u> times the heat losses, because heat losses are a function of I^2, or current times current, or $(2)^2$, or 4. Right? So, the higher the EV's pack voltage, the less the current that needs to be delivered for the same amount of power, and the less the line losses.

Two more advantages to a higher voltage system: the less current drawn from the batteries, the less of a load that represents to them. Result? A longer life for the batteries. And, with a lessened current requirement from the batteries, the more capacity they'll deliver (see Rate of Discharge, this section). Which spells more range, acceleration, or torque.

Keep this information under control; you can go overboard on a high voltage system. The motor itself may be the limiting factor --- finding one or being able to afford it --- but this discussion is mostly meant to steer you away from the low voltage/high current motors that have flooded surplus stores. These starter-type motors may be inexpensive to buy, but the batteries, wiring, control circuits, etc., that you'll need to 'support' the load will be cost-prohibitive. Stay fantasy-sober!

BATTERY PACK

If we had six, 220AH, 6-volt batteries sitting on the floor, we could proceed to connect them up in about a thousand different ways. If, however, we had a 36 volt motor in our EV, there's only one way to hook them up to supply that 36 volts (see Fig. 3-1). Note that the positive terminal of one battery is connected to the negative terminal of the next in line. When we're finished, we'll have a 'battery' of 36 volts, with a capacity of 220 AH. Therefore, when we 'series' batteries, their voltage is additive, but the AH capacity remains the same as any one of the batteries comprising the whole.

If we were to 'parallel' the same six volt batteries, we'd connect positive terminals to positive terminals and negative to negative (see Fig. 3-2). In this case, however, the voltage would remain the same (six volts) while the AH capacity would be additive. Since there are six 220AH batteries, that'd be 6 times 220 or 1320AH of storage capacity. That'd take a long time to charge up, but it'd take a long time to deplete, too!

For batteries with 220AH rating, and a six hour discharge rate, we can expect a little more than 36 amps continuously, without exceeding the rating (220 ÷ 6 = 36.6). However, from our previous discussion of current requirements for even a two horsepower motor, we see that this isn't going to make the grade. Of course, we <u>can</u> draw more current from the 220AH batteries, but by exceeding the rating, we're only shortening the service life. We can go to a higher AH capacity, say 350AH, to achieve a higher current rating; at a six-hour rate, a 350AH battery will deliver 58 amperes of current. This would be sufficient for a 2 HP motor, but still too low for higher motor HP requirements. However, we might be in trouble with 36 volts of 350 AH batteries. Don't forget about the weight! Depending on the make of battery, this could be 720-900 pounds and, compared to 350-420 pounds for 220 AH batteries, that's quite an increase.

An alternative to the 'series' setup for high AH batteries is to parallel two sets of smaller AH ratings (see Fig. 3-3). This effectively doubles the total battery pack current rating; if you remember, paralleled batteries have additive AH ratings and, therefore, additive discharge rates (in amperes or hours, but not both). In the final analysis, this has a number of advantages over the larger AH battery set.

1. You can usually get a better price per battery with quantity; buying twelve smaller batteries might turn out to be cheaper than buying six large ones.

2. There is a tendency in battery manufacturing today leaning toward a larger AH battery weighing more in pounds per AH, or conversely, a lower AH rating per pound. For example, a 350 AH battery from one company weighs 150 pounds, which is 2.8AH per pound. A 190 AH battery from the same company, however, weighs only 59 pounds, or 3.22AH per pound. If we were to get two of the 190AH batteries, and parallel them, we'd have 380AH worth of capacity; this is 30AH more capacity than a single 350 AH battery! As well, in a 36-volt battery pack configuration, the twelve smaller batteries actually weigh less than the six larger ones, by 42 pounds! That's what I call a deal!

3. Smaller batteries are easier to tuck away or distribute within the EV than large ones are.

4. Smaller batteries weigh less, which is easier on your back, right?

5. The batteries can be set up to run tandem, or separately; if you've set up batteries with a rated discharge of twice the required current of the motor, this can be a feature which will give you the extra mile, or a reserve pack for a point of 'no-return' indication.

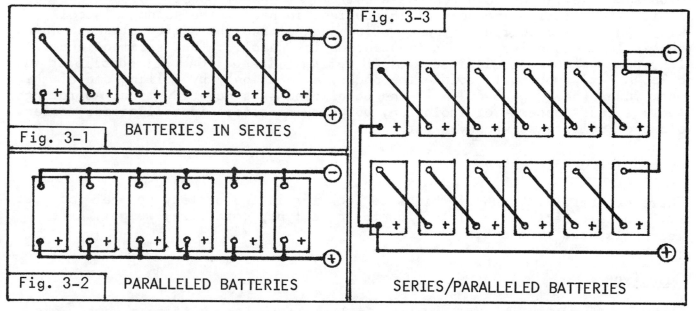

Fig. 3-1   BATTERIES IN SERIES

Fig. 3-2   PARALLELED BATTERIES

Fig. 3-3   SERIES/PARALLELED BATTERIES

6. High AH batteries like to be charged at a rate much higher than the smaller AH batteries. If your charging station con't deliver it, you can charge the batteries one set at a time, or series the entire battery set (at 72 volts for two 36 volt sets) and charge it at a higher voltage (if possible).

7. Since line losses are a function of resistance and current squared (I^2R), the batteries will have less tendency to heat (less internal resistance) and there will be fewer line losses (external connectors and wires) with

more batteries of smaller AH capacity.

    8. When you've determined the proper AH capacity for your EV, it's going to be easier to come close to it with paralleled sets than with a single set. The AH ratings for batteries available from one company are 190, 217, 250 and 350. By paralleling these you can come up with AH combinations (other than those four) of 380, 417, 434, 440, 467, 500, 540, 567, 600, and 700. By paralleling only 'like' AH ratings, you're limited to 380, 434, 500, and 700. Sometimes, lots of choices can be better than just a few.

If you do parallel two sets of batteries, give serious thought to the use of isolation solenoids (see Fig. 3-4) or isolation diodes (Fig. 3-5). The first has the advantage of independent operation of the sets, but both insure that the batteries in one set do not discharge into the other set. This happens because the batteries, of their own accord, like to discharge themselves; this is a process referred to as 'local action' and it's why batteries that have been sitting for a while "die" or become discharged. Because this process occurs at uneven rates, one pack will discharge at a different rate than the other, and the less-discharged set will try to charge the other set, discharging itself in the process. This goes on, back and forth, until both packs are discharged --- usually in less time than either pack would have discharged by itself. The relays prevent this from happening by connecting packs together only during use and re-charging (although you could use this circuit to charge only one pack at a time, if required); the diode circuit isolates the packs all the time.

Diodes and solenoids both consume a certain amount of power. Diodes heat up a bit, thus dissipating some of the current in heat. The solenoid's coil windings require current for activation and holding the switch closed. Which one is less expensive or less troublesome to install? That's situational. If you're using dissimilar sets of AH rating (like a 190AH set paralleled with a 250AH set), you must isolate the packs, even if only by pulling one of the pack fuses (see Fig. 3-6). If the paralleled sets have identical AH ratings, there's less concern for isolation, but play it safe: install diodes, solenoids, or pull fuses when you park!

OTHER BATTERY PARAMETERS

There are still a bunch of things to look for in the battery you get for your EV. In this section we'll look at the case type, case size, weight, type of terminals, and connectors.

Case Type

Batteries for wind-electric systems, telephone company batteries, etc., are available in clear plastic cases. (This is like buying food in glass jars instead of cans because you like to see what you're buying.) But clear plastic cases are not required in an EV, and will probably be of less strength than the standard black plastic cases of most car batteries. However, watch out for batteries whose sides are thin enough to push in easily with a finger. If the battery is the 'mobile' type, it usually has a reinforced case and a large space below the bottom of the plates to accommodate shedded plate material.

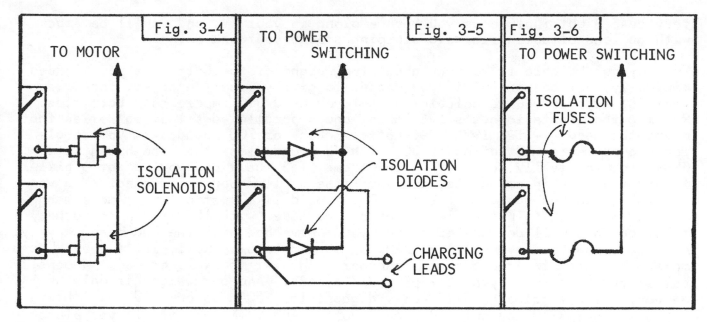

Fig. 3-4 TO MOTOR ISOLATION SOLENOIDS

Fig. 3-5 TO POWER SWITCHING ISOLATION DIODES CHARGING LEADS

Fig. 3-6 TO POWER SWITCHING ISOLATION FUSES

Case Size

Batteries come in different sizes, depending on the make, intended use, and other design characteristics; a different AH rating, however, doesn't mean a different battery size. One manufacturer that I know of has batteries ranging from 190 to 350 AH without so much as a quarter of an inch variation in just one dimension of the battery case. Here, he's built a case that will accommodate the bulk of the largest AH rating, and he fits smaller AH rating plates into it, leaving extra room around and below. One case for four batteries is a lot cheaper than making four cases for four!

EVs can generally handle the width and length of a typical battery; it's the height of the battery that may cause problems. So, watch out for this in the dimensions. About one foot (including the height of the terminals above the case) is a good height. Also, you might be wise to design the battery space for the next higher AH rating size of battery. That way, if you decide to go to a little more AH capacity with the next set when you get new ones, it'll fit with no modification. Or, it might allow you to fit another companies' battery, if you're changing brands. In the battery compartment, we'll be leaving spaces in between and around the batteries anyway for cooling, cleaning, etc., so you'll only need a little larger space to deal with the first batteries' size in an 'oversized' battery compartment.

Weight

Once you've got the design AH rating requirement, there won't be much that you can do to minimize the weight by more than 5% or so. I've already mentioned two tricks, but they were tucked away in another discussion, so I'll pinpoint them. Shop around for your battery; different companies have different cases. If one guy is using the same case for four different sizes, and you need the smallest he has, someone over at another place may be using the right size of case for the AH rating you need, and it's just that much lighter. Or, compare the weight of one large AH battery with two smaller ones that will make or exceed that rating. Don't get carried away by this process; a paper-thin battery case might rupture as you bounce along in your EV, and you'll be stuck with gallons of sulphuric acid slurping around your ankles!

You may not be able to do much about the weight of the batteries you'll need minimally, but be careful if you decide to give yourself a safety factor. That is, suppose you've calculated that you need 350 ampere hour batteries. Running the lightest that's available, and a paralleled set of batteries that meets the need --- two 190AH sets of six each, or 708 pounds --- you're already over design AH rating by 30, with 42 pounds less than the 350AH set. Okay, say you really scrimped on the frame (153 lbs.) and you've got a girlfriend that's skin and bones, and you gross at 1107 pounds running. You've got the speed you want, plus some. But, you'd like just a little more range. So, you're going to put a 217 AH set on one side (with the 190 on the other) figuring that will add the 42 pounds you'd have had with the 350AH set anyway. And, wow, now you have another 27AH, or 407 AH total. Well, let's see. Let's make both sets 217 AH and that's another 27AH over the 407, or 434. Whoops, better check that ... yep, 217 plus 217 is 434. And our weight is only up 84 pounds, for a total of 1191. Well, doggone it, 250AH on one side will bring it up another 37AH and only 54 pounds more. And ... stop it! If you piecemeal it like that, the next AH rating will always be tempting. But you've got more than that to do when you add weight. Like, re-calculating the rolling resistance and checking it out in the speed/power equation. And, you've got to call it quits somewhere.

Terminals

You'll find two major types of terminals on batteries: the tapered-round or a square post. The former is used on batteries for automobiles and other applications and it's made for a snappy connect and disconnect. The only good thing about this post is that it's usually easy to tell which is the positive terminal and which is the negative. That's because the positive is larger in diameter than the smaller, negative terminal. That's good to know if the battery case and terminal are not marked, and you removed the connectors without noting which went where. If you get this type of battery, you can use a conventional, automotive-type terminal to interconnect battery posts, or hook up wires.

The square-post terminal is conventional on heavy duty batteries. It has one or more holes drilled in it for a bolt, and the interconnecting straps have a flat-stock lug with a corresponding bolt hole. This is the preferred terminal post for a battery that is used in an EV. Some manufacturers solder flat lugs with right-angle bends to the square post for varied types of connectors and applications.

Both types of post are lead and, during extended use of the battery, these get soft as the heat accumulates. With the tapered-round post, you'll have it shrinking inside the terminal and this will give you a high resistance contact, a place for corrosion to set in, and maybe a spark. At the very least, it's a hot spot. Both of these conditions are bad for a gas-filled compartment. The square post is a much better way to secure terminals as tighter connections can be achieved. Care must be exercised in hookup to the square post as it's easier to get lots of surface area contact (considered desirable) with the tapered-round. The bolt should be plated to resist corrosion.

Connectors

The choice of battery connectors, or straps, is important. They should be very heavy wire, multistrand if possible, with a good thick insulator to avoid shorts. The wire should be molded (in lead) to the terminal, or soldered. Crimped connectors are no good; there's simply too much chance for the terminal lug and wire to part, fray, corrode, or become a high-resistance connection.

One way to avoid the wire and lug arrangement of connectors between batteries is to use 'bus' bars, just like the big boys in the industrial applications do. Where they might use copper or lead straps, this would be inconvenient for our purposes. So, try a copper tube. If you measure off the correct distance separating the lugs, and note the point of any necessary bends, you could cut a section to fit out of 1/2 inch or larger copper tubing. Then, by squashing the ends and drilling holes, you'd have a first-rate connector strap. You'll need to insulate it, but it's easy to tape. Or you can slip some thin, flexible plastic tubing over the copper tube; put it on beforehand or you'll not get it on over the flattened portions. Another excellent insulation is heat-shrink tubing; it's a spaghetti designed for covering wires and, when exposed to the heat of a closely-held match, soldering gun, or heat gun, it shrinks to about 1/2 its original diameter. If that doesn't pan out, get some spray resistive compound (or the brush-on type) and apply it to the connector straps. This is the same stuff they put on circuit boards to seal them from the effects of moisture and to prevent shorts. Trouble with using it is that it's invisible to the eye, so you can't just look and see that you do or don't have some insulation or any particular part of the strap.

Oh, for any kind of connector, don't forget to build in some 'give'. Everything is going to get hot during extended or heavy use, and heated things like to expand. If you are stingy with the copper tube, I can't really blame you, it's expensive. But, if you make them as short as possible, when they've heated and cooled a few times, you might find them building up some pressure, breaking or bending connectors, etc. So, give them room to expand and contract.

MAINTENANCE

You'll have more to do than get, install and use your EV's batteries; if you want them to last a long time, they will require maintenance. This may be something as simple as an inspection, or it may involve hydrometer checks and other handiwork. Maybe you'll do this instinctively, or maybe you'll need to set up a schedule; either way, it must be done. Too often, maintenance is like a New Year's resolution --- we tend to forget it as time goes on.

Much of the stuff that might be placed under the heading of Maintenance is listed under the battery section in the chapter on Safety. It lists do's and don'ts according to what is dangerous to you or parts of the EV, whereas this section will be concerned with things which will keep your batteries alive longer.

Battery Water

Batteries require periodic water addition. During normal operation of the battery, water is dissociated, a process whereby electrical energy separates the water into its two component parts --- oxygen and hydrogen. Since these are free gasses, they 'vent' from the battery, and are lost. So, we need to add some water. How much is dependent on many things, so we just have to check it once in a while. It's a little hard to figure the 'depth' of the solution in the battery as we peer down the fill-hole (after removing the vent cap, of course) but the aim here is to keep the stuff above the lead plates but below the full 'line'. Once you've worked with a battery for a while, you'll acquire a knack for this.

It's necessary to have battery gasses --- hydrogen and oxygen --- vented from the battery cell, but battery acid slopping out of the cells is undesirable. So, we use vent caps. These have an inner chamber which gets both gasses and solution, but the gasses pass through a tiny hole above and the solution runs back into the cell. If the cell is gassing --- a rapid dissociation of water akin to boiling --- some solution may be blown out of the vent hole in the cap, and spray over the battery case. Since this is readily identifiable, it's an indication that we are overcharging or overdischarging the battery, or that we have a bad cell. An attempt should be made to determine which of these events is occuring and have it corrected because we're not only losing water, but sulphuric acid as well. But, it will also mean that we must add some water.

The battery will be only as good as the water that's added to it. If you take it from the tap, you're asking for trouble. Nope, it's got to be high-test water. Premium. Distilled, in other words. What you get for your irons will do just fine. But not just treated water or good ole country well water. Not rain water. Distilled water.

Never add acid to your battery. Not unless you're going through a special revitalization process or have dumped out the old. This is not to say that the there will never be an occasion in which acid should be added to your battery, just that it doesn't dissociate itself or need replenishment during normal use.

Hydrometer readings

A wise EV owner has a hydrometer. This is a simple device which will measure the specific gravity of the cells in the batteries. Since acid is driven out of the plates during charging, and the higher specific gravity is an indication of more acid in the acid-to-water ratio, it should make sense that we'd be able to tell when the battery is charged by comparing the reading that we take with the original value. In operation, the hydrometer is a squeeze-bulb-and-tube affair which is used to suck some of the battery acid into the tube where it gives buoyancy to a small float. How much buoyancy is the measure of the specific gravity, and there's a convenient scale on the float to translate its flotation into a precise reading.

If the water in the cell is low --- some of it having been dissociated and vented as hydrogen and oxygen --- this will throw off the reading. If water has just been added, it will not have had time to mix with the rest of the battery acid, and this will throw the reading off. If the battery-acid temperature is lower or higher than 80°F, this will also render the reading in-

You've heard of auxiliary gas tanks? Well...

accurate. Don't fail to learn as much as you can about batteries and hydrometer readings (see References); it's not difficult to assimilate or put into
practice, and it will allow you to make a lot of sense out of whatever readings you do take. Hydrometer readings are the only inexpensive and accurate
way to know if your batteries are charged; that's information that you cannot
be without if you're trying to maximize battery life.

Get yourself a good hydrometer (see Sources). Auto parts stores carry them,
but most are worthless. Two desirable features of the hydrometer are temperature compensation and .005 increment read-out. Most hydrometers have readings ranging from 1.100 (very low charge) to 1.300 (very high acid and very
high charge). This scale should be displayed on the hydrometer bulb (which
floats in the measured fluid) so that you can read specific gravity to the
nearest .005 with ease. The temperature-compensating portion of the hydrometer involves the use of a small thermometer, which on one side has a scale
reading from -30°F to 160°F. On the other side is a scale which reads the
number of points (to the nearest .002) which must be subtracted or added to
the actual hydrometer reading to compensate for the temperature deviation from
the standard reference: 80°F. Actually, a temperature-compensating hydrometer is a misnomer; it does not actually do the compensation for you. But then,
what do you expect for $5? Univac?

The Maintenance Schedule

One effective way to insure the batteries will not run out of water, or that
the batteries are getting a proper charge, is to set up a schedule of maintenance. Initially, you will probably perform inspection checks too frequently. Don't worry; this is natural. But don't do as some will, stopping them
altogether. Battery trouble may be sudden, but it's more frequently a slow
buildup and easily detected in its earliest stages. If you're obviously doing
it too frequently, then do it less. Establish that you'll do it after so many
charge/discharge cycles, or after so many miles of use, or after a certain

number of weeks --- this can be extended until it feels right. If you carry whatever schedule you have in the EV (figuring that it's not all in your head), then you can carry out impromptu inspections or checks. Note when you did it, and also note when you should do it again. Such records will provide you with a lot of information: how many miles you actually can go on a charge; how much water the batteries dissociate per mile, week, or charge/discharge cycle; how long it takes to build up a certain amount of dust on the batteries, etc. It puts you in tune with your EV.

May I suggest a schedule? (See Fig. 3-7). Make several carbons, or use a ditto master to make the original, and you'll have copies enough for a long time. Or get some xeroxs of the original before you use it. Mark dates, mileage (if you have an odometer), number of charge/discharge cycles --- as much or as little as you wish. It's your record, so tailor it to what you will really fill in and use. Keep it simple, or you'll find yourself unable to bother with it each time something needs to be filled out.

If you hate paperwork and despise having to take your car in for a tuneup, you might consider some shortcuts. You'll also shortcut on the information you'll get, but it's better than nothing. First, once you've taken hydrometer readings on the batteries you've installed, find a pilot cell. That is, when the batteries are charged, find the one that reads the lowest. By using this as a reference, you can then know that when that battery is charged, all the rest must be. This saves taking hydrometer readings on all the batteries' cells each time you want to check the 'stage of charge'. Of course, it's just a sample, and limited to the information that sampling one cell can give you. But it's a fair assumption that, without going too long between reading all of the cells, it will be representative.

If you start out taking good notes, there's a lot that you can do to cut down on the paperwork. Always measure the amount of water that you add to the cells and note which ones needed how much. Finally, you should be able to see how long you can go before adding water to the batteries by noting one. Again, there are assumptions that you make in following this method, but it beats waiting too long if you simply cannot bring yourself to regularly maintain the batteries.

Hydrometer readings and adding battery water are not the only checks that must be made on the batteries. Always look for cracks in the insulation of connecting wires, corrosion about connections or the battery terminals, and accumulated dust. Once in a while, you may get a lump of something right on top of the batteries. In either case, clean the batteries and keep them clean. With higher voltages, the accumulated dust and spilled acid provide a high-resistance 'pathway' for electrons, and they'll 'leak' away into the night. You can't pop the clutch to start an EV whose batteries are dead, like you can with a car!

THE BATTERY COMPARTMENT

Since the batteries represent the power source in the EV, their placement deserves some careful consideration. Okay, maybe you tuck them wherever you can fit them, or wherever you have the best center of gravity or distribution of weight. But, there are a few features that will enhance working on them later.

EV BATTERY MAINTENANCE	BATTERY #	1			2			3			4			5			6		
	CELL #	A	B	C	A	B	C	A	B	C	A	B	C	A	B	C	A	B	C
HYDROMETER READINGS — DATE 3-12-73 / ODOMETER 00370 / CYCLE # 23		1280	1285	1270	1285	1275	1280	1275	1270	1275	1285	1280	1285	1270	1275	1275	1280	1280	1275
DATE 4-28-73 / ODOMETER 00502 / CYCLE # 24		1285	1290	1280	1280	1270	1280	1275	1285	1270	1280	1275	1280	1275	1280	1270	1275	1280	1280
DATE / ODOMETER / CYCLE # 25																			
ADDED WATER in CUPS	23	–	1	–	–	½	–	–	½	⅓	–	¼	–	–	–	¼	–	–	–
	24	–	–	⅓	–	–	¼	–	–	¼	–	–	⅓	¼	–	–	¼	–	⅓
	25																		

NOTE: Test batteries approximately 8 hours after equalizing charge. Temperature-compensate all readings.

Fig. 3-7

One desirable feature is battery access. That means you don't have to remove half the vehicle assemblies to get at your powerpack. The first time this will prove a benefit is when you put the batteries into the EV. You'll know that you've done something right when you don't wake up sore in the morning from the contorted, yoga-like positions you had to attain to weasel them through frame, under axle, by steering column, and over brake-lines. The second time that you will reap the benefit of proper placement is when you perform an inspection, wanting to add some water to some needy cells, or take some hydrometer readings. The third time you'll thank the earth for your brilliance is when you need to wash the batteries, to remove accumulated dust, leaves, stowaway insects, toads, and the neighbor's hamster. And the fourth and final delight will come on a hot summer day, after an arduous hour or two of EV travel, when you exit the EV and notice the pungent fragrance of hydrogen which you did <u>not</u> find yourself having to breathe <u>inside</u> the EV's passenger compartment.

It won't be an accident that the placement of the batteries will be such that all of these factors are accomodated. Wrangling with 60 pounds or more of battery is no fun. Maybe you will only need to install or remove them once during their lifetime, but if you have built your EV around them, it'll probably mean that it's difficult to get at them for water addition and hydrometer checks. It's no wonder that they won't get checked if it takes a long time just to get 'access'.

Because of the nooks and crannies around the vent caps and terminal posts, and with the connector straps so close to the top of the battery cases, it's a lesson in patience to clean them of dust and battery acid (which can spray out of the vent cap during gassing). It can be done, but so that you will do it more often (or more cheerfully when you do), try to place the batteries so that you can just douse them with water or play a hose over them. That's easy enough to do, but I mean without having to install a bilge pump to get rid of the water afterward! Small drain holes will prove a nuisance here. Opening the whole bottom of the battery compartment, however, is not necessarily a good solution to always-getting-plugged drain holes; this may let in the very dust that you're trying to avoid accumulating. If that's true, a compromise may be in order. How about installing a battery pan, mounting the batteries on a rigid framework (which you must do anyway) and attaching a sheet metal 'undercover', easily removed and replaced? Figuring that you will be period- ically soaking the batteries, wires, and compartment with water, be sure to use materials which will not rust. Locate any items which musn't get wet --- wires, equipment, switches, etc. --- away from this exposure.

Proper battery gas venting is necessary for safety, both to the EV and its occupants. I'll not say much here because the section on safety discusses the do's and dont's of battery gasses, and the Equipment section of this chapter deals with the subject as well. Do you get the feeling that I'm trying to tell you something? Good!

CONTROL

Control of an automobile is subtle. Do you remember when you first learned to drive? Think about it. First of all, there were all those processes that had to be learned. Take, for instance, starting the engine. Put the key in the slot-provided-for. Put the shift lever in Park (for an automatic), neu- tral (for a stick shift), or it didn't matter if you pushed in the clutch, provided that you remembered which of the eleven pedals down there on the floor was the clutch. If you were on a hill, you didn't want to push in the clutch unless the emergency brake was engaged, or you started rolling. Oh, yes, but you could put the stick shift in neutral, step on the brake pedal with your left foot (doggone it, where is the brake pedal?) and operate the gas pedal (which was esay to identify because it's different from the others) while the engine was started. Now, where were we? Oh, yeah, key in the ig- nition. Now, rotate the switch one increment to the right and, gee, look at those lights that come on, under ALT and TEMP, whatever they are! And one more notch. Scared ya, didn't it! Whrrr-whrrr-whrrr-whrrr-whrrr and whr-whr whr-whr-whr-r-r-r-r-r-r---and you let go of the key---and vaarrrooooommmmmm- mmmmmmm---foot off the gas pedal and chug-chug-wsssll-pop-shimmy-chug-chug- chug-vrop-chug and on and on.

Then there was the process of adjusting mirrors, fastening seat belts, get- ting the vehicle into the proper gear (forward or reverse), looking behind and to the side, working the gas and clutch, and, whoops, the window is fog- ged, so on with the heater and defroster, and maybe the windshield wipers and turn signals, and Gee, I need a cigarette, so you push in the lighter.

These processes are automatic now. You probably don't realize at all how much you impress your own kids who've just entered high school Drivers' Ed and have to 'do it' themselves. Oh, sure, you've trucked them around for years and they can see what you've been doing, but 'tis another thing to actually do it. We don't realize that our eyes sweep frequently over the speedometer and gas gauge (and oil pressure, water temperature, and ammeter gauges, if you have them). We intuitively know when the engine is about to start; the hand reaches for the turn signals at the proper moment; we shift or downshift, and can detect slight changes in the 'feel' of the vehicle; we know when it might be time to have something checked over at our favorite garage.

If you decide to own an electric vehicle, you will have the chance to experience all this again. It won't be as mysterious and panicky as learning to drive the car for the first time, but that's because many of the controls of the EV are similar in location, function, and appearance to those of an automobile.

Every electric vehicle, regardless of size, shape, and function will have two distinct components of control: power switching and operator controls. In a manner of speaking, the operator control switches, levers, or pedals are 'master' controls which operate the 'slave' controls in power switching. Power switching is concerned with the smooth handling of motor current, and will include relays, solenoids, SCRs (silicone controlled rectifiers), contactors, transistors, or some combination of these devices. In the battery motor-assisted bicycle, Class 5 or 6, this may be simply a switch which turns the motor On or Off; that's the extent of the power switching circuit. The operator control might be a simple, mechanical lever which brings the motor's drive wheel in contact with the bicycle wheel's rim or tire. But with larger EVs, the system's voltages, currents, and motor factors --- horsepower, torque, rpm, etc. --- will be equivalently higher. Consequently, the master/slave circuits will become more diversified and the overall sophistication of the system will increase to insure its own safe and efficient operation.

It might seem as though we could just jump into the control circuits that are used with a motor, but we can't. Why? First, remember, we have different motor types. Second, there are different methods of control, and which is best to use for a particular type of motor depends on many factors. And third, before we discover the ways and means of motor control, we must have a common understanding of what the term means. Let's take an example.

You already know something about the series motor from its introduction in Chapter 2. If we make the rate voltage available to the motor, it will 'draw' its rated current, and deliver its rated RPM, torque, and horsepower. This translates into, for the EV in which it's mounted, a certain speed under a given set of conditions --- load, slope of the terrain, battery charge, etc. But what if we want to go only one-half as fast? Well, it should make some sense to suggest that if we were to provide only one-half as much voltage, the motor would draw only one-half as much current, and deliver only one-half the RPM, torque, and horsepower. Well, almost. The relationship is true, but the proportion, as we shall see, isn't one for one.

Control, however, goes beyond this simple illustration. What if one of our switches or solenoids sticks On or Off? Or we have a locked motor, or an uphill start with a heavy load? What protects the batteries, motor, and control

circuits? There's much to learn before you hit the drawing board. But let's
get started, dealing first with some of the conditions we must provide for,
irrespective of the motor type. Then, a close look at the control techniques.
Next, we'll apply them to specific motor types, And, finally, we'll evaluate
them in the light of all that information. Even if you're going to get someone to design and construct your EV, or maybe to maintain or repair it, you'll
be much better off with a working knowledge of what makes it tick.

BASIC CONTROL REQUIREMENTS

There are things that we want our EV to do. Go when we want it to go. Stop
when we want or need it to stop. Reverse directions, as required. These are
basic control requirements. But there are some subtle aspects to these functions. First, we want them to happen in increments. We don't want to peel
out at every start, or skid to a stop everytime we hit the brakes. When we
say we want the EV to Go, we mean at a rate which we will select each time we
want to Go. And we want to have the option of braking slowly, or fast, or in
between. That's one of the implicit definitions of Control. There's another
one too --- the converse. Yep, don't forget the converse. When we don't want
these things to happen, they shouldn't. If you're boppin' down the road at
25mph, you do not need the EV to suddenly go into reverse. First, you'll be
skidding and fishtailing to maintain control. Second, it's awfully rough on
the motor, which will be internally hemorrhaging with overcurrent. And third,
it'll generally ruin your day.

Besides the obvious Go, Stop, and Reverse functions, there are other things to
contend with. Let's deal with each of these factors more specifically, and
introduce pertinent terminology.

Breakaway Current

Any motor under load draws more current than when it's not under a load. And
most motors draw more current under excessive load than they do under a normal,
rated load. So, it should make some sense that when a motor starts, it draws
more current than when it's at its rated speed, operating under its rated load.
After all, when it starts, it doesn't have any speed (rpm), right? The amount
of current that it actually draws during start-up is dependent on the motor
type and the mechanical advantage it has in respect to the load. This amount
of current is called 'breakaway' current. ('Breaking away' from a dead stop.)
For most motors, this could represent as much as two or three times the rated
motor current. Sometimes, it's several multiples of that.

Why do we have to concern ourselves with breakaway current? Surely, if the
batteries are of the lead-acid type, there's no worry there; they'll deliver
the current or they won't, but their internal resistance will protect them in
any case. But, the motor is not so lucky. It can't take 'pure' breakaway
current. See, most motors have a built-in capacity to avoid overcurrent; it's
called back-EMF. But when a motor is just starting, it hasn't had the time to
develop this protection. So, we must provide some external protection. How?
I'm not trying to generate any suspense, but you'll have to wait until the
next section (Control Techniques). But I'll give you a clue! We have to
'limit' this current. And, no, it won't be with fuses. They'd only blow every
time we tried to start the EV!

Speed

This is sort of synonymous with the Go I was talking about at the beginning of the section. While some smaller motors could handle the On or Off routine for Go or no-Go, that method won't work with medium to large EVs. It's just rough on everything --- batteries, motor, drivetrain, tires, circuits, and you --- and who needs that kind of punishment on machine or Man. (Or Woman either, I better add!) So, we do it in increments. Or, rather, we design some control circuits that will allow us to do it in increments. The How of it will be described in detail in the Control Techniques section but, just as in the case of 'breakaway' current, the process will involve the limiting of current or voltage to the motor itself. However it's done, it should smoothly correspond to the depression of the accelerator pedal.

There's one other part to the speed control: anti-speed. It's unique to an EV but it's very important that you understand it. In an automobile, you accelerate with the gas pedal. If you hit the brakes, you can slow down or stop. But that's not the only way you slow down! Sometimes all you have to do is to take your foot off the accelerator. Unless you're going down a very steep hill in high gear, the vehicle will slow down and, in some instances, stop. Not so in an electric vehicle. If you take your foot off the accelerator, the power is disconnected from the motor and it will 'freewheel'. Sure, you'll slow down. IF you're going up a hill or on a straightaway. But, unless you've got a lot of rolling friction (which you shouldn't have), you'll go a long way before you stop. And, if you're going downgrade, you'll have gravity accelerating the vehicle.

Let's face it, this 'coasting effect' can be very economical in an EV. To use it in your automobile, you need to put the transmission in neutral or shove in the clutch. Either is illegal for a motor vehicle. In an EV, it may or may not be legal. You're still in gear. You haven't put the Fwd-Neutral-Rev switch into neutral. You've just stopped accelerating. It just so happens that you can't 'compression-brake' a DC motor. But if the codes eventually require it, or rule against it when you have it inspected, or you simply want the vehicle to slow down a bit at times when you take your foot off the pedal, provide for it in the circuitry. It's not difficult, and it'll keep you from having to ride the brake whenever you need to slow down. As well, it might be feasible to convert some of the EV's inertia into some useful electricity for recharging batteries! (See Special Circuits, this section).

Motor Reversing

When you want to travel in the reverse direction in a car, you put the shift lever in Reverse. What have you done? You've shifted some gears, reversing the directions of rotation for the driveshaft respective to the engine. The engine, however, always rotates in the same direction, irrespective of the car's motion backward or forward. If you install a gearbox in the EV which has a reverse position, you can do it the same way the Detroit gang does it. You'll feel right at home.

But, you don't need a gearbox in the EV to reverse the EV's direction of travel. If it's a DC motor, you can reverse the motor instead. This involves a little bit of wire-switching, which solenoids can handle easily. Which wires depends on the type of motor. A nice advantage to reversing the motor's direction of rotation is that you'll have all the same gears in reverse, rather than just one, as in the internal-combustion automobile. Or, if you have only one gear, you have all of the increments of the accelerator pedal for speed variation.

The simplest way to rig an operator's control for reversing is to use a three-position switch. On Earthmind's UTLEV, the Forward-Neutral-Reverse Switch takes the place of an independent master and slave control; it's a high-current switch. An alternative method is to use a small DPDT (double-pole, double-throw) toggle switch which energizes a hefty relay equipped with 'normally-open' and 'normally-closed' contacts. In the un-energized position, the 'normally-closed' contacts have the motor wired for EV travel in the forward direction. By energizing the relay, the 'normally-open' contacts close, and the motor wiring is in a 'reverse' mode, and the EV travel is to the rear, or backward. The second method is more expensive but works better for a limited-space situation on the control panel. Using the first method, the hand-operated power switch, requires a switch with a substantial rating and it may be hard to come by.

Notice the Neutral position between Forward and Reverse. This is a good idea, particularly if you are accident-prone and might 'elbow' the switch out of one position and into another. With a neutral between them, you have to 'bump' it through two positions to have your 25mph vehicle go bananas. Since I don't want to underrate anyone's capacity for bungling, may I suggest the installation of a 'Fail-Safe' method of switching from one to the other? Earthmind's UTLEV has little metal pins to prevent the switch from being shifted by a blow to the switch. To shift its position requires bearing down on the handle, then turning it sideways, and letting up. Admittedly, you can still go from Forward to Reverse when you try to go into neutral, but we've never had it happen unintentionally. Nevertheless, it might be wise to arrange it, even if you were to use two separate switches, so that it's impossible to do it unless you want to. The pins in our UTLEV also prevent the switch from being knocked accidently into either Forward or Reverse from Neutral, which is also a nice feature.

Reversing the motor, with the exception of the permanent magnet motor, is achieved by reversing the 'polarity' of the field windings with respect to the armature windings. Only the permanent magnet motor can reverse its direction of rotation by simply reversing the polarity of the batteries. While the Practical Circuits section of this chapter will concern itself with the details of motor reversing, among other things, 'proper' motor reversing involves reversing the armature (respective to both the batteries and the field windings) instead of the field windings. This has to do with field discharges (collapsing inductive coils), the seriousness of losing field control (runaway or overspeed problems), and the loss of potential dynamic-braking (see Practical Circuits, #8) with the field 'open'.

Overcurrent

It's essential to provide some kind of protection for too much current. The problem is not so easily solved by just sticking in a fuse that's rated a little more than the motor requires. We also have to allow for the current requirements under a heavy load, or the breakaway current. If we fuse it for breakaway current, we may end up stewing the motor in its own field coils because it's drawing more than it should under rated load, but not more than the breakaway rating. A true dilemma!

In reality, we take a chance. We install an ammeter (see Monitor, this chapter), which we read as frequently as we check the speedometer when a 'black-and-white unit' is following us. That will give us a telltale sign, because we learn what's normal, and thereby, what isn't. We fuse the motor for breakaway and we make it a slo-blo fuse. If, perchance, we exceed the fuse's rating momentarily, it won't blow. If you're no-nonsense about it, make it a straight or fast-blo fuse, and 'nurse' the motor current by the meter. You'll never have nightmares, and you'll always get the maximum range out of the EV and the batteries' service life.

If you feel that you cannot hold yourself to this responsibility, put in the slo-blo and hope that you don't get a partial short. And hope that you didn't underrate the motor's horsepower; an underpowered motor will heat excessively and most likely draw more current than its rating under all conditions.

The fuses in the EV are there mainly to provide for an out-and-out short, which is going to quickly shut down the EV systems when it occurs, slo-blo or fast-blo fuses installed. Get DC fuses and try to find some for the EV's pack voltage. No kidding! If you're on a 12, 24, 36, or 48 volt pack, check out marine hardware places or surplus equipment, and set yourself up a supply; they're not that common. But they'll work better if they're properly rated, and made for DC. Otherwise they'll blow high or low depending on what you get, and that might not be good enough. Most of the time it will. As I said, fuses usually start blowing when there's trouble enough that most <u>any</u> fuse will blow.

Don't forget to use the proper size wire, for the particular job. It'd be silly to have your wires melt before the fuse blows, wouldn't it? Don't just string your EV with anything that you happened to find in the garage. There is a limit to the beauty of recycling materials; if you substitute your hands for your brain, you can get into trouble. Know the size of wire you need to handle the current. You should know what it will be for everything in the EV --- motor, lights, horn, etc. --- or you haven't done your homework. Wire size should be twice the required rating, so that you can keep those I^2R loss losses down!

A fuse panel should be located where it's readily accessible; it makes the fuses easy to replace, to look at to see if they need replacing, and to pull out. Particularly the last reason. Sometimes things go into a partial short; if you can reach the fuse, you can shut down the function quickly. Most of the fuses in the EV will be small ones, at least smaller than the one you use to protect the battery pack or motor. So, you might want to install the 'big' fuse closer to the action --- near the batteries or motor --- and the rest in the cab. Just keep them all accessible!

Breakers can be used instead of fuses in the EV. They're more expensive, but you don't have to replace them if they 'pop' out. They double as a switch, too, which you can open or close if you really want to have things under control. Less of a chance to get an electrical burn or shock; as well, if you have to pull the fuse in a hurry, it might get kinda hard to find, safely. But you can also put a large knife-switch in line with the fuse, for a lot less money than a breaker. And, if you're scrounging up breakers, don't get (or use) AC breakers. They'll fail on you first time out. And they don't 'pop' at the same current, on DC as they do AC, either. DC breakers it is, folks, or stick with fuses!

CONTROL TECHNIQUES

The most important control requirement in the EV is the motor. There are three techniques for four motors. Amazingly enough, all of the combinations work. But, in the highest probability, after you've read through all of the information, you won't have much of a decision to make. That's because many of the other circumstances which represent your particular situation will choose it for you. You're only a pawn in the game.

So, what are the three techniques? First, there's resistive control; it does its job by limiting motor current. Second, there's voltage-taps; this controls motor voltage and, hence, current. And finally, there's the famed 'chopper' circuit; it does it all with mirrors and smoke. Or, more specifically, by controlling both motor voltage and motor current.

Actually, I lied. There are four control circuits for these four motors. The one I didn't mention is On-or-Off. In larger EVs, it's known as a chiropractor's ricebowl. In smaller EVs, it's okay. And, since small is beautiful, let's start off with it.

On-or-Off Control

On-or-Off is self-explanatory. When you want to Go, you turn it On. When you want to not-Go, you turn it Off. If you've got good manual dexterity or motor-response, you could flick it on and off, and achieve the human version of the 'chopper' circuit. For <u>very</u> small voltages, currents, and EVs, this is a good alternative. It's cheap, easy to install, effective, and really keeps the console clear. If you <u>have</u> a console. The big part here is a switch. It can be a pushbutton, a toggle, a rotary, or a knifeswitch. I prefer the pushbutton. That way you don't have to hit-and-miss to get it to the Off position as the curb looms before you. A pushbutton switch makes for the same arrangement as trains use: a Deadman's switch. In theory, if you die at the handlebars of your electric-powered three-wheeler, you'll be relieved in the hereafter to know that your EV won't go careening onward, chalking up other statistics.

Get a switch that will handle your EV motor's current with ease and, again, get a switch that's rated for DC. Switches can actually survive ten to twenty times the amount of current they're rated for, when they've been turned on and left on. But, the moment of truth arrives when you turn the switch off. There's something about those fast-moving electrons; they just don't want to stop, trying instead to jump the 'drawbridge' as the switch contacts open. And that arc is what destroys the contacts, and thereby, the switch. DC is worse than AC in this regard. The arc is longer and hotter for the same voltage and current. The contacts in DC switches, therefore, are beefier --- and there's usually a little more spring in the switch, so the contacts move apart faster.

If you can't find a switch with the proper current rating, try to find a switch that's actually two or more switches ganged together; if you can find one where, by adding together the ratings of each part, you can total the same or more current rating than you need, you've got an alternative. Don't 'parallel' the switches, as might seem to be the solution; 'series' them. It's the only way the current ratings are additive!

Resistance Control

Resistance control is a good, widely-used method of motor control. Some folks think of it as the poor-man's circuit, but I'm not so sure that's accurate. I think that its main drawback is that it's simple and isn't electronic. Nowadays, if it ain't electronic, it's 'primitive.' But ... you decide for yourself.

With resistance control, motor speed and torque are regulated by inserting a resistor in series with the field, the armature, or both, depending on the type of motor. Great! you say. And what is a resistor? Well, they're devices which resist current flow, like a faucet which, depending on its setting, limits the amount of water (current) flowing through it to a certain rate. If you want less water, you turn down the faucet. If you want less current, you get a larger resistor. Not larger in size (at least, not necessarily); larger in value, which is in ohms. You can get variable resistors so that, like a faucet, you can select the amount of current you need. Or you can get fixed resistors, which have values corresponding with almost every position that you can set with the variable resistor. The value and physical size of the resistors, or the number of them, will depend on the application; we'll discuss them later on in Practical Control Circuits.

Resistive Control of Armature Current

If you remember the discussion about regulating breakaway current, you'll want to study this section. As well, some of the motor types will actually regulate armature current if the resistive control method is used. So it's important stuff.

To regulate the motor's speed, torque, power, RPM, etc., a resistance is inserted in series with the armature (see Fig. 3-8). In this manner, the motor 'sees' less voltage/current/power because the resistor 'consumes' some of it. How much the motor gets and how much the resistor gets depends upon the total value of resistance in series with the motor. If we want less motor power, EV speed, etc., we increase the value of resistance. If we want more, we decrease the resistance value. Sounds like a good place for a variable resistor (see Fig. 3-9), doesn't it? True. But, watch out; there's a slight problem.

I've already said that the resistance we insert will 'consume' some of the power. Since we don't want to be in violation of some basic physics laws, we must realize that that power goes somewhere. And it does: it becomes heat. So what? Well, here's the thing which determines the physical size of the resistor: the wattage rating. I^2R losses apply to resistors as well as wire,

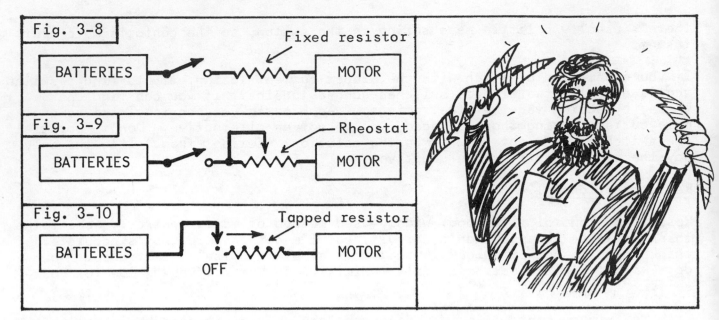

Fig. 3-8 — BATTERIES — Fixed resistor — MOTOR

Fig. 3-9 — BATTERIES — Rheostat — MOTOR

Fig. 3-10 — BATTERIES — OFF — Tapped resistor — MOTOR

and I^2R is a 'power' formula. We know two out of three of the values ---
wattage (power), current (I), and resistance (R) --- we should be able to find
the unknown one.

You could use a large-wattage, low-ohmage variable resistor, called a rheostat;
but even if you could find one, it'd be very expensive. A frequently-used
arrangement is to put several resistive coils in series with each other and
provide a 'stepping-switch' to bypass each coil (see Fig.3-10). Then, when
you depress the accelerator pedal the first little bit, the maximum amount of
resistance is in series with the motor, and the least amount of power reaches
the motor. As the accelerator pedal is further depressed, consecutively more
and more of the resistive coils are bypassed until, with the pedal to the
floor, full battery power is reaching the motor, and all the resistive coils
are bypassed.

This simple arrangement has a number of advantages. There's smooth acceleration
and precise speed control, if you've provided enough 'steps'. This is easy on
you, the drivetrain, and the motor. But there are a few disadvantages, too.
Battery power is wasted as heat, dissipated by the resistive coils. How much
depends on how much of the time the vehicle is operated at low speeds (minimum
to just shy of maximum pedal depression). As well, with less-than-normal
current flowing through the armature, particularly if it's got a series-field
(a series motor, that is), the motor's torque is greatly reduced. This not
only results in inefficient use of the power that's available, but happens exactly when power is needed the most, too --- at low speeds. There are three
different ways to design a resistive control circuit for armature current;
they're listed in Practical Control Circuit and differ only in the types of
components they use.

Before we look at resistive field control, let's deal with breakaway current.
Since each of the motor types must deal with this aspect of control, this is
one more reason that a resistive control circuit for armature current is attractive. That is, by limiting the current to the motor, it not only controls
the motor but limits the breakaway current. Since you have to provide this

protection each time you start from a standstill, why double-up this system with another? The only thing you have to watch out for is the guy or gal who puts the pedal to the floor in the parked EV, bypassing this motor protection. For situations where a motor would be destroyed immediately if breakaway current wasn't limited, stepping timers are used. They force the slow bypass or the armature current resistances, allowing the motor to come to speed and develop its own back-EMF protection.

If you're able to control yourself (and others who might operate the vehicle) it's sufficient to slowly depress the accelerator. If you occasionally 'forget', making fast-as-it'll-go starts, check out a motor manual for the timed-sequence bypass circuits. Or better yet, install a fuse that will allow you a slow buildup of speed, but won't allow the vehicle to peel out. Maybe Pop drives conservatively and maybe he thinks his son, who's the spittin' image of himself, will too; but wait until the kid gets Pop's EV two blocks away!

Resistive Control of Field Winding

This doesn't apply to series or permanent magnet motors, but most assuredly to the other two. Other than breakaway current protection, the shunt motor and the compound motor can be controlled exclusively by the amount of current flowing through the field coils (see Fig. 3-11). This is ideal. Unlike the high current requirements of the armature windings, the field coils use very little current. This means that when using a resistive control circuit to limit the

field current, we can use relatively low-wattage resistors. Better yet, they can be variable, avoiding the need for relays, solenoids, or slide switches, and the array of resistive coils. An example is given in Section B of the Cubbyhole for determining the value of resistance needed for a particular motor's field windings.

Once either of these motors have reached their rated speed, it is possible to further increase their rpm by weakening the 'field'. In practice, then, a full field (maximum current, no in-line resistance) may bring about a strong motor torque but, as the motor approaches its rated speed, the field saturates, limiting the armature's rpm. By limiting the field current (inserting resistance), we 'weaken' the field, permitting the motor to reach even higher rpm. For some motors, this can be as much as 25% above the rated speed.

Resistive Control of the Armature and Field Windings

It's not unusual to find both the field windings and the armature equipped with separate resistive control circuits. While you can't do this in a series motor (its field is in 'series' with the armature) or a permanent magnet motor (it has no field windings, only permanent magnets), the shunt motor and the compound-wound motor may sport this arrangment. All in all, it handles the breakaway current protection, maintains precise motor control under all conditions, including overspeed (see Fig. 3-12). And, while it does have the disadvantage of requiring the maximum amount of control circuitry at whatever cost it figures to, it does allow for anyone's ignorance of what amount of control is really sufficient in the EV. I'm reminded here of the statement by EV drivers, particularly those who converted a regular IC-engined-car over to electricity, to the effect that the clutch was not really necessary. Other EV drivers, though, use theirs. Force of habit? Or is there enough difference between people that some will require it and some won't? If it turns out that you _can_ do without it, you've got a useless assembly on-board, taking up room, adding weight, and consuming precious wattage. If you can't do without it, it's okay that you added it, and a pain to dissemble and add if you didn't. The point is: Nobody knows what's going to work just for you. If you add in those extra circuits, you may end up not using some of them. But it's not a real

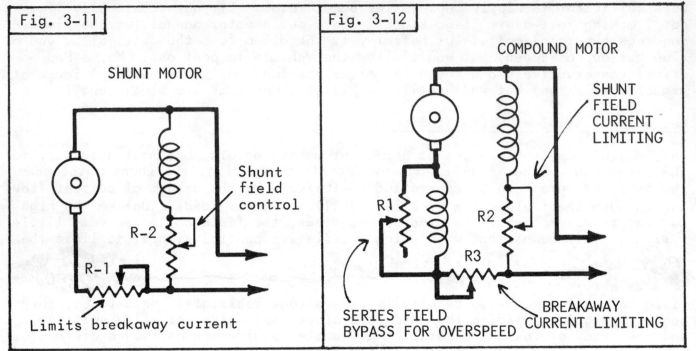

Fig. 3-11

SHUNT MOTOR

Shunt field control

R-2

R-1

Limits breakaway current

Fig. 3-12

COMPOUND MOTOR

SHUNT FIELD CURRENT LIMITING

R1

R2

R3

SERIES FIELD BYPASS FOR OVERSPEED

BREAKAWAY CURRENT LIMITING

loss because you arrived at what worked for you by checking out a variety of circuits. Sometimes we don't know what's enough until we have too much. Or, at least, more than we need.

VOLTAGE-TAP CONTROL

Another frequently-used method of motor control is the voltage-tap. It differs from the resistive control idea because it controls the voltage available to the motor rather than the current. The simplest demonstration of this method is to 'tap' the battery pack at the interconnection between the batteries and, by suitable switching, have more or fewer batteries connected in series with each other and their power routed to the motor (see Fig. 3-13). For low speeds, therefore, only a few batteries are connected to the motor; the others do not contribute any power. As the accelerator pedal is further depressed, more of the batteries are brought 'on-line' until, with the pedal to the floor again, we have all of the batteries in series with the motor, delivering power to it.

The first thing you should notice is that we aren't wasting any power; batteries are brought on-line as required and there are no resistors to dissipate the batteries' energy. As well, breakaway current is limited because the motor is not 'hit' with the pack's full voltage, and resultant current. With

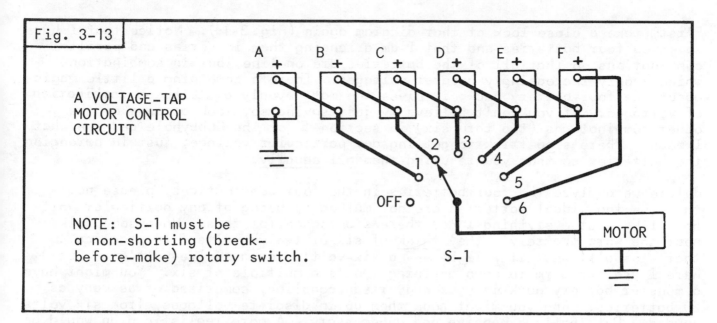

Fig. 3-13

A VOLTAGE-TAP
MOTOR CONTROL
CIRCUIT

NOTE: S-1 must be
a non-shorting (break-
before-make) rotary switch.

all of the advantages of the resistive control method and the extra advantage
of no loss of battery power in heat, it might seem that the voltage-tap method
has it 'hands-down'. But ... it has one major disadvantage of its own. Can
you guess what it is? Look at the schematic (Fig. 3-13). Study it. The voltage-tap method discharges the batteries within the pack at a _dissimilar_ rate!
(Of time and current.) Battery 'A' is supplying power _anytime_ the vehicle is
motored (regardless of the pedal position); it's the 'anchor' battery. Battery
'F', however, only supplies power when the pedal is full-depressed and maximum
power is being applied to the motor. It should be just as obvious that batteries 'B' through 'E' will be discharged at rates different from one another,
but somewhere between the discharge rates of A and F. So, some batteries work
harder or more often than others; they'll have to be replaced sooner. As well,
it's a real nightmare when you try to charge the pack, and nearly impossible
for the batteries to receive their proper charge. Under- or over-charging a
battery destroys its service life. At today's battery prices, even if you
ignore tomorrow's, that's a serious disadvantage.

There are a few ways to get around the dissimilar discharging problem of the
voltage-tap method. One that's been proposed is to have a switching circuit
which automatically changes the 'anchor' battery each time the vehicle stops.
So, the next lineup would be B, C, D, E, F, and A. And the next would start
with C and end with B. And so on. This assumes, of course, that the vehicle's
pattern of use is consistently and equally unchanging. Which would be a ridiculous assumption for most situations. And the circuitry involved would be
staggering!

Another, more feasible technique in the voltage-tap method of motor control
which does eliminate the problem of dissimilar discharging is the ganged batteries approach (see Fig. 3-14). Here, multi-contactors and solenoids are
arranged to parallel and series the batteries in discrete voltage ranges to
vary the voltage while insuring that all the batteries are being equally discharged. It's fun to figure out on paper, but there are a few subtle problems
involved with doing this. Quite frankly, they've caused me to disallow the
use of this method in any EV that I design. Let's see if they bother you.

First, take a close look at that diagram again (Fig. 3-14). Notice that I have selected four batteries and that I am arranging them in series and parallel combinations so that all of the batteries are on-line, but in combinations which supply increasingly greater voltages. There's something a little magic about the four-battery pack; it gives the most evenly distributed combination of voltages. If you don't believe my just saying so, look at some of the other combinations (two thru six) in section E of the Cubbyhole and see what I mean. There's no trick to getting any particular voltage, just in arranging the batteries so that you're using them all equally.

Before we analyze the four batteries in the four combinations, please note that the individual batteries are not marked as being of any particular voltage; like most everything I do, there's a reason for this. When some folks hear the word 'battery', they think of six or twelve volts. In practice, that's usually what it will be --- a six-volt'er or a twelve-volt'er. But here I use the term to mean anything that's a multiple of six. You might have a monster battery pack in your converted Econoline, comprised of as many as 20 batteries. And you might hook them up in discrete voltages, from six volts upward. But that's expensive and unnecessary. A more realistic plan would be to hook them up in four packs of five batteries each, or 30 volts per pack. Or maybe you decide to make it five packs of 4 each, or 24 volts per pack. Then, again, you might not have that many batteries, but it doesn't really matter. Please realize, however, that each 'battery' represented in the drawing might be a 6, 12, 18, 24, or 30 volt 'battery'.

Okay, looking at Fig. 3-14, note that part (a) shows all the batteries paralleled. Assuming that each of the batteries has the same voltage and the same AH rating, there's three things we know. This is 1/4th the total voltage of the pack. The AH rating available to the motor in this position of the accelerator pedal is four times the AH rating of any 'battery'. And, of course, all the batteries are used equally.

Part (b) of Fig. 3-14 shows the next 'arrangement' as the pedal is depressed to the second position. Here, we have paralleled two batteries and wired them in series to another set of paralleled batteries. The voltage available to the battery has doubled (it's now 1/2 the total pack voltage), the AH rating is only twice that available from just one battery, and we are again using the power from the batteries at an equal rate from each battery.

I'm going to skip to part (d) for a moment. Notice that here we have all four batteries in series with one another and we are supplying 100% of the pack voltage to the motor. The AH rating of the pack is the same as any one battery and, again, the batteries are equally discharging.

But here's the first sign of trouble. Back up and look at part (c). With four batteries, there is no way to arrange the pack so that we are equally discharging the batteries in the pack, and yet supplying 3/4 of the pack's voltage to the motor, which is the logical increment between 1/2 and full pack voltage. In fact, you won't get anything between them, no matter how hard you arrange them. Well, let's try a different combination of batteries, say 5 discrete batteries. Or two. Or three, five, six, nine, or ten. (See section E of Cubbyhole for these arrangements). Keep it up, but you'll find that you can

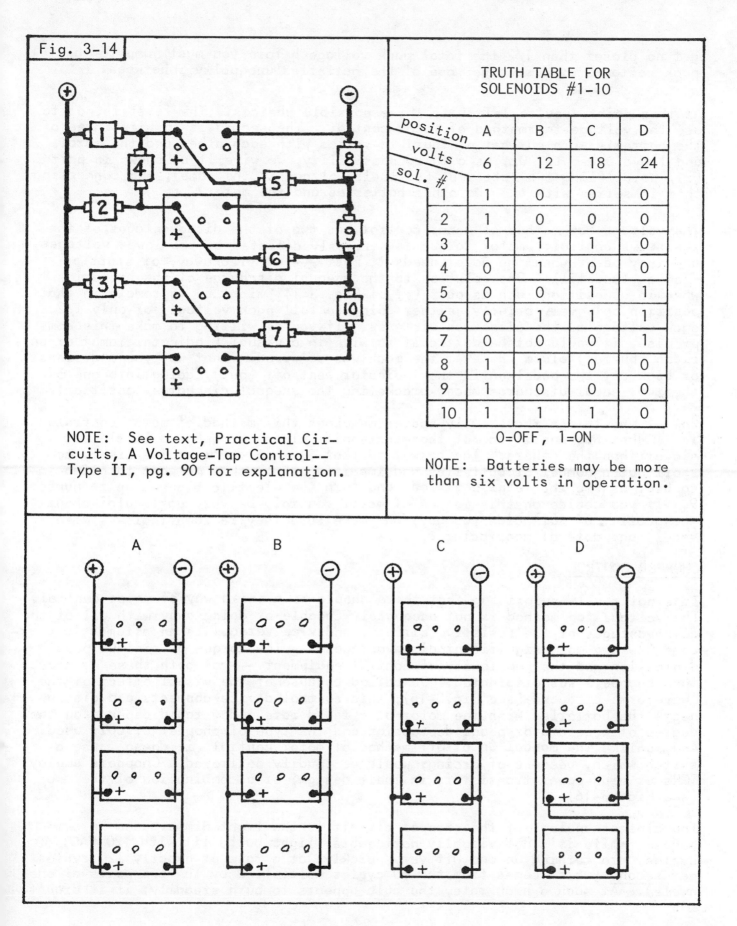

Fig. 3-14

TRUTH TABLE FOR
SOLENOIDS #1-10

position	A	B	C	D
volts	6	12	18	24
sol. #				
1	1	0	0	0
2	1	0	0	0
3	1	1	1	0
4	0	1	0	0
5	0	0	1	1
6	0	1	1	1
7	0	0	0	1
8	1	1	0	0
9	1	0	0	0
10	1	1	1	0

0=OFF, 1=ON

NOTE: See text, Practical Circuits, A Voltage-Tap Control-- Type II, pg. 90 for explanation.

NOTE: Batteries may be more than six volts in operation.

get no closer than 1/2 the total pack voltage before you must jump to the full pack voltage, or discharge some of the batteries unequally inbetween.

At this point, you're left with three possible choices. The first is not to use the voltage-tap method of motor control. The second is to wire three of the batteries (in our set of four) in series with each other and the motor, and leave one out. Or, as a third possibility, we wire it as shown in part (c), paralleling two batteries (so their voltage is the same), and connecting them in series with the two other batteries and the motor.

The voltage-tap method of motor control has two of the disadvantages of the resistive control: motor torque is seriously affected by the lower voltages, and they occur when the motor needs it most --- at breakaway, or starting from a standstill. One solution to the unequal discharge of the batteries when in a position such as part (c) of Fig. 3-14, might be to remain in that position only very briefly, either going to full pack voltage, or only 1/2 pack voltage as the situation dictates. If you're willing to make this compromise, it would not be difficult to wire in a visual (indicator lamp) or an audio (buzzer) alarm whenever the pack was so wired. That way you'd depress or back off the pedal until the indicator went off (out), going into one of the two, equal discharge modes bracketing the unequal discharge 'position'.

One of the things that really scares me about this method of motor control is: "What happens if one of those solenoids closes or opens a little bit slower than the others?" The answer to that is that you're quite likely to short out a number of batteries and imagining that makes me want to climb into bed, assume the fetal position, and turn the electric blanket up to number 9. If you decide on this method of motor control, be very particular about the quality of solenoids you buy, and make sure they're identical --- make, model, and date of manufacture!

CHOPPER CONTROL

It's not really surprising that there should be a third way of motor control. The voltage-tap method is not adequately capable of doing away with all of the disadvantages of the resistive circuit, and vice versa. In an attempt to overcome the two most significant disadvantages --- low torque at minimum pedal depression and the complexity of control equipment --- of both these methods, the 'chopper' was originated. So-called because of the visual effect of the 'waveform' produced (see Fig. 3-15), this control device connects and disconnects the batteries with the motor at a rapid rate. How rapid depends on the degree of accelerator pedal depression and the type of chopper circuit used. And, unlike the manual On or Off method of motor control, it doesn't use a switch which, because of arcing, would be readily destroyed. Choppers employ SCRs or high-power transistors in their design, or a combination of the two (see Fig. 3-16).

The closest analogy of the chopper circuit is the light dimmer used in some homes. While it's not visually noticeable, light bulbs lit with 120 VAC, 60 cycles, are turning On and Off very quickly, at a rate of exactly 120 cycles per second (which comes from the 60 cycles multiplied by the two parts of one cycle). At such a high rate, the bulb appears to burn steadily; if it didn't,

80

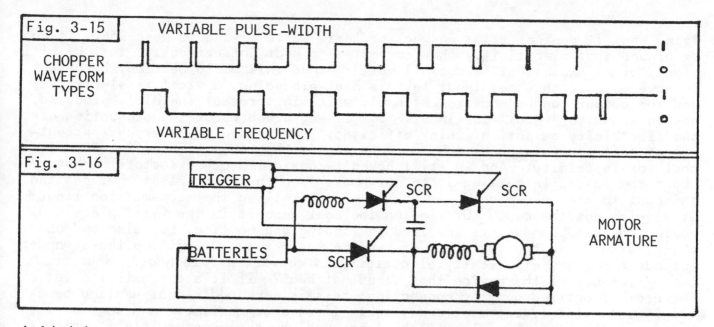

Fig. 3-15 CHOPPER WAVEFORM TYPES

VARIABLE PULSE-WIDTH

VARIABLE FREQUENCY

Fig. 3-16

TRIGGER

SCR   SCR

BATTERIES

SCR

MOTOR ARMATURE

it'd drive us crazy in short time. A light dimmer, inserted between 'wall' current and the light mounted in the lamp, 'chops' off some of the time the bulb is On; by varying the ratio of On to Off time, the light ranges between fully Off and fully On. The light dimmer's knob adjusts this rate, and allows us to control the lamp current from maximum (bright), through average (dim), to minimum (Off).

The chopper designed for DC motor control is a little more sophisticated, but the principle is identical. There are, however, two variations in chopper design: the variable pulse-width chopper (see Fig.3-15) and the variable frequency chopper (see Fig.3-15). Neither seems to hold a clear-cut preferability to the other, but if you're out shopping for a chopper, mentioning the terminology here might save some 'word-shock' then.

The chopper circuit can be used with any of the four motors that we've discussed, and it may be used to control either the field or the armature, although more frequently the latter. The operator control is still the accelerator pedal, but the linkage is a straight-forward connection to a slide resistor --- the only external part of the chopper control itself --- which is contained in a 'black box' and heat-sink mounted against the EV frame.

EVALUATING CONTROL TECHNIQUES

In the next section, we'll tangle with actual control circuits, but I'd like to first evaluate the four control methods --- On-and-Off, Resistive, Voltage-Tap, and Chopper --- in light of such intangibles as efficiency, compactness, technological sophistication, torque, components, troubleshooting, smoothness of operation, and the impact (or the lack thereof) on the batteries, motor, EV, and your body. As well, we'll consider the tangible application and its requirements, the cost and idiosyncrasies which may be defined as individualistic. If you have a propensity for tromping down on accelerator pedals, you must install circuits to protect your EV against you!

Efficiency is one of those words we throw around a lot without, perhaps, realizing that it depends a lot on what criteria we're trying to describe. It can be argued that electricity, when converted to heat intentionally, is 100% efficient, or so close that it doesn't matter. And this would be true, because we have defined that our input to this heat-producing 'device' is electricity and the output can be measured as heat, which in terms of the BTU's produced, can be shown to 'equal' the input. But if we talked about the production of the electricity as part of this 'efficiency', we'd have to lower our percentage of efficiency to about 40%, because that's the conversion efficiency of coal to electricity. And we still haven't considered other factors! What about the losses in getting it to our house from the power plant? Or getting the coal to the powerplant? Or making and installing the transmission lines? Or digging out the coal? Or finding the coal deposit in the first place? Or paying the people who are involved in finding and hauling, building and operating, or billing the customer, or reading the meter? Or writing those wonderful ads about how efficiently electricity is converted into heat? What about the efficiency of the device that uses that heat? If it's a toaster, a lot of the heat is carried away by convection; this is some additional heating benefit if it's winter, but most undesirable if it's summertime. And some of the heat from the heating coils will be 'consumed' by the toaster itself, which is certainly depriving the toast of some additional toasting. Or what if it's space heating that we're using the heat for? If the house is so efficient, why does the furnace keep turning On? When we consider what happens between the time we figure we want to go out and find some coal to make our toast in the morning, we've gone a long route. And, if the overall efficiency of that process approaches 1/10th of 1%, I'll eat the coal instead of the toast!

The efficiency of any one control method is dependent on how much of the time the control unit is in operation. When they're Off, they're all efficient (input equals output equals zero), although it's not considered cool to divide zero by zero. When they're full On, they're also fairly efficient, well within 2% of each other. If we look at what's in between, where control is really in play, we'd have to vote for the chopper as making the best use of the energy from the batteries. The voltage-tap method is next in line, with resistive third. On-or-Off doesn't play in this ballgame; it doesn't do anything in between On and Off, unless you can do a fast 'jig' on the toggle.

What about good motor torque at low EV speeds and low motor rpm? For the first pedal position, it's definitely the chopper control; it's a characteristic of the motor and intrinsic to the thory of the chopper circuit that this type of control gives high torque at low power. Of course, as you press down on the accelerator pedal progressively more, the resistive and voltage-tap control methods reach a greater proximity to the chopper's torque-giving control. They're all identical when we get to full On.

Compactness? The chopper fits into a little black box one-half the size of a cigarette carton (not a pack). The On-or-Off switch fits into half a cigarette pack. The resistive method's components will generally fit into the space consumed by two cartons of cigarettes. The voltage-tap control components will be 1-1/2 to 2 cartons worth of space. It doesn't sound like space is going to be a problem for any of the methods, does it?

Technological sophistication? If you're into high-tech stuff, the chopper will be just the thing. On-or-Off is the crude-but-clean control method. There's lots to show and tell if you use solenoids with the resistive control method, because you get 'clicks' and some heat from the coils when they're in use. The slide switch, resistive control doesn't have 'clicks' like the voltage-tap method, but it does give an impressive 'light' show occasionally, with the arcing at the contacts, with a slight 'headiness' due to the ozone's titillating your olfactory. If your chopper gives out on you as you're playing roulette on the LA freeway, you're going to have a bear of a time getting home. If the others have a problem, you've got a good chance of 'jury-rigging' (also known as 'bubble-gumming') the control to work until you're back on home territory. I don't know of a bobby-pin that can 'fix' a chopper transistor.

Troubleshooting means finding trouble when you have it. When you need to do this, you want it to be an easy process. Too often 'things' are built to many design specifications and little, if any, thought is given to repairing the device easily. As though not thinking about it will prevent it from becoming necessary to do so. Or, let whoever's working on it deal with the problem. After all, he/she is getting paid by the hour, right? Having worked as an electronics technician for many years, I've developed a lot of love for design-work which makes finding trouble and replacing parts a snap. Sure, it means extra effort when you design, build, and install the thing but if you're not thinking ahead, why build it at all?

It'd be difficult to say that one control method's circuitry and components are easier to 'troubleshoot' than the other. Fewer parts means fewer parts to go wrong, so the On-or-Off control gets the blue ribbon in this category. Since any trouble is likely to be only one component, the chopper-controlled EV will be easier to troubleshoot because it shouldn't be too difficult to figure out if the chopper control itself is the source of the problem. Beyond that, isolating the problem in the chopper is going to be hardest of all of them because it will take fairly sophisticated equipment (multimeter, VOM, O-scope, etc.) to pinpoint the malfunction within the chopper control box. On the average, the components in the chopper circuits will be cheaper than those involved in either the resistive or voltage-tap control circuits, although the required parts may be easier to obtain for the latter.

Smoothness of operation is worst in the On-or-Off and best in the Chopper. The remaining two methods approach the chopper's smoothness of operation with a sufficient number of discrete steps in the accelerator pedal. The roughest part of control is the start because the static (immobile) friction is greater than the dynamic (moving) friction. So, when we push the accelerator pedal to where the vehicle will move, it suddenly loses a large percentage of the friction and, at that pedal position, will really 'fly'. Hence, the little 'leap' when you start. If you can do some fancy footwork on the pedal, you can eliminate a lot of this effect, but it's not nearly as bad as all of the attention that I'm giving to it implies.

How about cost? Well, it's about time that we looked at this! The least expensive system is the On-or-Off, requiring only a simple switch as the single component. If you've got even a fairly good-sized current requirement, this should only run $10. It'll be more if you buy the first thing that you find, and a lot less if you've developed a fine sense of scrounging.

The voltage-tap control system may run around $60. That's figuring the extra wiring, and five solenoids. Of course, if you use aircraft-specification or NASA-grade solenoids and connectors, you're going to invest some real money. Resistive control components will run a little more than this if you use the solenoids to affect wire resistor bypass, but a little less if you have just the slide-switch and coils.

If we don't talk about cost, the Chopper seems to have it over the others, but when we do, it meets its armageddon. You might find one for as low as $200, but the present state of the art puts it at $400 and up if it's going to give you troublefree operation for many years. Unless the EV in which it's mounted is exposed to a lot of stop-and-go usage, it just doesn't pay its way. At least, not in the way I define a cost-benefit ratio.

PRACTICAL CONTROL CIRCUITS

This is the nitty-gritty stage, transforming the varied control or motor characteristics into something you can sink your teeth into, or wire into reality in your EV. The circuits will range from simple to complex. There are several things you might notice. One is that the more complex circuits are sometimes just combinations of simpler ones. Another is that these are not the only circuits that might be used; an astute designer could further re-combine them into other versatile control systems.

1. A Simple On-or-Off Speed Control

Fig. 3-17 diagrams the On-or-Off method of motor control. A good, beefy switch will simplify the setup, but you might have to use a small switch to turn on an electrical switch (a solenoid --- see Fig. 3-18); this is the ole 'master-slave' control. If you don't have a solenoid or a relay big enough to handle the current rating, gang a few solenoids together (see Fig. 3-18) in series; this makes their current ratings additive. Make the master switch (the one you'll mount in the cab or on the handlebars) a pushbutton type, and you'll find it safer and faster to use.

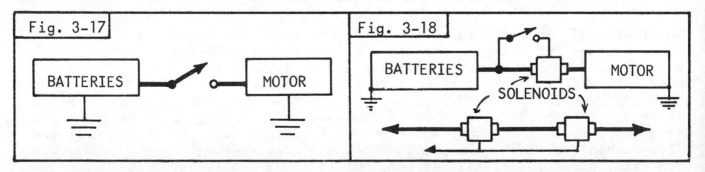

Fig. 3-17   BATTERIES   MOTOR

Fig. 3-18   BATTERIES   MOTOR   SOLENOIDS

2. A Slide-Switch, Armature Current, Resistive Speed Control

If you can scrape up some nice copper flat-stock, make yourself a handy slide-switch and, winding your own resistive coils, install a slide-switch, resistive coil armature current control (see Fig.3-19). The copper bars should be spaced within one-sixteenth of an inch of each other. The copper brush, which is attached to the sliding arm activated by the accelerator pedal through linkage, should also be copper flat-stock and wide enough to short from one bar to the next (a make-before-break situation). You don't want to interrupt motor

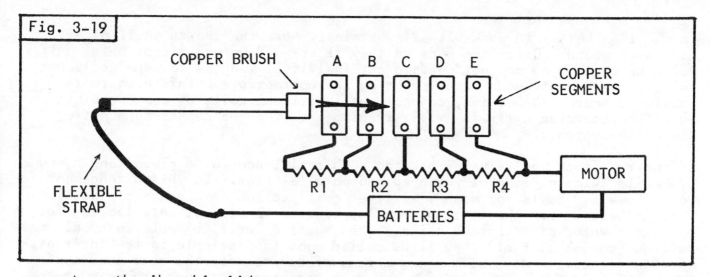

Fig. 3-19

COPPER BRUSH

A B C D E

COPPER SEGMENTS

FLEXIBLE STRAP

R1 R2 R3 R4

MOTOR

BATTERIES

current as the 'brush' slides across copper segments. By drilling holes at the ends of each of the copper segments, you can secure them to the insulated board (micarda or what have you) and also make the necessary connections for the resistive coils. Since the latter will be large and bulky and the copper strips narrow and close, you may be better off mounting them side by side and connecting the resistive coils to the copper segments by lengths of wire. This is the time to decide whether to mount the resistors where you can make some use of their dissipated heat, or to have them out in the open for cooling.

Before we work out some construction details, let's see what happens in the slide-switch type resistance control. When the accelerator pedal is not depressed, note that it is not in contact whatsoever with any of the copper segments and we have no current flow. Bearing down on the pedal and bringing the copper brush over and in contact with the first segment (a) provides the necessary closure of the circuit and current flows from the batteries, through the flexible strap and the copper brush, down the copper segment (a), and through resistors R-1, R-2, R-3, R-4, and to the motor. Maximum resistance in series with the motor and minimum current flow. As the copper brush travels to the next copper segment (b) with further pedal depression, everything is the same except that resistor R-1 has been bypassed and no current flow occurs through the (a) copper segment. As the pedal goes through the remaining positions, resistor R-2 and then R-3 are bypassed until finally, with the pedal to the floor, the copper brush is in contact with segment (e) and all resistance is bypassed and the motor current is maximum.

Making a resistive coil is one of the most exciting parts of building your EV's control system; don't deny yourself this experience. You'll need a form; this can be anything that will not deform as you wind the small diameter rod about it to form the coil. Even though I've provided an example in our section F of the Cubbyhole for determining these values, there are many factors involved --- the rod material, the required resistance values for smooth motor control, the amount of space allotted for housing the resistive coils, etc. --- and you should be prepared to wind them again, or change their values to suit your situation.

A large broomstick or a piece of 1-1/2 to 2 inch pipe or dowel is very satisfactory as a form. Once you've approximated the length, wind it around the form. It's better to work with if you simply mark the length until after it's been wound. Dress the ends so they'll screw down under some bolts. If you plan ahead, you may not need to cut individual lengths for the coils but, rather, run a continuous loop, securing the appropriate points down to the insulated board. Otherwise, connect the individual coils at common points where you can also affix the wires running over the the copper segments of the slide-switch.

If the rod-stock you're using has too much resistance for a given length, make two coils twice as long as you need and parallel them. In this arrangement you'd have two coils for each resistive 'coil' called for in the application. This is better than short, single coils, because we are not only looking for a certain value of resistive coils. They must, as well, be able to handle the wattage (amount of heat) they'll be called upon to dissipate in the interests of motor control. More wire means more surface area for the same amount of heat, which is good. More wire means more resistance, though, so we must combine the wire coils so we get lots of wattage capability and little resistance. Since identical resistors wired in parallel have one-half the resistance of just one resistor (to the batteries, anyway), we can use this setup to solve our resistance/wattage dilemma.

Always make the resistors a little longer than you might think/guess/calculate. Hook them up, and give your EV a trial run. If it's too much resistance, particularly if you can't start the EV from a standstill without going to full pedal-depression, it's fairly easy to decrease the resistance --- just snip off some of the wire, maybe even a full loop of the coil. If it turns out that your original estimation of resistance values is too low --- i.e., there doesn't seem to be much speed control, the vehicle leaps off the line with the first bit of pedal depression and you don't seem to have any speeds between stopped and going --- then you're going to have to make up new coils, because it's too much trouble to add on to coils that are short.

The resistive coils will get warm during use. If you stay in a low-speed position for very long, they'll even smell a bit, cooking leaves that fall on them, etc. Check this situation out after the control system is installed. If proper precautions are observed, it wouldn't really matter if the coils got red hot.

If they get so hot they sag, distort, or melt, go to another size or type of rod for the resistive coils, or add some in parallel. Remember, if they move around, they can touch and ignite something or some of the loops might short out, making the rest get still hotter and giving you that much less motor control.

A good all-round investment will be a wiring manual or some other publication --- mechanical or electrical or electronic publications --- which provides resistance values for so many feet of various types of wire --- steel, copper, aluminum, etc. I always recommend scrounging materials but there are limitations to the benefit derived from using wire that you've found wrapped up in a dusty corner of your root cellar. Even if you've gotten some wire tables from somewhere, how do those figures relate to what you've got in your grubby mitt? How often have you computed resistance values, wound coils, installed wiring, etc? Have you ever burned your hand on an electrical stove? A resistive coil control unit is a disguised mini-stove and it will give you something to feel (a burn) and remember (a scar) if improperly tackled. By no means am I wanting to scare you off from this fun job. But do yourself a favor and get in some homework time on the related subjects beforehand (beforehand gets burned).

3. A Solenoid-switched, Armature Current, Resistive Speed Control - Type I

This is pretty similar to the unit described in #2 above (see Fig.3-20), but solenoids are substituted for the slide-switch and a rotary switch is added; through mechanical linkage, it is connected to the accelerator pedal just as

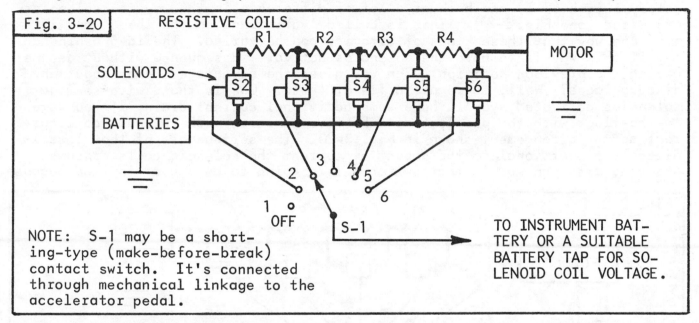

Fig. 3-20

NOTE: S-1 may be a shorting-type (make-before-break) contact switch. It's connected through mechanical linkage to the accelerator pedal.

TO INSTRUMENT BATTERY OR A SUITABLE BATTERY TAP FOR SOLENOID COIL VOLTAGE.

the slide-switch is. Other than these components, resistive coils are still used, connected in the same way, and bypassed one-by-one. Let's look at the operation.

With the vehicle stationary, and your foot off the accelerator pedal, switch S-1 is in position (1) and no juice is flowing. Gently, you depress the pedal, and the wiper-arm of S-1 is moved into contact with position (2). Current flows from source of S-1's current (the instrument battery --- see Monitor, this chapter --- or a voltage tap from the batteries) into solenoid, S-2 and it activates, allowing main battery current to flow through itself, and resistors R-1, R-2, R-3, R-4, and on to the motor. This is lowest power position of the circuit, where maximum resistance is inserted in series with the motor.

Okay, we depress the pedal further, the wiper arm of S-1 goes to position 3, we energize solenoid S-3, we de-energize solenoid S-2, and battery current flows through S-3, through resistors R-2, R-3, R-4, and on to the motor. If the values of the resistive coils are identical, we've just decreased the in-line resistance by 1/4th by bypassing resistor R-1 and the motor is getting more current. This sequence continues until we're at full pedal depression, S-1's wiper arm is at position 6, solenoid S-6 is activated, and feeding main battery current directly to the motor. All resistors are bypassed and all other solenoids are de-energized. Nothing to it, right?

If we want the sequencing of these solenoids to be smooth (no interruption of motor current), we __must__ get a 'shorting' type rotary switch for S-1 (make-before-break). Then, as we pass from one position to the next, two solenoids will momentarily be on simutaneously, one that's just energized and one just about to de-energize. Don't worry; the electrons know which way to go and nothing will be hurt.

4. <u>A Solenoid-switched Armature Current, Resistive Speed Control</u> - Type II

This is very similar to #3 above (and Fig.3-20), involving the same number of components (solenoids and switches) but one slight difference in the type of rotary switch (S-1) and heck of a lot of difference in the way the solenoids are wired (see Fig.3-21). This is called 'variations on the theme' and it's just one way that these kinds of circuits can be varied. The idea behind doing it this way is to have the solenoids activate in sequence <u>without</u> de-energizing the previous position. Can you guess the advantage? What about any disadvantages? Well, there are a few of those. One is that, with so many solenoids activated, you'll have some additional current drain; if you were to-the-floor with the pedal, that'd be five times as much solenoid coil current as the arrangement shown in Fig. 3-20. The seriousness of that loss is directly proportional to the amount of current the solenoid coils consume. A second disadvantage is that switch S-1 is going to be a bear to find because

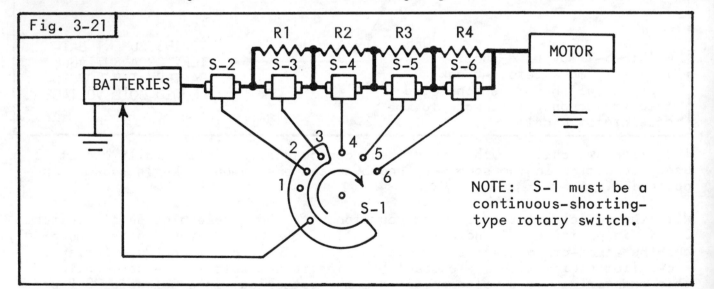

Fig. 3-21

R1 R2 R3 R4

BATTERIES

S-2 S-3 S-4 S-5 S-6

MOTOR

1 2 3 4 5 6

S-1

NOTE: S-1 must be a
continuous-shorting-
type rotary switch.

it must be a 'continuous-shorting' type (make-but-don't-break). In case you haven't yet figured out the advantage of this circuit, note that the solenoids are all in series. Any clues? No? Switches in series have additive ratings, right? Solenoids are just sophisticated switches. With this circuit, you don't have to have any with a rating higher than 1/5th the maximum motor current (figured on 5 solenoids).

I don't recommend using this setup. Even if you did have a situation where you might have lower-than-necessary-value solenoids and could find the switch (S-1), I wouldn't recommend it. To my mind, a control circuit should not draw more current than absolutely necessary. One of the reasons that I've mentioned it is because someone is bound to figure it out, and he or she would probably get blinded by the uniqueness and not think of the disadvantages.

5. A Field Current, Resistive Speed Control

If the motor can be speed-controlled through limitation of the current in its shunt fields, a variable resistance such as that provided by a rheostat can affect this regulation (see Fig.3-11). While you should exercise proper caution by calculating the necessary wattage rating of the rheostat, you'll find it to be a relatively small value.

Controlling the field strength by limiting field current is a bit different than the other controls we've talked about. In them, we have the condition of maximum resistance initially, decreasing to zero as our EV gains speed. In resistive control of the field coils, however, we want a strong field at the beginning which means full field current, or minimum resistance. After the starting circuit has brought the motor to its rated speed, the motor will govern itself to that speed because its field has saturated the armature. To increase motor and EV speed, we must then weaken the field. We do that by limiting the field current and that's where the rheostat comes into play --- we increase its resistance.

Please observe that I mentioned something about a starting circuit. Actually, it's just a circuit identical to those discussed in #2 or #3. Hey, does that mean you have to install one of those, too? Yep, you do! While the rheostat will do a beautiful job of controlling motor speed, it cannot be used exclusive of some method of armature current control. Here's where the ole breakaway current exerts its influence. If either type of motor --- shunt or compound --- was being started under load, it would only require the smallest bit of armature current resistance during breakaway. If it's direct-coupled through gears to the wheels, it's just too much of a load. Sorry! If you have got a transmission in your EV and a clutch, you might be able to bring the motor to speed, and then slip it into gear. But don't figure that this lets you off. A rheostat in the field circuit simply cannot provide armature current protection, even at no load. You still have to have a resistance in there, although it might be of lighter duty if you never tried to start the vehicle without bringing the motor to speed first. And don't think that you can just weaken the field initially and have the motor start up slower. It doesn't work that way and only makes things worse!

All kinds of problems present themselves when we try to come up with a neat circuit to incorporate both the starting and speed control aspects necessary to these motors. If we try to do it all through the floor pedal, the first increment that we reach in stepping on the pedal must do two things: give full field current to the motor and insert the maximum resistance in series with the batteries and motor armature. Then, with the next two to four increments, we need to retain full field current as we gradually decrease the resistance in series with the armature. Only when we have unresisted armature current can we begin to decrease the field strength by increasing the resistance to current flow in the shunt field coils. One of the hurdles is how to rig the linkage so that a standard rheostat, which normally turns through about 300° of a revolution, can be made to move through this space with only a few inches at most of pedal depression.

At this point, you're either scribbling madly away, trying this and that, accepting the challenge of the circuit whether you will use it or not. Or you're ready to go on to the next circuit, hoping that you'll find in it a better understanding, an easier solution, or the perfect, already-worked-out wiring diagram with parts list. But it's all unnecessary. The circuit isn't difficult; it's just involved. One solution to the 'rotation' problem of the rheostat is to use a slide-resistor (this is different than the slide-switch in circuit #2). The solution to the combination armature/field control on one accelerator pedal is two pedals. No, seriously --- use separate copper segments if you're using a slide-switch (circuit #2) or use a double-wafer rotary switch if you're intrigued with solenoids (circuit #3). Things get less complex quickly if you substitute a few small, fixed resistors for that rheostat in the field. Just make sure that you do not begin limiting field current before you've got all of the armature resistances bypassed. And don't run a pedal switch for one and hand control for the other! That's not only cheating; it'll get you into lots of trouble. Neither motor can handle breakaway current and a low field strength at the same time.

6. A Voltage-Tap Control - Type I

You've already seen one voltage-tap control circuit (see Fig. 3-13) but it has the disadvantage of your needing to replace the switch every week because it arcs itself to death. So, let's use a little rotary switch to activate some beefy solenoids (see Fig. 3-22).

I got tired of explaining down which paths the amperes were flowing, so I've put together a small chart with the drawing to help explain things. Read over the notes above the chart so that you'll know where I've come up with the values of motor voltage. Also note that the source of control voltage for the solenoids and that rotary switch, S-1, should be a non-shorting type (break-before-make). This is not absolutely necessary because we have diodes in the circuit to prevent shorting out the batteries should two solenoids be energized simultaneously. But ... theoretically, if the diodes were not there and you had a break-before-make rotary switch (S-1), two solenoids couldn't be energized at one time, and that's a bunch of muck. Diodes do short out occasionally, through over-voltage, over-current, overheating, and just plain orneryness. By doubling up on the safeguard and pretending that you don't have diodes to help you, your start will be a bit jerky, but always safe. You'll be almost as safe if you install twice- or thrice-rated diodes (voltage and current), but understand that unless you put fuses between the solenoids and batteries (one for each) a main battery fuse will <u>not</u> blow if one of the batteries is shorted by the solenoids because you had a make-before-break switch and a blown diode.

In Fig. 3-13 I've indicated that anywhere from one to all six batteries could be brought on the line, whereas in Fig. 3-22 I show only three of the batteries on line with the first pedal position. This is simply to indicate that an EV motor may not start on 1/6th or 1/3rd of its rated voltage; it may take as much as, or more than 1/2 the motor voltage to start. I can't speak for all cases, but do be aware of it; it might save you a lot of extra components --- solenoids, wiring, etc.

7. A Voltage-Tap Control - Type II

While the circuit described in #6 above (Type I voltage-tap control) is

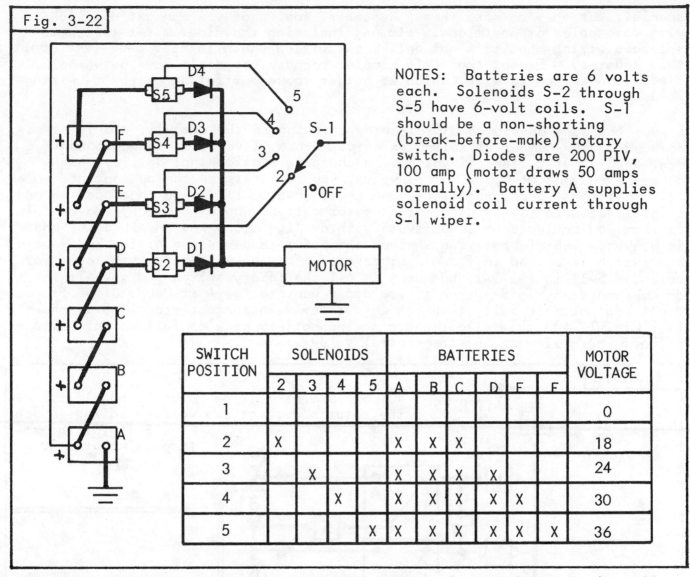

Fig. 3-22

NOTES: Batteries are 6 volts each. Solenoids S-2 through S-5 have 6-volt coils. S-1 should be a non-shorting (break-before-make) rotary switch. Diodes are 200 PIV, 100 amp (motor draws 50 amps normally). Battery A supplies solenoid coil current through S-1 wiper.

SWITCH POSITION	SOLENOIDS				BATTERIES						MOTOR VOLTAGE
	2	3	4	5	A	B	C	D	E	F	
1											0
2	X				X	X	X				18
3		X			X	X	X	X			24
4			X		X	X	X	X	X		30
5				X	X	X	X	X	X	X	36

straightforward and simplistic in design, construction, and use, it has all those built-in disadvantages attributed to the voltage-tap method surveyed in Control Techniques, this chapter. To eliminate the most serious one --- unequal discharge of the batteries in the pack --- requires a more complicated maze of solenoids and some interesting sequencing to correct. One such circuit is shown for the four-battery pack, which I've found to be one of the easiest to work with because it gives three battery pack voltages at equal discharge rates and only one that's unequal. Through a monitor function, it would not be difficult to know when you're in that mode and to go higher or lower, eliminating an unequal discharge (Fig. 3-14).

I've accompanied the drawing with a 'truth table' for the four voltage-steps: 6, 12, 18, and 24 volts. There are ten solenoids called for in this circuit and they are listed as well. I've used a one (1) to show them energized and a zero (0) to show them de-energized; note their state in each of the four voltage groups. The accelerator pedal will be attached to a rotary switch which has five positions (including an Off position) and at least 10 wafers; this would be called a five position, 10-pole switch. Sounds weird and

special, but they do make them. Remember, too, that you can get a switch
with more poles or positions. I'm not including the diagram for switch-to-
solenoid wiring, but it's not unlike the wiring shown in Fig. 3-32 (see Monitor,
this chapter). Except that it's simpler because you don't have a two-pole,
8-position switch to wire (which is harder to keep straight as you're wiring
it).

I have the same phobia about solenoids sticking in the circuit, and it's com-
pounded by the number of solenoids used. Hence, I've added some diodes (see
Fig. 3-23). Of course, if you have a charging station that delivers high-
amperage current at 6, 12, or 24 volts, you can energize the appropriate solenoids for those pedal positions, and charge away. If you do this, add an additional solenoid (S-11) as a master motor current shutoff switch. Maybe this
is what you activate or de-activate with an 'ignition' key on the dash, and
it prevents vehicle motoring whether the pedal is depressed or the Fwd-Neutral-
Rev switch is placed in forward or reverse. By the way, the truth table for
solenoid S-11 is 1-1-1-1, but keep it off the rotary switch and save it for
an emergency shut-off switch if you don't want to 'key' it On or Off. If you
don't add solenoid S-11, then put in a relay with contacts to close as shown
(see Fig. 3-23); this allows charging the battery pack at full normal voltage
without energizing any of the control relays.

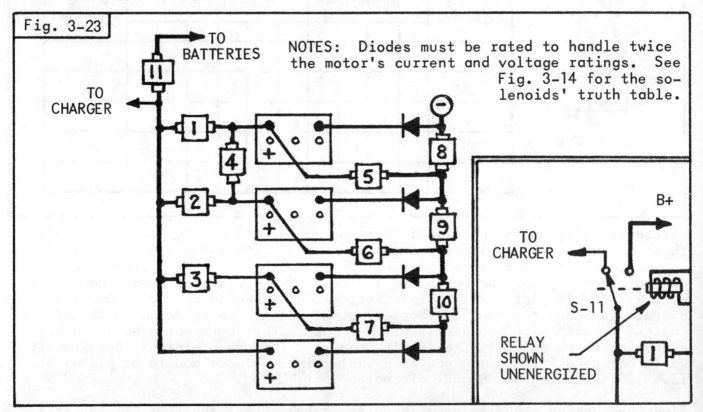

Fig. 3-23

TO BATTERIES

TO CHARGER

NOTES: Diodes must be rated to handle twice
the motor's current and voltage ratings. See
Fig. 3-14 for the so-
lenoids' truth table.

B+

TO CHARGER

S-11

RELAY
SHOWN
UNENERGIZED

If you choose a voltage-tap method of motor control, use this circuit (instead
of the one shown in Fig.3-22). Once you've got the solenoids wired, and they
are connected to the rotary switch, use some small lantern batteries in place
of the big batteries and a voltmeter in place of the motor. Now, run through
the pedal positions. You should see 6, then 12, then 18, and finally, 24 volts
displayed on the meter. If you don't, find the trouble. Don't be too sure of

yourself and your wiring capability and stick the big batteries in for the test. They have a name for the process of 'doublechecking' your own work; it's called wisdom. And they have a name for those who ignore such a precautionary setup: Whiz-Dumb.

8. A Series Motor Reversing Circuit

Our own electric truck has a hand-operated, mechanical reversing switch for the motor, as described in the section on Control Requirements. Its job is to switch the field windings or the armature windings in respect to the batteries, but not both. As it turns out, it follows the universal preference, switching the armature windings instead of the field windings. Understand that simply reversing the battery polarity with respect to the motor will not reverse the motor's direction of rotation. If the motor's armature windings are inaccessible, switch the field windings (see Fig. 3-24).

While the mechanical switch has the advantage of a middle, neutral position, you could use a relay to perform the reversing function. This appeals to me because it eliminates a large cumbersome reversing switch mounted in the dash or close at hand in the cab. And, if the relay's un-energized (normally-closed) contacts are used for the Forward wiring polarity, the relay will not draw any current until the vehicle needs to back up.

The size of the switch or switch/relay will depend on your driving habits. There'll be lots of arcing at the contacts if you're trying to reverse while the vehicle is still moving (under power). If you can faithfully keep your foot off the accelerator pedal as you switch forward to reverse, or vice versa,

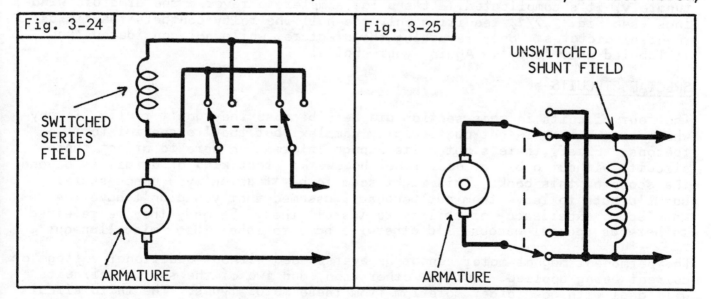

Fig. 3-24
SWITCHED
SERIES
FIELD
ARMATURE

Fig. 3-25
UNSWITCHED
SHUNT FIELD
ARMATURE

the reversing switch will only need to be rated at half of normal motor current; that's because the other control systems are pulling the arc as they shut down motor current.

9. A Shunt Motor Reversing Control

In a shunt motor, either the armature or the field windings can be switched

93

for changing the direction of shaft rotation, but the preferred method is to switch armature windings (see Fig. 3-25). This is a crying shame because the switch required to reverse field windings in a shunt motor is tiny compared to

the switch or switch/relay combination needed for the armature windings. But, when I run across a word like 'preferred' in the text of a DC motor manual, I take it literally. And, in opening up my three shunt motors and finding all of them with reversing setups that involve the armature windings, I just can't grab hold of anything to argue about. Put it this way. I'm not going to recommend switching the field and I'm not going to do it myself in any switching circuits I design. You can do whatever you want!

10. A Compound-Wound Motor Reversing Control

Because both series and shunt fields are involved in the Compound Motor, we have to be careful when we figure out ways to reverse this motor. The simplest expression of awareness might be: don't reverse the shunt field and the series field with respect to each other. So, if you switch the 'field', this means you switch both of them.

The preferred method of reversing the compound motor is to reverse the windings of both fields (respective to the armature and batteries --- see Fig. 3-26). This opposes the general rule in motor reversing, but it's written in the books, and it's the only way I've ever seen the reverse wires connected. And, unfortunately, it's complicated. It's a lot simpler to reverse the armature windings (see Fig. 3-27), requiring only one-half the relay contacts the fields' reversal dictates. But, reversing the armature, while not considered 'bad', is labeled only 'okay'. Again, your choice!

SPECIAL CIRCUITS

The four circuits in this section are here because they don't really fit anywhere else. They're not particularly complex, but they're special for two reasons. First, there's not quite enough information here to affect these circuits without a bit of additional homework; that kind of detail is beyond the scope of this book. This might seem to be 'teasing' you unnecessarily; but I'd hate to leave them out because I assumed that you didn't have the knowledge, experience, or ability to install them. Second, they're referred to here as special because I'd otherwise have to label them 'miscellaneous'.

The permanent magnet motor cannot be overspeeded without additional voltage or current being applied. But the others can, and two of the special circuits will deal with how to get more rpm from these motor types. The third circuit describes dynamic braking. And the fourth is the often-heard-of, but grossly misunderstood, regenerative-braking circuit.

11. A Series Motor Overspeed Circuit

If you want to achieve higher-than-the rated speed (rpm) of a series motor, it involves messing around with the field strength. You can't just put a resistor in series with it, however, because that limits the armature current, too.

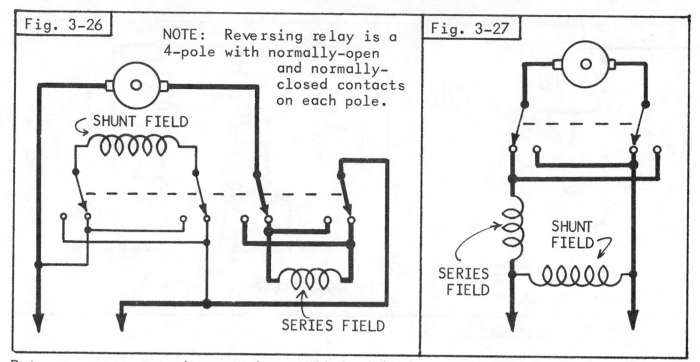

Fig. 3-26

NOTE: Reversing relay is a 4-pole with normally-open and normally-closed contacts on each pole.

SHUNT FIELD

SERIES FIELD

Fig. 3-27

SERIES FIELD

SHUNT FIELD

But, you can put a rheostat in parallel with the series field and, once the motor is at its rated speed, slowly decrease this resistance until some of the armature current is bypassing the series field winding. If we went all the way --- rotating the rheostat until its resistance was zero --- we'd entirely bypass the series field winding. Depending on the amount of residual magnetism and the load, the motor might stall or seriously overspeed. Since the motor should not exceed 25% of its rpm rating anyway, we must limit the amount of effectual bypass. This might be a 'stop' on the travel, or degrees of rheostat rotation, or it might involve replacing the rheostat with both a rheostat and a fixed resistor in series. That way, even if we fully rotate the rheostat, there's always some amount of resistance in-line (see Fig. 3-28).

If you find the idea of overspeeding the motor a bit intriguing, get hold of a DC motor manual and obtain the necessary information for determining the values of the resistance required. I wanted you to know it could be done, but you'll have to take the ball from here; it's beyond the scope of this book to deal with it further.

12. A Compound Motor Overspeed Circuit

To achieve rpm above the rated value for a compound motor involves both series and shunt field regulation. Since the compound motor approaches the similarities of both the series and shunt motor, we can install a resistive bypass for the series winding. We can expect, once the motor has had a hefty series motor 'start', to inactivate the series winding; the motor will assume the characteristics of the shunt motor at higher EV speeds. Fig. 3-29 illustrates the components and their respective positions for a compound motor with series field bypass (R-1), shunt field current limiting (R-2), and a breakaway current limiter (R-3). Wouldn't it be nice if the resultant circuit was as simple-looking? By the time you arrange for all of these control functions adjoining operator controls, you'll wonder what manner of beast has taken refuge in your EV's control system!

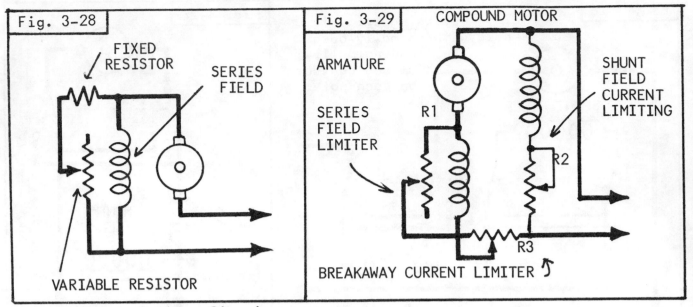

Fig. 3-28

FIXED RESISTOR

SERIES FIELD

VARIABLE RESISTOR

Fig. 3-29   COMPOUND MOTOR

ARMATURE

SERIES FIELD LIMITER

R1

SHUNT FIELD CURRENT LIMITING

R2

R3

BREAKAWAY CURRENT LIMITER

13.   A Dynamic Braking Circuit

Because the tendency of EVs to coast when the accelerator pedal is released, a method of braking which does not need mechanical or hydraulic brakes might be nice. I suspect that, with the proliferation of electric vehicles, the vehicle codes will change, requiring the automatic applications of dynamic braking when the foot is off the accelerator pedal. But, until then, your state's vehicle codes **may** permit its application at the driver's discretion.

The simplest method of dynamic braking is to insert a low resistance across the armature windings (see Fig. 3-30), after the battery power is disconnected. This, then, provides a load for the motor, which has become, in essence, a generator. The effect is that the resistor dissipates the produced current, and the motor loses speed. And, since the motor is coupled to the gearbox and wheels, the vehicle is 'braked'. To have a more pronounced effect, sometimes the motor can be simply shorted out, and its own internal resistance serves as the load (see Fig. 3-31).

Either method of dynamic braking has its limitations. First, only the permanent magnet motor can be simply loaded. The stock series motor, if used for dynamic braking, must have its field windings reversed. The shunt and compound motors both require full field excitation for dynamic braking, and this gets mucky, trying to put power to the fields and keep it off the armature. Second, the braking effect is most pronounced at high motor rpm (high EV speed). It then diminishes quickly to very little braking effect at lower rpm and EV speed. Which is just backward from what we need! If dynamic braking is automatically activated when you remove your foot from the accelerator pedal, this could be dangerous, decelerating the EV at a rate similar to when you hit the brakes in a panic stop. And, at lower EV speeds, the effect would be barely discernable, so additional braking becomes a must.

These disadvantages don't say that you shouldn't use dynamic braking. On the contrary, it saves using the mechanical brakes all the time, and will make us feel right at home like we do with 'compression-braking' in an internal-combustion engine'd car. But, I hope that my argument persuades you not to connect this control function to your accelerator pedal, which is overloaded with dealing with breakaway current and speed control, anyway. Rather, make it part of the brake pedal. In most vehicles that I've driven, the brake did not activate immediately when the brake pedal was depressed a bit; it has to go down several inches before the brakes were really on. Gee, with some cars I've been in, you could put the brake pedal all the way to the floor and nothing happened. But, if you micro-switched the brake pedal so that at the teeniest bit of depression, it put a load across the motor, you could achieve the necessary braking without using the mechanicals (or hydraulics). To keep from flying over the dash at high speeds, maybe you could rig a stepper-switch on the pedal, inserting a high resistance at first (minimum loading and minimum braking effect) and then progressively go to lower resistances until, say, the motor was shorted out. Further depression, then, would activate the mechanical brakes, to bring the vehicle smoothly or quickly to a halt. With this arrangement, if you ever had to do a panic stop, you'd have the brakes <u>and</u> motor working at maximum to kill momentum, and that beats what happens in a regular car!

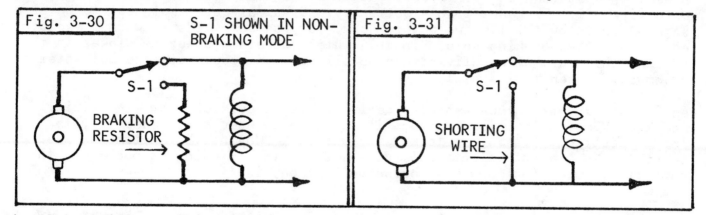

Fig. 3-30   S-1 SHOWN IN NON-BRAKING MODE

S-1   BRAKING RESISTOR

Fig. 3-31

S-1   SHORTING WIRE

An alternative to activating dynamic braking at the brake pedal is to incorporate it in a switch, toggle or rotary (depending on the number of steps), and mount it on the dash. A DPDT switch can be used; with the up position, you can get half the effect that results when you throw it down (it's off when the switch is in the center position). Since it's handling motor current, this will only activate a solenoid which does the real switching. I suggested a double-pole switch because you must, when in either of these positions (low or high dynamic braking), insure that the accelerator pedal is de-activated. Otherwise, you're going to depress the pedal and put pack voltage across the dynamic braking load resistor. Or, if you've been using the motor's internal resistance as the load, you've just shorted out the battery pack. How silly of you! Lemme see, I saw some batteries for sale just last week over at ...

If you've got a tiller for a steering wheel, it'd be easy to set the dynamic-braking switch right by your fingertips, as close as the little bell on your old bicycle (the one that went 'thriinnggg-thriinngg') used to be. If it's mounted there, it's easier to reach than the dash and you don't have to take your hands off the steering wheel. But, you won't have to in a real emergency, because you'll foregt all about dynamic braking and just hit the ole mechanical or hydraulics. Dynamic braking is best used for things like hills or maneuvers where you need to have the EV slow down any time you take your foot off the accelerator pedal. Which means that you're forewarned and don't have to frantically reach for it, wherever it is.

14. Regenerative Braking

It's always a shame to see the inertia of a moving vehicle 'wasted' when we bring it to a stop by applying brakes, whether they're mechanical, hydraulic, dynamic, or the rock-and-rope method. When that's done, the energy is dissipated in heat, thereafter lost for useful work. This doesn't have to happen. It does happen because, in the final or first analysis, it doesn't pay to try to recover energy that's this low-grade. 'Pay', however, is a relative term. There may come a time when something will not be so quickly taken for granted and thrown away.

One such method of energy recovery is regenerative braking. While the term is often used hand-in-hand with electricity, it's far more inclusive than that. To regenerate is to be "formed or created again, restored to a better, higher, or more worthy state, to utilize by special devices heat or other products that would ordinarily be lost." So, we could capture the energy in the vehicle's momentum by storing it for re-use. How? By tightening a spring. Or speeding up a flywheel. Or generating electricity. Or simply use that heat to bake some biscuits by the time we got to work. Or, as some kids to whom I explained regenerative braking said, "Install water-jackets around the brakes in the car and that way, after driving around all day, you could use the hot water for a shower." Aren't kids silly?

An EV is a rather unique vehicle, deriving its propulsion from electricity. And the EV motor is unique in that it can also be used as a generator, to 'make electricity'. So, we look twice and say, "Why not?" Anytime we need to brake, we generate electricity at the same time, feeding it back into the batteries. Gee, that's almost perpetual motion, isn't it?

It's hard enough getting what we pay for, much less any more. There's no doubt, however, that we can reclaim something from regenerative braking. That may only hold true for some kind of EV that's using enormous amounts of energy in the first place. But irrespective of the type or size of EV, there are limiting factors to the 'gain' by regenerative braking. Let's look at a few.

1. Generating electricity with any one of the motors we've discussed so far requires a higher rpm than the one we achieve by simply bringing the motor to speed, even if completely unloaded. That's because the motor must develop a higher potential (voltage) than the battery pack in order to charge the latter.

2. The regeneration of electricity will occur for only that length of time that the motor rpm remains above the battery pack level. Okay, this sounds like #1 above expressed another way. But, what's meant is that both a generator and a motor will grind down to a halt, but a generator, having fallen below the electricity-generating stage, will have long ceased to produce any power.

With the obstacles imposed by #1 and #2, a fast solution might seem to be: shift down. Meaning, go to a lower gear so the generator rpm remains high respective to the wheel rpm. Well, true. But you're going to be downshifting like crazy, trying to grab a few AHs and expending more energy (human) than you're getting (electrical).

3. Regeneration of electricity doesn't necessarily offset the need for electricity. If you're driving down the road, flat out, and it's level all the way, regenerative braking hasn't done a thing for you. Or, if you drive down a mountain in the morning, using the regenerative braking to charge your nearly-depleted batteries, you'll never get back up the hill without additional charging. The lighter your vehicle, the less inertia you have. Since the expression is mass times velocity squared and you're limited to 25 mph top speed, you don't have a fourth of the inertia that a 50-mph vehicle has.

If someone offered $100,000 to come up with a practical method of regenerative braking for an EV that meets all the criteria of the cost/benefit ratio --- low cost, simple, easy to install, easy to use, etc. --- it'd probably be on our doorsteps in a few months. But in solving each of the above difficulties, fresh problems arise, and it seems beyond a good solution. It's a good idea, and one that should be pursued until it's solved, but how involved do you intend to get with it? If you've got stop-and-go traffic to contend with in the space-hippie Econoline you want to convert, regenerative braking should be seriously considered. If you've got a lightweight, spartan-class, lowspeed EV, your efficiency rating is already so far beyond the others that trying to incorporate regenerative braking would be a conspicuous attempt at perpetual motion.

End-of-Section Comments by the Author

I don't want to unduly influence you through my preference of one circuit type or another, or how I'd combine them, but a brief glimpse into the intended control circuits for our upcoming PASEV and UTLEV is given in the chapter on Vehicles.

MONITOR

There are all sorts of indicators of things happening in the EV when they happen. If you push down on the accelerator pedal, the EV will move forward (or backward, depending on the setting of operator controls). If you're occupying the driver's seat, so will you. You see the movement, however relative, of the environment toward you (looking ahead), past you (looking sideways, or out the corner of your eye), or away from you (if you're looking at the rear-view mirror). You hear the sounds of the wheels on dirt or pavement and the motor whine. You feel the vehicle moving, the wind in your face, and the vibration in your hands. If you're traveling at really high speeds, you can even taste the event, particularly if your mouth is open (whether laughing or screaming with excitement) and it's that time of year when there are a lot of bugs flying about. And, if you're going in reverse, you might smell the hydrogen from your batteries, or the ozone as your slide-switch resistive circuit is arcing. Many 'senses' acting together to tell you what's happening.

But can these senses tell us in which direction we will travel when we depress the accelerator pedal? Or what the motor RPM is? Or the amount of current drain? How about battery voltage? Vehicle speed? The answer is: No! Or, rather, a qualified "No". No, unless we extend the senses' capacity by using

them to 'read' other devices which transform the given effects --- RPM, voltage, current, and vehicle speed --- into something which our senses can detect,
interpret, and understand. A car has many of these devices but they fall into
basic groups --- indicators and gauges.

INDICATORS

Indicators are generally lights which go On or Off to signify that something
is or is not happening according to plan. In a car, there may be a light
which goes On if the temperature of the engine has exceeded a safe limit, or
another light will illuminate if the alternator stops charging, such as can
occur if the alternator belt were to break. In an EV, indicators can be used
to show switching sequences, a low battery voltage condition, or that other
accessories are On (which might get left On, if you don't have an indicator
to tell you that it is still On). For important things, however, it's best
to shy away from using indicator lights. First of all, they have a nasty habit of coming On too late to be of much use. Or the filaments have burned out
on the bulb and it won't come On in any case. Second, they don't tell you
very much; they've earned the name 'idiot' light in automobiles because the
manufacturers felt that gauges were too confusing for the 'idiot' consumers
to understand. Or that the driver would not notice a gauge reading as likely
as a red light. I'm probably being rough on the Detroit guys; it's more likely that they decided in favor of indicator lights because gauges were too expensive to install.

GAUGES

Gauges are the way to go, whenever and wherever possible. Gauges fill the gap
between knowing nothing (no reading) and still not knowing much (indicator's
On) but being scared to death. Instead of getting a light that says something
like, "trouble-trouble-trouble", you get to see a temperature reading; what's
better is that you will have seen it creeping up to Hot, so you won't be
caught with your pants descended. In the EV, you'll have as many as six
gauges to install; they are: ammeter, voltmeter, speedometer, tachometer,
temperature gauge, and an odometer.

AMMETER

The ammeter is one of the most important of the gauges in the EV; it reads the
motor current flow in amperes. If this was the only gauge that you had in the
control panel, you could tell when your batteries were beginning to get low; I
daresay that, after using your vehicle a while, you could almost determine how
much or how long you had to go before a recharge with just a glance at its
reading. You should know beforehand what maximum amperage you can expect from
the motor circuit under worst conditions --- starting up, under maximum load,
or on an incline (up). You'll want to get a meter that reads at least 25%,
but no more than 100%, more than this value at full scale pointer deflection.
Meters read the most accurately in the center of the scale, and least accurately at both ends. If you've wondered why auto speedometers read up to 120 mph
even though you normally operate around 70mph maximum, now you know. The larger the meter movement (in inches and across the face), the better the resolu-

tion and the easier it is to read quickly. With some, you'll be able to read down to the nearest ampere, and with others, you can only read to the nearest 10 amperes.

With the kind of high currents present in the motor circuit of an EV, the meter you will get for it will have a shunt; this device passes 99.99% of the current, and the rest (0.01%) of it passes through the meter. The shunt may be inside the meter case but, for higher currents, they sometimes put it outside; after all, it will dissipate some heat. If the shunt for your meter is external, this is good because you can put it somewhere close to the batteries and put your meter at some distance away; this saves having to run heavy wires over to, and behind, the control board. Don't worry too much if the shunt is inside the case; the savings in wire or I^2R losses is not that much. Unless you've done it before, don't go into the meter movement to try removing the shunt.

If you buy a current meter second hand, make sure that it has a shunt inside or if it doesn't, that you're provided with an external shunt. Check! The meter face may show a full-scale reading of 1000 amperes but, if you put 120 amps through it, it'd explode! Shunts are expensive (if your meter didn't come with one) but they can be made out of copper or nichrome wire and calibrated very close to the real thing. Get someone to help; amateur radio folks or any electronics man worth his stuff can do this.

VOLTMETER

While it's convenient to have both a voltmeter and an ammeter, you can make do with just one or the other. The voltmeter is convenient because it will also tell you when the batteries are getting a mite low. But a good voltmeter is less expensive than a good ammeter and can be used to take readings when the vehicle is not in motion (see Fig. 3-32); the ammeter only does its 'indicating' when the motor is drawing current. As well, with a suitable wiring circuit, it's possible to tell how each battery in the pack is doing (see Fig. 3-32); this can be helpful in isolating a battery which is not being charged to capacity or is not performing as it should. For these reasons, the voltmeter will be used only if one meter is allowed.

You can select and use a voltmeter which reads only slightly above the battery pack's voltage when fully charged; unlike the ammeter, the voltmeter's readings will only decrease from that point, during operation. The same rule of mid-scale readings for highest accuracy applies, though; if you want to read the battery pack voltage and the individual batteries (one at a time), you must try to keep the pointer away from the ends of the scale. For a total battery pack voltage higher than 12 volts, you cannot use the same meter range for pack and individual battery readings. If you've got the money, you can go luxury class: two meters. For those with an eye for adventure, use one meter but two ranges for the two different readings, and a switch to select one or the other (see Fig. 3-32).

Voltmeters don't use shunts because, for the readings they take, very little current is required. Increasing the voltage that a particular meter can read is simply accomplished by the addition of a resistor in series with the meter;

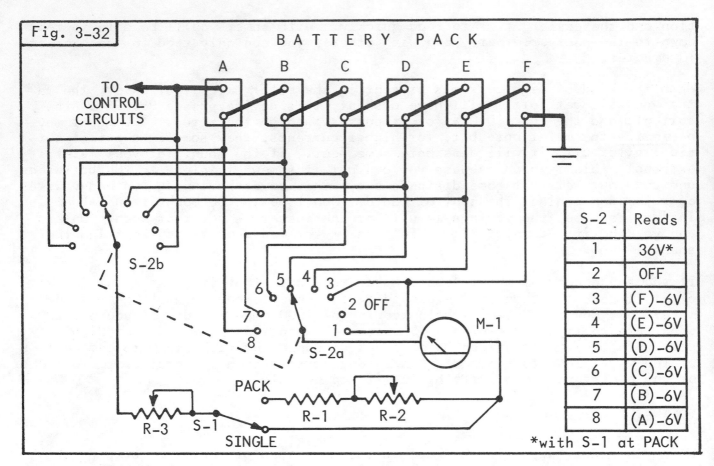

Fig. 3-32

BATTERY PACK

TO CONTROL CIRCUITS

S-2	Reads
1	36V*
2	OFF
3	(F)-6V
4	(E)-6V
5	(D)-6V
6	(C)-6V
7	(B)-6V
8	(A)-6V

*with S-1 at PACK

for fine adjustments to odd voltages, or to compensate for out-of-tolerance resistors, the more common procedure is to insert both a resistor and a variable resistor (called a potentimeter, or pot) in series with the meter. If you need two ranges, you can buy a meter which conveniently reads a little more (full scale) than the highest voltage possible in the lower range of voltage, and then, by flipping a switch, insert the resistor and pot in-line, to read the upper voltage range.

Let's consider an example. You have a 36-volt battery bank in your EV and you wish to monitor this as well as each individual battery, in sequence, under load conditions, (see Fig. 3-32). You've found a voltmeter which reads 10 volts full scale, in one volt segments. Okay, with switch S1 in the indicated position, S2 may be rotated to monitor each battery in the pack, whether under load or with the vehicle stopped. By switching S1 to the other position, resistor R1 and pot R2 are inserted in-line with the meter movement and will, according to the wiring circuit, read the voltage of the pack. With proper selection of the values of R1 and R2, the meter can read 100 volts full scale, (with 10 volt increments) or to read 50 volts full scale (with 5 volt increments). With this latter arrangement, you'll always be multiplying the reading (in your head) by 5, but you can get used to it. Mark the control panel in such a way, however, as to prevent confusion for other persons who might operate the vehicle.

If you've got an electronics friend with some experience, you can get him to open the meter case (if it's not glued together), add some curved tape on the meter face, and write in the secondary scale readings below or above the other, using the same spaced increments (if linear). If it's marked in a different color to that used originally on the meter face, you can color code the switch positions to give a visual aid to figuring out which scale is in use. Don't attempt mucking around with the meter yourself, unless you've done it before (successfully); it's really easy to mess up the movement bearings, damage the pointer, and otherwise destroy a good, maybe expensive, meter.

You can place the same curved tape outside, on the meter face glass, and mark the appropriate readings for the second scale, but this presents a few problems; if the meter is read from an angle, you don't know what the pointer is pointing at. As well, the tacked-on scale will fade, smear, or peel off eventually and then everyone will get to guess what it used to read.

One other thing. Switch S2 in Fig. 3-32 must be a twin-wafer, multicontact (at least one 'position' more than the number of batteries in your vehicle), rotary switch. The most important part of the design of the switch is that it be a 'non-shorting' type; this means that, as the switch is rotated from position to position, the wiper arm in the switch does not 'make' contact with the next position before it 'breaks' contact with the previous position. If it were to 'make before break', wired as shown in Fig. 3-32, this would cause a few sparks, because momentarily, one battery in the bank would be 'shorted'; it's a nice show, but it'll cost you your switch.

SPEEDOMETER

The speedometer is a nice thing to have in a PASEV, but useless in a UTLEV. If you've got a 4-wheeled EV or are otherwise operating your vehicle as something other than a motorized bicycle, you will have to check on the Vehicle Codes to see if you require one. In California, there is no mention in the codes of the word speedometer. So, at least in California, you don't have to include one as standard equipment. However, unless your vehicle's top speed is below the speed limits, it might be nice to know how fast you are going, particularly when there's a Highway Patrol unit tagging you. Even if you decide not to install one, you might at least have a friend 'pace' you in his vehicle so that you can learn approximately what your speed is under varying conditions, or flat out and stripped for a time trial. Have him follow you or lead. Don't have him alongside; you'd never live down trying to explain to the judge that you really weren't drag-racing!

If your state's codes insist on the installation of a speedometer, try to find one that's matched to the wheels you've got on the EV. This might be an easy process if you're using something like motorcycle wheels, but a tough position if you've cannabilized your kid's little red wagon. Check with the specific wording of the codes; they might not require one on a vehicle with your classification.

ODOMETER

The odometer is the device that records the miles the vehicle travels. A motorized bicycle does not require one. The California vehicle codes do specify that, if your vehicle is equipped with an odometer, it must be connected and functional. They do not say that a vehicle must be equipped with one originally. Check your state's codes for applicable information regarding odometers and study closely the working of anything they do say; inference is not the same as 'gotta have'.

If for any reason you want or need an odometer, it can be built. Of course, if you install a speedometer that's actually calibrated for your car, it'll probably have an odometer as part of the mechanism, and you're home free. If not, all you need is a counter mechanism which will record the number of revolutions of your wheels and will, when reaching a predetermined value (a mile divided by the circumference of the tire), advance a low-voltage, DC counter one step. Again, this is the time to renew (with vigor) your friendship with anyone you know who's into electronics. If that appears too complicated, get a VW speedometer, with cable; they have a nice, direct way of hooking it into the rotating, front left wheel, for a readout. If you can get a tire diameter equal to the 15" rim and wheels they use, it's going to be right on --- both the speedometer and odometer. If not, calibrate it by getting a friend to 'pace' you, and paste the conversion numbers for different speeds --- about every 5mph --- right on, or next to the speedometer/odometer unit. There hasn't been a vehicle code that I've seen yet which specifies that your speedometer/odometer can't have conversion scales; they're mainly concerned with making sure that someone doesn't change an odometer reading and in no way falsifies what the reading should be, and they're only trying to prevent misrepresentation of sale where used cars are concerned.

TACHOMETER

The tachometer is a nice addition to the control panel in an EV, but useless if you have (a) a fixed gear ratio, and (b) a speedometer; in this combination it's doing the same thing as the speedometer. Actually, it's a luxury unless you don't have, or can't get, a speedometer; it may be an acceptable substitute if properly calibrated. If you've got two or more gears in your EV, the tachometer can be used in conjunction with a speedometer, helping under various conditions by insuring proper shift-up or shift-down for proper torque and speed ratios.

The difficulty you experience in hooking up the tachometer, though, is the deciding factor of whether you'll use it or not. If you've begged, borrowed, or stolen a tachometer which is normally used in a gasoline-fueled engine, you've got a problem. Normally, tachs connect to the distributor, counting the pulses to give you the RPM reading. EV's don't have a distributor, or anything resembling it. You might be able to count pulses out of the motor's commutator, but you'll get no help on that one from me; I haven't done it before. Or, you can attach a magnet to the shaft of some rotating part, and get pulses from a reed-switch or a magnetic diode, and count or average them for meter readout. But, these tachometers are meant to work with thousands of RPM (up to around 8,000 RPM). The fastest thing going in the EV is the motor, and it's only around 1000 - 2000.

There's one other possibility for wiring a tachometer: Don't use a standard one. Get a meter movement (milliammeter or millivoltmeter --- that's 1/1000ths,

104

folks), start off with the magnet and reed-switch idea (which is the least expensive), and go from there. If it seems to be getting too complex too fast, forget I wrote anything at all; you'll have enough to occupy your time in building an EV.

TEMPERATURE GAUGE

This is more a suggestion than a necessity, but it might be nice to have a temperature gauge in the control panel of your EV; after continuous use, there will be a lot of heat build-up in the batteries. Assuredly, with a good design of venting, whether just an air passage or a blower system, hydrogen-oxygen gases and battery or controller heat should dissipate. However, batteries are not very good radiators and will not dissipate their accumulated heat that quickly; this being the case, it might be nice to know when they are getting hotter than you'd like them to be (125°F is tops). That way, you can pull off and sit for a while; if you've got a blower unit, you can keep it on to keep circulating the air for even faster cooling.

Insofar as the battery compartment itself might be quite cool while the batteries are not, the best arrangement would be to epoxy or glue a thermistor to the exterior wall of one of the batteries; if it's buried in the epoxy, it will not be affected by blower cooling, and read ambient, rather than battery, temperature. Thermistors can be obtained very inexpensively and cover wide ranges of temperature; they are, in fact, small resistors which are greatly affected by temperature, lowering or raising their resistance in proportion to temperature rise or fall. Which way they go depends on their temperature coefficient --- positive or negative. For this application, you will want one with a negative coefficient so that, as the temperature increases, the resistors' value will decrease, causing a greater deflection of the pointer in an appropriate meter. Then it's a matter of calibrating the meter in order to readout the various temperatures a battery experiences.

If you're in snow country, it might be wise to detect temperatures into the cold range as well; it's not difficult to find thermistors that will run the gamut --- reading between 32° and 212° --- but meter calibration or accuracy may pose a difficulty for this wide a spread. If you want both hot and cold readings, consider using two scales with one thermistor, or switch between two thermistors, one handling the low end and the other the high end, and mark two scales on the meter face. A good thermometer will suffice for the calibration; just make sure that both thermistor and thermometer are exposed equally to the heat (or absence thereof) and allow them sufficient time to stabilize before marking them down on your 'paper' scale. Oh, and don't just take a few readings! Thermistors aren't necessarily linear and neither are many meters; taking a high reading and then a low one and dividing the difference into equally-spaced segments and marking them with increments is a no-no. Anything worth doing is worth doing right --- the first time!

INSTRUMENTATION POWER

As main battery voltage varies, so will the instrumentation readings. There goes accuracy! If you're going to run a lot of meter stuff, consider the use of a single, separate battery for its operation. This isn't really such a bad

idea, because it can also serve as an 'emergency' battery. If you have a de-
pleted battery pack on the road or other main battery problems, you'll have
some auxiliary 'juice' to power warning flashers, signals, a trouble-shooting
light, a radio, your CB, or your vibrator. The size of the battery will vary
depending on how much of this you want it to do. If you're going to throw caution to the wind, get a small motorcycle battery just for the instruments.
Unless you can get one used, it might be more expensive than a regular old
car battery or an extra six-volt unit, but it will certainly be a lot lighter.
If you're running very little instrumentation, with a small current drain, a
lantern battery may suffice. You should make provisions to read its voltage;
it would be a shame to have it run down and mess up your readings. After all,
you're getting it just so that won't happen. An extra position on the rotary
switch used to monitor the various pack voltages will take care of checking
this battery's voltage. If it's a rechargable one, make certain that you wire
it in so that it'll get charged with the others.

EQUIPMENT

There are at least four different categories of equipment: legal, safety,
functional, and luxury. In a Detroit machine, it might be difficult to dis-
tinguish among them because they're standard equipment, rather than extras ---
and the automotive electrical system, including battery and generator/alterna-
tor, is capable of handling that power. In an EV, however, you must pidgeon-
hole what you'll install. It may fall into more than one category, but the
predominant one decides. A horn, for instance, falls into two of these areas
--- legal and safety --- so you put it on. Turn signals, however, are required equipment only in Classes 1, 2, and 3 of vehicles; in the remaining vehicle
classes (all motorized bicycles), they are not required. But, safety-wise,
expecially if you're working through some traffic, they'll enhance your chances
of survival. A luxury item is anything that doesn't contribute to the function, safety, or legality of the EV; that's CB radios, radios, cigarette light-
ers, TVs, Quad sound, and pom-poms. If in doubt, ask two questions about the
thing: Does it consume battery power, and does it weigh anything? If it's yes
to either, it's dispensable. It's absurd to spend extra money and time to
prevent 25 watts of power loss in some bus cables by installing larger wire,
and then install and use a cigarette lighter!

Instrumentation (monitor) and controls (operator-type) have been discussed, so
the equipment section covers the general 'what's left?' Keep thinking about
the big four --- legal, safety, functional, and luxury --- for your own situation, and mark them off as we go by. I'll reference to the California Vehicle Codes for MVs (motor vehicles, classes 1, 2, and 3), MBs (motorized bicycles, classes 4, 5, and 6), and BCs (my term for bicycles). Check your own
state's codes for its rulings/laws/wording on the same items. If the code
differs or you can meet it some other way (with other equipment), fine! However, refrain from installing a different item or the right item a different
way without checking first with the DMV or Highway Patrol (or an equivalent
authorized body); what's important is not your interpretation of these codes,
but theirs.

Note: As we go through the various items of equipment or accessories, I'll refer you to the California code section that's applicable. If you'd like, turn to the specific section and look at the fancy wording. The vehicle codes for California that are applicable to electric vehicles are listed in section A of the Cubbyhole in numerical order. So that you can also find the proper code by its subject, I've listed them that way, too. You're getting your money's worth! Oh, for purposes of clarity and to prevent the needless repetition of 'see section so-and-so', I will merely indicate code numbers with a (#) prefix. Example: " . . . require a horn (#27000) but . . ." Got it?

HORN -- All classes of motor vehicles (MVs and MBs) need one of these (#27000) but BCs do not. Surprisingly, the codes don't specify that it be an electrical one. I know of one chap who mounted a squeeze-type kid's air horn on his big motorcycle. It passed inspection! That was original. Also, very funny. And, then, it seemed kind of scary. I mean, can you just imagine the 'tragedy' as some old guy who's hard of hearing steps off a curb into the path of the motorcycle, and that driver's squeezin' that horn like crazy? Maybe it's 'legal', but it's hardly 'safe'. As well, remember that the horn is not on there just for other folks; maybe it's going to get your 'behind' out of trouble sometime.

Electrical horns are a dime-a-dozen (figuratively speaking) at auto salvage yards. Sure, they draw a lot of power, but when you need it, you won't really care if it depletes half your battery capacity. Anyway, it's only for a few seconds, unless you're the type who likes to lean on it, and get about 20 beeps to the mile. But, be careful if you decide to install something other than the electrical horn. An air-horn (compressed-air type), for instance. The code also says, "... but no horn shall emit an unreasonably loud or harsh sound." So, maybe that nearly-deaf old man hears you; but if he has a cardiac arrest, you haven't helped much!

WIPERS -- This applies only to MVs (#26706 and #26707), unless you equip your MB with a windshield (#267000 and #26703), in which case, you might have to install wipers. It probably wouldn't apply if it was a motorcycle-type windshield, but that might only work for a Class 6 vehicle, and leave Classes 4 and 5 having to install wipers. Note that some commerically made EVs (like the CitiCar) have only one windshield wiper, so keep it narrow (the windshield, that is) if you want to try for that chance. Otherwise, if the windshield goes in, you'll have to install two windshield wipers. Volkswagen windshield wiper motor assemblies are good units to work with because they're easily adapted to different situations. With a hacksaw, you can decrease the distance between the wipers for a tight fit. Don't forget the blades!

MIRRORS -- You'll need two for a MV, none for the BC, and it's unclear about the requirement for a MB. That translates to, "you'd better install them." Class 6 will maybe get away without having to have them, but Classes 4 and 5 will get snagged for sure. It's just as well; anyone with a vehicle over a few inches in width would be nuts to drive without them. And that goes especially for EVs. Why? Because most EVs, unless in Class 1, are moving slower than normal traffic. In front, things are moving toward you at a slower rate, meaning that you have time to manuever, brake, decide, etc. But going slowly also means that what's behind you is coming up fast; one of the worst dangers that you face in an EV is being smashed into from the rear. So, you're going to spend a lot of time watching what's happening behind you, relative to the guy who's going so fast that nothing is 'threatening' from behind. And if you've got to be looking in the mirrors often, they should be big ones. If you can cope with the distortion, also get some of those round, convex mirrors installed; if your mirrors are tall and wide enough (see Fig.   ) you can get the stick-on kind, and just add them onto a portion of the mirror.

The codes say that you need two mirrors. One of them has to be on the left side and the other can be located on the right side or in the center of the vehicle. Don't put a plain/convex combination mirror in the center or you'll get busted; they're strictly for the sides.

SPARE TIRE -- Detroit is getting chintzy --- in their late model cars, they're not including a spare tire anymore. Costs too much, I guess. As though it were a luxury! If you are building an EV, don't forget it, or you might not allot room for it. And it's functional and safety-oriented. Functional, because while EVs look light (since they're small), they're not --- and they get flats just like everyone else. Safety, because they get flats in the most god-awful places and you can't just walk away and get some help. Since it's such a must, you might as well use it as packing material to give your EV some 'collapse distance' in the event of a collision. So, put it between you and the weakest side of the frame; it might be just enough to keep someone else's car from 'leaking' into the cab.

There's nothing in the California codes about having a spare tire, but they do have one (#35413) which concerns the proper securing of a spare tire at the front of a vehicle. If they get you for this, they've saved your life; a tire falling off the front of your vehicle while it's in motion is going to cause you to lose control! Oh, and don't forget the tools for changing flat tires! Find a nice, out-of-the-way, yet readily-accessible spot for these.

TURN SIGNALS -- All types of vehicles must have turn signals, but for MBs and BCs, they let you use people-powered ones: your hands! But a MB is wider than a BC, so stick 'em on there; it's not that difficult. You don't have to use them (and have that battery power consumed), but it's nice to have options when it starts getting dark. It'd be safer to use them than not to. Look at the applicable codes (#24951 and #25952); you have to get ones that are approved, so if you know what kind of vehicle you stripped them off of, it'll help. You also have to get the right color of lens in the right place, and the lamps must be mounted within a minimum and maximum distance from the ground. It's not really that much hassle. Fig. 3-33 illustrates a simple wiring diagram using a standard automotive steering column switch. If you don't want to support the auto parts industry, check out the circuit and switches in Fig. 3-34. Remember, anything you install must be kept in operable condition, whether it's required or not.

HEADLITES -- Watch out here! MVs (Classes 1 thru 3) need two headlights (#24400), multiple beams (#24406), proper lighting for the upper and lower beams (#24407), properly-adjusted headlights, properly-working headlights (#24252), a high beam indicator (#24408), taillights (#24600), and a license plate light (#24601). That adds up to a lot of work and a lot of power con-

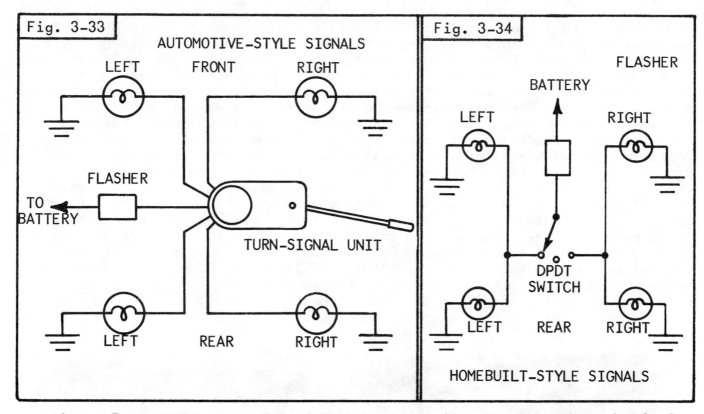

Fig. 3-33

AUTOMOTIVE-STYLE SIGNALS

LEFT   FRONT   RIGHT

FLASHER

TO BATTERY

TURN-SIGNAL UNIT

LEFT   REAR   RIGHT

Fig. 3-34

FLASHER

BATTERY

LEFT   RIGHT

DPDT SWITCH

LEFT   REAR   RIGHT

HOMEBUILT-STYLE SIGNALS

sumption. For a 2HP motor-powered EV, that can add up to as much as half of what the motor current is. Little wonder that you won't find many MVs on the road with a motor horse power less than 2HP; when the lights are on, the motor is starved for power, and the vehicle slows way down.

But ... the MB (Classes 4, 5, and 6) and the BC don't need any of this equipment, unless they're (caught) on the road after darkness (defined in #280). And, if it's desired to mount the equipment for such a contingency, only a single headlamp is necessary (#21201). If this isn't enough light to suit your idea of safety, check into motorcycle headlights (#25651). Besides reflectors (which are discussed below), none of the rest of the equipment listed for MVs is needed. If, however, you install a headlamp, you might as well put in a few taillamps. They don't draw much current. They'll let whoever is coming up on you from behind know that you've got some width (if you install two), and they'll make you a little easier to see. Reflectors are required, sure; but they're only as good as the other guy's headlamps. If he's got one out, and the other's splashed with mud, you're going to get creamed.

As with any other after-darkness lighting you may want to install, just ask yourself this question: "How much time do I plan to spend driving around after dark?" On the one hand, if you install it, it's there for use anytime you need it. You must, however, keep the equipment in good working order and it must be approved equipment. On the other hand, if you don't have the equipment installed, you can't operate during darkness. You might get away with a detachable headlamp if mounted properly, but temporary mountings usually require more design and construction effort than fixed ones. At any rate, the thing you will want (or at least I do) when driving at night is to SEE and BE SEEN.

STOPLAMPS -- You'll need them to be legal in a MV (#24603), but not in a BC or
MB. But they're an easy addition in the MB, particularly if you're going to
install taillights, because you can get a combined unit. Again, you don't
have to use them; a switch on the dashboard can cut them off when you're running around during the day. If you install just brake lights (not taillights),
and you're pulled over by a Highway Patrol unit, they will probably not like
the idea that you can switch them off, and, consequently, defeat the pedal
switch; so, be ready for that contingency. You can explain that you're <u>not</u>
required to have them, but you've installed them for safety reasons and <u>you</u>
<u>are</u> able to demonstrate that they <u>do</u> work when you <u>want</u> them to, but you don't
keep them on <u>all</u> the time because you're battery-powered and it's a drain on
the battery. If you're smug, that explanation will get you nowhere; if you're
unlucky to get someone who's a stickler for the code (which can be interpreted to mean the brake lights go on anytime the brakes are applied), you might
have to explain it to the judge. Or just check that rearview mirror and flip
the switch on when you see Smokey (that's CB lingo for Highway Patrol and not
kosher to use when talking with one). Or, to heck with the switch, and just
have them activated any time you depress the brake pedal. If you don't install brake lights, don't forget to use the handsignals instead!

REFLECTORS -- Every vehicle on the road needs reflectors to be legal: MVs (#24607 and #24609), MBs and BCs (#21201 and #21201.5), and all three --- MV, MB, and BC --- check #25500. In the event of a power blackout, these are all that can save you from imminent destruction on the road, whichever class of vehicle. Get the right colors in the right places and don't get stingy with the size or number you install!

VENT FAN -- This is not a legal requirement for EVs (yet!) but neither is it a luxury item. So, that leaves safety and functional. The vent fan, incidentally, is what I call an electric fan or blower which removes gases and heat from the battery compartment. "What compartment?", you ask. "My batteries get lots of air; they're out in the open!" Okay, ignore this section. Some of us, however, perfer to keep dust, metal objects, and little children's fingers off the batteries. To do this, we stick the batteries away, into the EV's darkened interior. Unfortunately, gases and heat will pocket there. In not wanting to risk explosions or choking hydrogen fumes at 25 MPH, we make sure the compartment is vented, and depend on the movement of air to disperse the heat and gases. However, this type of venting will not disperse the heat and gases from (a) a recently-stopped but heavily-used vehicle, or (b) a recently-charged vehicle. Hence, we install a blower.

The blower fan should be mounted in front of the vehicle (to suck in air and blow it into the battery compartment), and behind a filter (which is removable and cleanable, or replacable) so that dust and other airborne matter is filtered out. Furthermore, we seal the battery compartment so gases cannot escape except through one vent located in the aftmost position of the vehicle. We install two switches to turn on the fan; one is automatically engaged when the vehicle is put in motion (activated by the accelerator pedal linkage) and the other is a manual bypass (a toggle mounted on the dashboard). Or simply wire it on the motor 'side' of the power switch if you don't want to hassle with one more item on the accelerator pedal linkage. But don't forget that manual bypass. We check the fan frequently, or, in some manner or another, assure ourselves of its proper operation at all times. Maybe we do a cockpit check (I'm serious) by switching it on and listening for the wwhhhhrrrrrr or sswwwiiiishshshhhh.

If we want to impress our friends, or 'play' ignorant, we install the fan at the rear of the vehicle, having it suck out the gases and, in effect, suck in outside air through a filter up in front. Upon reaching the fan's motor, a spark is sure to ignite the gases and --- voila --- an Afterburner! Just like the big Jets in the sky. Life expectancy for the blower is approximately 1.3 seconds. And there is the very exciting prospect of blow-back, or flames rushing back into the battery compartment. Warning: The EV god has determined that Death is Hazardous to Your Health.

HEATER FAN -- This is not a legal, safety, or functional thing, but if you live in cold country, it won't really be a luxury, either. For those with 'chopper' or 'voltage tap' controls, sorry! They're too efficient to be of help. But for us poor folks with resistive coils, here's where they start to earn their keep. If specially mounted, the controller can dissipate its heat to the environment normally, but when it's cold, vents can be shut so that heat is confined to the environment of the cab. If a small, normally unused

111

fan is stragically installed, it will send those little wafts of warmth all over your frigid body. Of course, you don't get any heat unless you're underway, and moving slow (so the coils are dissipating power), but it works.

This isn't going to be a lot of heat, but it's not chickenfeed either. If you wanted to increase the heat in the cab, you might have installed a housing for the motor and gearbox, and have their heat vented inward on this special occasion. But, if that seems like a lot of work, then just add a few resistive coils (particularly down by the feet), and, with the flip of a heavy switch, bring them on-line for some real warmth. It wouldn't be difficult to figure out the current drain and how many miles you've just taken off the range for that charge, but maybe you've got it to spare, huh?

If you come out on a cold morning, having left your EV outside, don't be too perturbed if it seems to be 'sluggish' when you start off; this is perfectly normal. When lead-acid batteries get cold, their internal resistance increases enough to prevent normal 'delivery' of the power. This doesn't mean that it's lost any of its capacity; only that it can't deliver it. As soon as some amperes start flowing through the cells, they will warm up. If it's cold, it will take time, but they will warm up! Here's where it would be nice to go out, flip a switch, and start heating the cab with the spare heating coils. In doing so, not only will it be comfy when you're ready to go, but in having to supply current, the batteries will also be 'warming up'.

Don't be tempted to route battery compartment air into the cab. The heat would be nice, and the oxygen from the batteries can be refreshing, but both are inseparable from the hydrogen, and another Hindenburg no one needs!

INTERIOR LIGHT -- Maybe this seems like you're begging for trouble, but rather that than be begging for a trouble lamp. At the worst possible moment, you'll probably find that your flashlight is dead, or mysteriously absent. So, you've got a cab light, but you can't see anything in the control compartment or under the vehicle, etc. Enter the trouble light. This handy-dandy cord and light (safety glass or safety-shielded, right?) plugs right into the charging socket of the EV, and gives you daylight. Whoops, you might have a battery failure, so maybe you don't have juice on that terminal. No matter! Plug it into the 'instrumentation' battery charging socket. Let there be light! Make the cord long so you can carry it around, over, down and under. Have part of it covered, so that it doesn't blind you all the time; put a thumbwheel switch right there near the bulb. Have something to grip on to; if you've got it On for very long, and it's a cold night, it might feel nice, but the smell of burning flesh is not. Have a place to store it where you can reach it groping blindly; that's usually the typical scene when you need it.

BATTERY COMPARTMENT LIGHT -- This is synonymous with having a light under the hood in a car; if you've had the experience of needing to stop at night and do something under the hood, you'll never forget the convenience of a light mounted there. No flashlight to try to set down so that it will shine where you want and not roll away, fall, break, and be lost forever. So, whether you have some troubleshooting to do or just some late-night battery water checks to perform, have a switch and light reserved for the battery compartment. If you live in bitter cold country, make it a substantial wattage bulb, and it can double-up as a battery warmer.

For that matter, don't be afraid to put a little bulb into every compartment you have in your EV; if they're all low-wattage bulbs, you can replace the toggle switch (you'd use for each) with a rotary switch (for them all); this would keep the expense low and keep your control panel from looking like a Cape Kennedy Launch panel. It might be a hassle to add into a Detroit clunker, but don't forget that you are designing and constructing this vehicle and you deserve the very best of everything. Once you've figured out the wiring diagram, it's 'cable-laying time' and one or two extra wires won't matter. Run 'em now; you can decide whether to install the bulb and switch later, as desired.

You don't necessarily need the switches for these lights in the cab or on the control panel; they can be located just inside the compartments. One neat possibility is to install microswitches that 'trip' the light on when the panel or hatch is opened. But there are three things you will want to consider. The first is that a switch's arc can ignite gases, if it's located in or near the battery compartment. Second, if the door or panel opened, the light would be 'On' without your knowing it, which might give you a discharged battery bank if it sat for a few days. And, third, microswitches are expensive!

CHARGING

Some EV owners will have no problem charging their vehicle's batteries when it becomes necessary to do so. Just break out the ole charger, plug one end of it into the EV and the other into the wall socket, and come back tomorrow. Well, it can be just about that simple for any EV owner, but there may not be a handy-dandy wall socket to plug into. But, how about some alternative charging methods for your alternative vehicle? First, we need to know what we need, what's available and from where, how to convert more specialized power into EV power, and some other conveniences we might wish to incorporate into the overall charging scheme.

CHARGING REQUIREMENTS

The EV battery pack will need DC (direct current); AC (alternating current) won't charge batteries. And, depending on what the batteries like to see as a _minimum_ rate of charge, the source must be able to deliver at least that much current. And, if we're wanting to charge the EV in a short period of time, the charging source may have to deliver several multiples of that current. Furthermore, we must consider the voltage of the battery pack itself. The charger will need to produce that much voltage, plus some, if we want the electricity to flow from the charger to the batteries in the first place. And, finally, we must have some way of tapering the rate of charge, so that we don't waste the charging source's energy, overcharge the batteries, or dissociate more battery water than necessary, when the batteries are nearly charged.

Actually, a lead-acid battery can accept a very high initial charging rate.

The only real requirement of the charge rate is that it be one below the rate where the electrolyte begins to gas. However, you would rapidly have to back off this charge rate, to prevent the battery from gassing. A better way is to deliver current at a rate which does not exceed the rated discharge if the battery is rated at a 6- or 8-hour rate. If it's a 20-hour rate, you'd be safe to double the discharge rate as a charge rate. For maximizing the life of each battery, however, you should not charge the batteries at a rate which is <u>less</u> than their discharge rate, except for the taper charge at the end, as the batteries reach full charge. So, we're talking about a charge rate somewhere between 10-50 amps, for batteries that are rated between 200-400 AH with 6-20 hour ratings, and a taper charge rate of 1-10 amps, respectively. Now let's examine some sources of that electricity.

CHARGING SOURCES

Although the AWS (American Wall Socket) will be the source of power for most EV battery packs, there <u>are</u> alternatives. One is the automobile. Yeah, no kidding! Another is a gas-fired standby generator. And then there's that nearby stream, or the wind that blows daily across your land. Let's start with the AWS source first, though.

Utility Charging

If you've got access to utility power for your EV's batteries and have no scruples about using it for your alternative transportation, do it. It's a straightforward process to use the AWS but you will have to convert the 110-120VAC, 60 cycle form of the electricity into whatever voltage you're using in the EV. Since AC won't charge a battery, the first thing you'll need is a rectifier. This is an electronic checkvalve about the size of a boulder marble which converts AC to DC. If your battery pack totalled to 110 volts DC, all you'd need is just a diode (see Fig.3-35). Most EVs, however, will have battery pack voltages between 6-48 volts. There are a few different ways to get that 110 volts down to any of these other voltages, but there's only one efficient way: by using a transformer. I'm sure you've heard the term before. Maybe you've seen one of these up on a utility pole; the wires from your house are probably connected to one. As well, if you were to open up your TV set, or radio, stereo, etc., you'd see an ominous black, lumpy thing. Hark, the transformer! If you want to learn more about this efficient voltage/current converter, you'll have to look it up in an electronics text; we'll be concerned with its ratings rather than its design or theory of operation. Nevertheless, if your voltage requirement is different than what utility supplies to you, you'll use the transformer first (stepping down the voltage) and then the diode (to change the AC to DC). We mustn't put the diode in front of the transformer; transformers work only with AC. If you plug one into DC, you get lotsa smoke!

There are commercially-made battery chargers available (see Sources) which will deliver varying voltages and currents, but you may not find one for your EV's voltage. Or its current requirements. Or at a cost you can afford. With this in mind, I'll describe the essential ingredients so you can build one (see An EV Charger, this chapter). They're not all that difficult; if you mastered the wiring and control system for the EV, this will be a snap. But, if you've

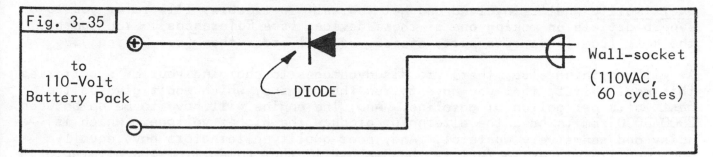

Fig. 3-35

to 110-Volt Battery Pack

DIODE

Wall-socket (110VAC, 60 cycles)

failed miserably to construct even the simplest of Heathkits in your day, read through the section, and armed with the vital information, search out a manufactured unit with those ratings. Good luck. It might be easier to design your EV around a particular charger!

When you get the charger, be sure that it's a constant voltage type unit, and not a constant current unit. Most big chargers are of the first type, but it's what you want, so make sure. That way, when the battery nears its full charge, the charger will automatically taper the charge rate. This assumes, of course, that the battery charger and the batteries are matched. If they're not, you must check them and adjust the rate of charge. Or use a timer. Or connect a voltage sensor in there to disconnect the charger from the batteries once they are nearly charged. There are plenty of electronic watchdogs that can be used to insure a fast and safe charge rate, with the necessary taper charge; which one you use will be the one you can understand and afford.

Automobile Power

Maybe you didn't have an automobile in the first place -- but if you did, and replaced it with the EV, you can still make some use of the car, besides using it as a playhouse, greenhouse, or storage shed. More specifically, if the engine's electrical system used an alternator. When the engine is running, the voltage regulator limits the alternator's output to 14 volts; this way, it can charge the battery without over-charging it, and supply power to the lights, fans, radio, etc., in the car. If you were to bypass the regulator, or disconnect it, the alternator would supply power at much higher wattages and voltages. This is ideal for an EV's battery pack.

There are limitations to the amount of power the alternator will supply, but to give you an idea of what you might expect, let's try an example. Say, the alternator is rated at 55 amps. At 14 volts, that's 770 watts (14 x 55). At 60 volts, (for a 48 volt battery pack) the alternator will still be able to deliver very close to its rated current, 55 amps. So, we'd have 3300 watts. Eddy currents and friction will cause some heating, so we might not be able to get this much power, nor whatever we did get for more than a little while, but we could easily expect that the alternator would deliver half of this wattage continously. But, that's enough.

Here again you can buy kits which will allow you to bypass the alternator's voltage regulator when you need to charge the EV's batteries, but otherwise normally use the automobile, and have an operating electrical system. You'd be amazed at how simple the kit is to make yourself, but just so that you don't

<u>oversimplify</u> what's involved and get yourself in trouble, I'll refer you to a superb article on making one of these devices (see References). You can buy the kits from local auto parts stores, or mail-order them (see Sources).

As with anything else, there are disadvantages to charging your EV's batteries this way. First, that you have to run that engine, which won't give us the best watts per gallon of gasoline. And, the engine will have to be up between 2000-3000 rpm to have the alternator produce the higher voltage. Which is noisy and seems very wasteful. And, poor quality alternators have equally poor quality diodes to rectify the 3-phase AC that comes from the alternator; at higher voltages, they might suffer a 'breakdown' and require replacement. Fortunately, there are alternatives to using the automobile engine to power the automobile alternator.

Standby Generator Power

One way to use the applicable characteristics of the alternator to provide power for the EV's batteries (without all of the disadvantages of using a car engine to do it), is to connect that alternator to a smaller engine. <u>Now</u> you can use the automobile for a greenhouse without fear of disturbing your plants! And you won't waste gasoline, or make a lot of smog and noise. Well, there will be some noise and some smog, but not in the copious amounts you can expect from a car's engine.

One such engine to use for this purpose is a lawnmower engine. While the vertical shaft type of lawnmower engines are more prevalent, you'd have greater success with an engine that has a horizonal shaft. Of course, you wouldn't want to take the alternator out of your present transportation (although you <u>can</u> take it out of the greenhouse car), but alternators are easily obtained from auto wrecking yards. Then, by mounting the alternator and engine on the same stand, you can connect the two together by a V-belt, chain, or gearbelt and suitable pulley sizes (see Fig.3-36). By adding on some monitoring and control devices --- ammeter, voltmeter, field rheostat and toggle, fuses, and an adjustable throttle for the engine --- you're in business. Just add the oil and gasoline, connect the wires, and give a pull on the starter cord.

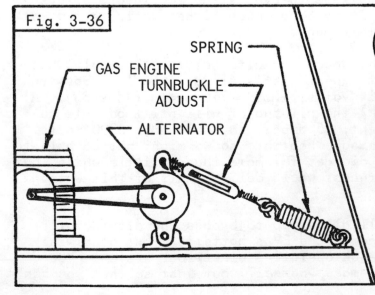

Fig. 3-36

SPRING
GAS ENGINE
TURNBUCKLE
ADJUST
ALTERNATOR

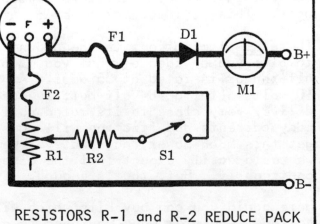

RESISTORS R-1 and R-2 REDUCE PACK VOLTAGE TO PROPER FIELD VOLTAGE RATING FOR THE ALTERNATOR USED.

One of the important considerations when selecting the engine for this standby generator is its rated horsepower. As in the discussion for selecting the EV's motor, you can expect some losses and, if you're wishing to achieve a particular wattage from the alternator, you must figure what engine horsepower rating is required, or be satisfied with what you get. A 50% loss is normal in the alternator, gears, and bearings. So, with every engine horsepower, we can expect only half a horsepower's worth of electrical energy out of the alternator. Or, just 373 watts. A 2HP engine, therefore, will give us 746 watts. For a 48 volt battery pack, that's only a maximum of 12 amps (746 divided by 60 volts). For a 36 volt battery pack, that'd be about 17 amps maximum (746 divided by 44). These current values aren't peanuts, but large AH battery ratings don't like to be charged at low rates. You may, therefore, need to get a larger engine. A 5HP engine-powered alternator will deliver somewhere in the vicinity of 1850 watts. For the 48 volt battery pack, this would supply over 30 amps and for the 36 volt pack, over 42 amps.

If you're inclined to make a standby generator, it's probably because you don't have much of an alternative, having no utility power. But a by-product of building such a device is that it can also be used to charge stationary batteries, and supply your modest habitat with a little electric light, at least. I won't suggest this too strongly, however; most Americans used to be sane in the amount of energy they consumed!

If you don't need to portable-ize this standby generator for charging your EV, there are ways to minimize the noise those little lawnmower engines make. Provided that you install a more efficient muffler, you might consider putting the engine in a box and burying it. Or just insulating the box. After a few chargings, an open-air standby generator with a lawnmower engine gets cursed a lot.

Standby generators can be store-bought (see Sources) but evaluate them carefully for the correct ratings. A 3000 watt standby generator may not deliver more than 25 amps at the voltage you need if it's designed to deliver that wattage at 120 volts. Most of them will probably seem like overkill for your EV's charging needs. But they, too, can be used for other applications, so evaluate them in the light of your whole situation.

Alternative Charging

If you've access to water flow, or have a fair amount of wind across your land, it might be time to think about some alternatives to fossil-fueled chargers. A hydroelectric charger provides an even output, but it must supply at least the minimum amount of power if it's to be utilized. The wind, on the other hand, will be variable in the power that it can supply for EV charging, but it has a higher potential for supplying the wattage requirement, depending on how much wind you experience, how large a machine you have, and how big your EV is. This is one of the sources of energy for our UTLEV (see Chapter 6 - Vehicles). Since we're also using stationary batteries a fossil-fueled standby generator is in the 'background', ready to taper the charge on the stationary batteries should it become necessary to do so. As well, it's available for the EV's batteries. Our windmachine produces voltages in excess of 40 volts, but it's used to charge batteries of varying voltages ranging from 12 to 36 volts, with the EV's pack also at 36 volts. The windmachine's generator is limited to 30 amps output, but this is sufficient for the 180AH batteries used in our EV.

Check the References and Bibliography listings for information on alternative sources of energy. There's nothing particularly new about the idea of using wind energy to power your EV, but it feels great when you're boppin' down the road on wind-watts!

CHARGING STATION

You might consider it a foregone conclusion that the EV's battery charger will be stationary, but I haven't and you shouldn't. There are pros and cons to the decision; let's looksee.

1. If the charging station is stationary, the effective range of the EV is one-half the total range, because before you're halfway through your battery pack's capacity, you must head back. Sort of a 'point of no return', beyond which you have to tow the EV home, or tote the charger to wherever it's stranded.

2. If you're using utility power to charge the EV, you can plug in wherever you go (unless it's up into the forest) by carrying a charger on board. Just because you're using an alternative method for charging the EV (normally) doesn't mean you can't also install another charger for utilizing another source, right? If you've got an on-board, utility-type battery charger, you've got extra weight to carry, which does reduce your effective range.

3. Anything other than a fossil-fueled standby generator charger, and whether it's on-board or not, --- you're outta luck if you run out of juice in the middle of nowhere. So, if you've got a small lawnmower-size engine and alternator charger on board, you're ready to go anywhere, provided that you don't mind waiting for your EV to recharge. A homebuilt standby generator will most often weigh less than stationary standby generators you can buy, but they've got some portable ones nowadays that are pretty light, and they'd tuck away very neatly into an EV.

4. An on-board charger may need to be dissembled so that it fits into the 'leftover' places in the vehicle frame. I say this because it'd be a shame to go out and pay good money for a commercially-built charger, and then have to take it apart to fit in your EV. So, leave room for it, or build your own. Actually, the only difference between commercially-built chargers and homebuilt ones is often said to be that "the homebuilt ones are just a little more spread out."

5. A PASEV will be in greater need of the on-board charger than a UTLEV, which stays around and relatively close to home and the stationary charger unit.

6. If you've an on-board fossil-fueled charger that can deliver at a rate of charge equivalent to the lowest current requirement of the EV's motor, when you do run out of juice, you can start the charger, and proceed along the way. Here, the charger is supplying power to the motor itself, with the excess (if any) going to the batteries.

118

AN EV CHARGER

Fig. 3-37 illustrates a simple charger that you can build for your EV, and Fig. 3-38 illustrates the control panel for it. The most expensive item will be the transformer (T-1), and it may be the hardest to find for your particular EV's voltage. It may be set up to provide one single voltage, but I think you'd be better off to have wiring 'taps' on both the secondary and primary; this will allow you to vary the charge rate, from start of charge to taper. Fig. 3-39 illustrates such a multi-tap transformer.

You can use one, two, or four diodes to rectify the low-voltage AC that comes from the transformer secondary into the required DC. The simplest method is to use a single diode (see Fig. 3-40); this is called a half-wave rectifier. This works well, but it only uses one-half of the transformer's capacity. While it doesn't waste the other half and the single diode is less expensive than several, it is a loss of almost one-half the charging rate you might have if you used two or four diodes. Since highcurrent transformers are expensive, using only part of one's capacity is more 'costly' in terms of the cost/bene-fit ratio than adding the diodes.

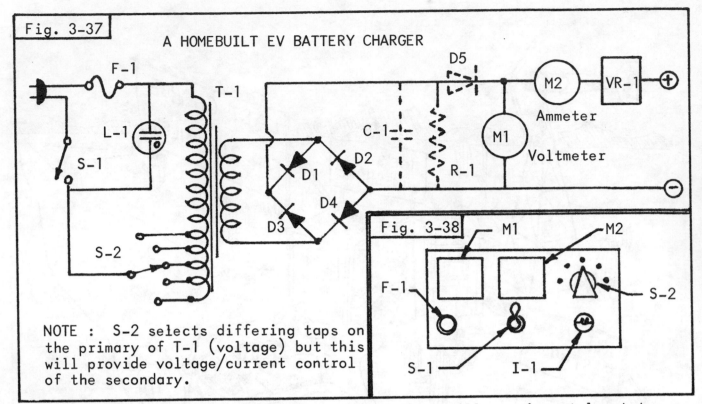

Fig. 3-37

A HOMEBUILT EV BATTERY CHARGER

NOTE : S-2 selects differing taps on the primary of T-1 (voltage) but this will provide voltage/current control of the secondary.

Fig. 3-38

Using both portions of the transformer's waveform will require at least two diodes (see Fig. 3-41); this is a full-wave rectifier, and it's used only if your transformer has a center-tap which can form the negative size of the circuit, and if the transformer is not used with multi-taps in the secondary. The best arrangement is to use four diodes and arrange them as a full-bridge rectifier (see Fig. 3-42). This gives the most from the transformer's design capacity and assures the highest rate of charge for the batteries. It is used with multi-tap secondaries, no center-tap secondaries, and ungrounded center-tap secondary transformers.

The diodes used in the charger must be rated for twice the expected current from the charger, or the next available value above that amount. A 20-amp charger, then, will have 40-amp diodes. You will also need to select a voltage rating, called the PIV (peak inverse voltage) and I recommend that it be twice the value of the unloaded voltage from the charger, or more. If you can't find a diode with the amp rating that you need, find two that add to more than that value, and parallel them. If you can't find a diode with the PIV value you need, get two that add to more than that value, and series them.

Diodes dissipate some energy or, in laypersons's terms, get hot. So, help them dissipate the heat; buy heatsinks. These are multifinned aluminum affairs to which to diodes are mounted; with a liberal application of heat-transfer cement you have effectively increased the thermal surface area of the diode. Or, rather, it stays cool. If you've got some thin metal in the EV in the proximity of where you'll mount the charger's diodes, these can serve the same function. But, the bond must be only a thermal one; if it's an electrical connection, the diodes will be shorted out, and won't do their job. So, how do you get a thermal, but not an electrical, connection? By using mica insulators designed for the job; get them with your diodes!

120

The capacitor, C1, is optional. Capacitors smooth out the pulsating DC and are needed wherever a ripple-free DC current is required. That doesn't really apply to batteries, but you can put one in there. Get one that's a few thousand microfarads (more than 1000MFD) and with a voltage at least twice what you expect the charger to supply with no load. If you install a capacitor, you must install a resistor, R1, to 'bleed' the capacitor of its charge so that it

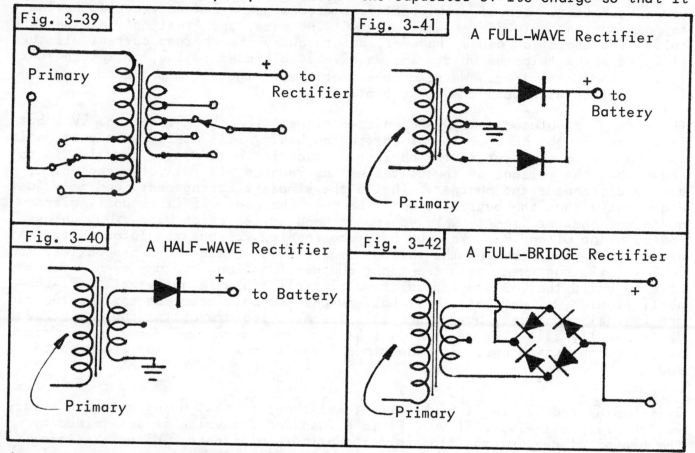

Fig. 3-39 — Primary — to Rectifier +

Fig. 3-41 — A FULL-WAVE Rectifier — to Battery + — Primary

Fig. 3-40 — A HALF-WAVE Rectifier — to Battery + — Primary

Fig. 3-42 — A FULL-BRIDGE Rectifier — + — Primary

doesn't rise to too high a voltage in use, and doesn't carry a 'shocking' charge after the charger is off. Its resistance value (in ohms) and its wattage rating (in watts) is determined by the current capacity of the charger; check with a power supply design manual for finding these two values. Or don't bother installing C1 or R1 at all!

It'd be smart to install a few meters (M1, M2, or both) to monitor the charging process. Connect them as shown (see Fig.3-37). Their values are determined in the same manner I described for the ammeter and voltmeter in the EV monitoring system (see Monitor, this chapter). A clever design would use the same meters for registering both monitor and charging. This would save duplication of equipment, and provide for on-board charging monitor irrespective of whether the charger itself was on-board.

If you do install C1 and R1, you should install an isolation diode. In appearance it is no different than the other diodes that you might use, but it serves a different function than rectifying the AC from the transformer; it 'isolates' the battery pack voltage from C1. This is important; when you connect the charger to the batteries, you won't get a flash as the battery pack

121

'charges' the capacitor. As well, should you inadvertently reverse the battery leads, you won't get a rush of current, either. And, if you install the charger on-board the EV, you can leave the charger connected to the battery pack; the isolation diode will insure that no current flows from the batteries into any part of the charger circuit. The value of the isolation diode should be at least twice the charger's peak current capacity, and four times that would be better. You see, the rectifier diodes get a 50% duty-cycle, having to pass current only for one-half the AC sine wave, and 'resting' for the other half. The isolation diode, however, has to carry the charger current all the time; it works twice as hard. So, we give it a higher rating, to insure that it can handle the load. We also make double-sure that it has a good heat-sink, able to dissipate the waste heat!

The voltage regulator, VR1, is connected between the charger and the EV's battery pack; if the charger is not carried on-board, it's pretty much your decision whether to mount it in the charger unit or in the EV. Its function is to sense when the voltage of the batteries has reached its full, charged value, and to disconnect the charger. That's the simplest arrangement, and it's just a guarantee that the batteries won't be over-charged. If it actually disconnects the charger from the EV, you won't need an isolation diode, D5, unless you're using C1 and R1. You can add more complex voltage regulator units. A nice feature would be for the voltage regulator to detect when the battery is 80-90% full, and then begin the taper charger function. In any event, you may have to build the voltage regulator you install; they're not exactly off-the-shelf items. Or, not yet. Most battery-charger manufacturers may incorporate one in their chargers, but, since it's the main feature of the charger, they don't usually sell them separately. That doesn't mean they don't or won't or that you can't find one. It means that I don't know of any to recommend to you.

Switches S1 and S2 aren't high current switches, so most any toggle and rotary switch, respectively, will do. F1 is a fuse and its value is determined by the amount of current the transformer's primary will need. Without getting heavily into transformer ratings, we can generalize the situation by saying that, if the secondary winding's voltage is smaller, i.e., you're plugged into 120VAC (primary) and you've got a 48-volt battery bank in your EV, you'll need as much as 60 volts in the secondary, right? So, the ratio of primary to secondary voltages is 120 to 60, or 2 to 1, right? The way transformers work is that if they step 'down' the voltage, they automatically step 'up' the current capacity. So, if we deliver 40 amps to the batteries, we only draw 20 amps on the primary. If this seems strange, go back and read this over again. It might seem that we're getting something for nothing, but it's not true. Any electronics or electrical book will tell you that one way to find power (in watts) is to multiply voltage times amperage. So, 120 volts times 20 amps is 2400 watts; that's the primary. And 60 volts times 40 amps is also 2400 watts; that's the secondary. Same, same. We've neither created nor destroyed energy. We're clean!

Finding the needed value of F1 becomes a matter of figuring the ratio of voltage in the primary to voltage in the secondary, and then dividing the secondary's current rating by that value. If the secondary voltage is less than the primary, the current in the primary must be less than the secondary. Doublecheck your calculations by multiplying each side, as I did. Increase the primary current's value by at least 50% but no more than 100%, and that's the fuse's rating. Make the fuse the slo-blo type if its value is close to the normal current flow in the primary, or if it's double that value, make it a fast-blo.

Indicator, Il, is just an indicator light which is On whenever the charger is plugged in and operating, which is helpful if you've got a blown fuse, and don't know it. Or, it lets you know that juice is getting to the transformer, which it might not if you've plugged into a wall socket that doesn't have juice to it.

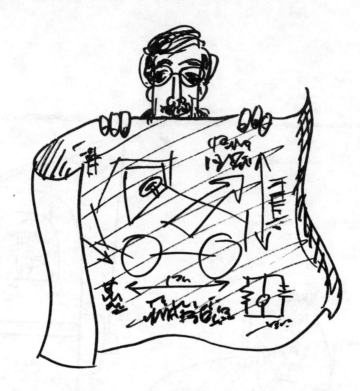

4 FRAME WORKS

The expression 'frame works' means a lot more to me than framework; it's also steering, suspension, wheels and tires, and brakes. And it's where you put the batteries, motor, and drivetrain. If you've planned ahead and properly arranged all of these different systems, it also means that you'll have a comfortable, roomy place for yourself and a passenger. Or, in a UTLEV, room for the cargo. And, when everything and everyone is tucked away, we 'skin' it with fiberglas, wood, plastic, or metal, and refer to it by an affectionate name, because it's part of the family.

But, whoa, let's go back and look again at the constituent parts. Slower, and in more detail. Steering is first.

STEERING

If your EV will have two wheels, you've plenty of bicycles and motorcycles to look at. I'll concern myself, therefore, with three- or four-wheel designs.

Fig. 4-1 illustrates the most basic wheel patterns for three- and four-wheelers. Six ways to steer your EV. And three of them will kill you! Or try their darndest to. Or wreck the vehicle. Can you figure which ones? Well, I won't leave you wondering; they're B, D, and F. Note that they're all rear-wheel steering types. Hence, it should not be difficult to remember that you only want to use a front-steering wheel.

Author's Note: The trouble with homebuilt versions of an EV is that some folks can't help but try to make the thing look really different from an automobile, or similar to the most streamlined, expensive cars. But, when you're doing it on your own, there are a few reasons to move slowly when exploring the possibilities of a new design. One is that you're traveling into unknown territory; blind-alleys, obstacles, and pit-falls await you. What you should realize is that others have traveled that path before you and there is usually a very good reason, if not several, for the design of cars used on today's highways. Sure, there's a generous portion of 'trend' and 'in' and 'new innovations', but beneath the body styling is the basic type of something which changes little, if at all. There are a number of reasons for front-wheel steering and rear-wheel drive; the problem of control is only one of them. If you've driven a car in reverse and noted the sharp veering that occurs when you cranked the steering wheel over (to turn), you'd understand the difficulty in controlling a vehicle with rear-steering. It's a whole lot to do with caster, camber, and moments of inertia, and it spells trouble for the unwary. It is possible to 'roll' a

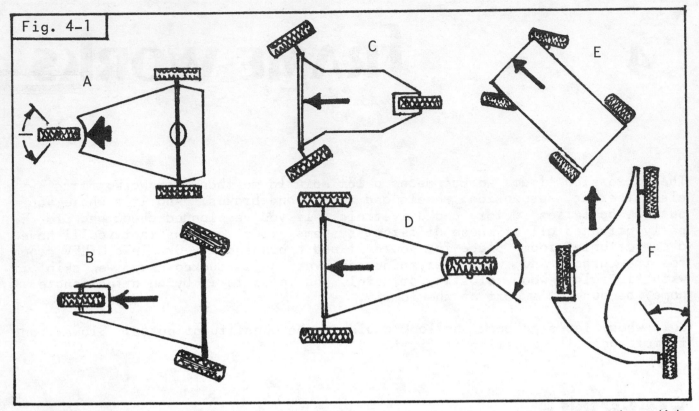

Fig. 4-1

car in a forward direction, with sufficient speed and steering angle, but did you know that you can roll the same car at about 10mph in reverse? Don't experiment to substantiate this, please! End of note.

Okay, three gone and three to go. One or two wheels to steer and one or two wheels for 'drive'. Which you'll choose depends on which class you can or will make, and meet requirements for. But let's first look at single-wheel steering.

SINGLE-WHEEL STEERING

Single-wheel steering is a simple affair if you do it bicycle-style. That is, you give it lots of caster, (see Fig. 4-2). This is what allows you, when riding a bicycle, to do the "look, ma, no hands!" bit. It's also referred to as "automatic steering". What happens is that when you turn the wheel, the front of the bicycle is lifted a small amount. Then, when you let go, it wants to fall back into the straight-ahead direction. That's not the only way you can arrange a single wheel; I've seen a lot of industrial trucks which use the true caster effect in single-steer wheels (see Fig. 4-3). In this arrangement the wheel is pulled, not pushed. For low speeds this is fine, but I wouldn't attempt this in a high speed PASEV myself!

TWIN-WHEEL STEERING

If you're contemplating a four-wheeled vehicle or a three-wheeler with two wheels to steer by, it doesn't have to be much more complicated than a downhill racer if it's a UTLEV that you intend to operate around the farm. You won't want to use the so-called 'bogey' wheel setup (see Fig. 4-4) for either, however; that's reserved for haywagons, your kid's little red wagon, or other drawn vehicles. But, if you're going to have something over 10mph and street-

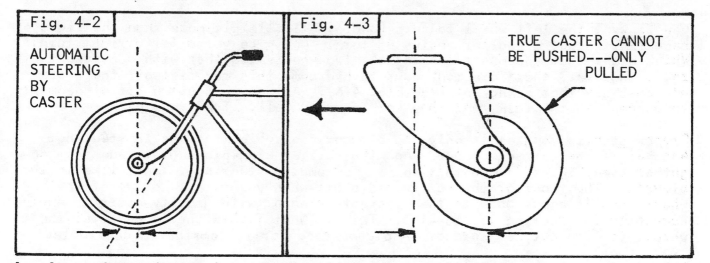

Fig. 4-2

AUTOMATIC
STEERING
BY
CASTER

Fig. 4-3

TRUE CASTER CANNOT
BE PUSHED---ONLY
PULLED

legal, you're going to have to do a bit of homework. I'll give you the basics,
but you shouldn't build it from just what I'll be telling you in the next few
pages. This is only meant to be an introduction to what's involved; have a
healthy respect for the relative complexity or involvement that the subject of
steering commands. It's my way of saying, "get something that's already designed" (off a used car, from a wrecking yard, etc.). If you really must build
it yourself, get one of the texts from the library on the subject and read it
carefully!

All right, some basic twin-wheel steering stuff. Two wheels are turning, right?
Both the same amount, right? Wrong! If you're turning left (see Fig. 4-5),

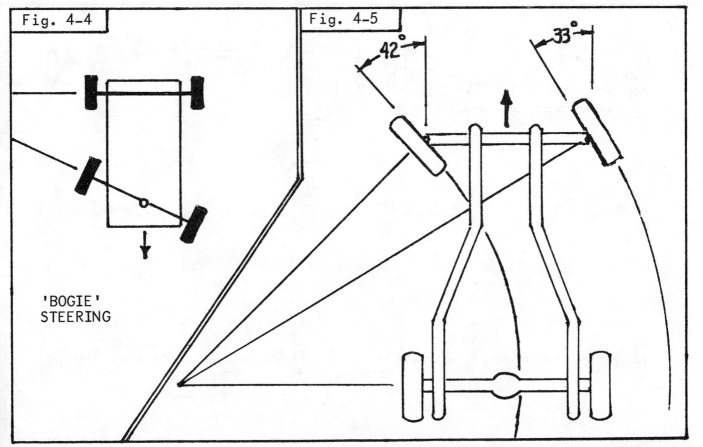

Fig. 4-4

'BOGIE'
STEERING

Fig. 4-5

42°

33°

you'll want the left wheel to turn (angle) a little bit more than the right one, because it's got a smaller radius of turn. And vice versa for a right turn. Which means that you don't connect the two wheels together with a straight 'tie-rod'. However, there are many ways to overcome this requirement; there are at least six that I know of (see Fig. 4-6). All of them use a bit of geometry to accomplish the task, and they work equally well. Take your pick.

Proper steering angles is only one of many desirable features in steering. Another is the correct camber. And the correct king-pin angle. Add them to-gether (see Fig. 4-7) and this spells 'automatic steering'. Just like in the bicycle. The front of the car raises a bit when you turn. Let go of the wheel, and it comes back to the straight-forward, with gravity-assist. Another necessity in steering is 'toe-in'. This is what fights the tendency of the wheels to turn out, or spread. A pigeon-toed car is considered desirable.

There are other terms you'll come into contact with in your pursuit of steer--ing knowledge: point of intersection, toe-out, pitman arm, drag link, tie-rod, relay rod, idler arm, adjustment sleeve, steering knuckle (and its angle), kingpin, etc. When you finally understand what they mean, where they go, and what they do, you're ready to design your own steering. The whole idea in steering is to maintain a slip-free traction with the road, under varying road and weather conditions, whether you're accelerating or braking.

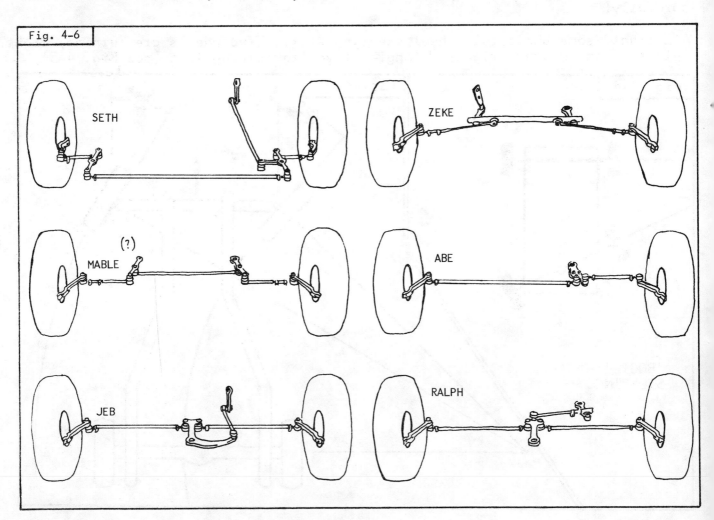

Fig. 4-6

SETH

ZEKE

MABLE (?)

ABE

JEB

RALPH

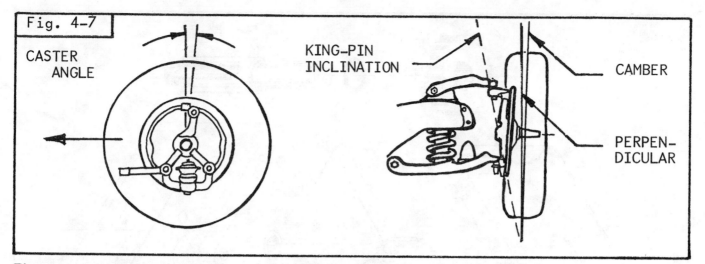

Fig. 4-7

CASTER ANGLE

KING-PIN INCLINATION

CAMBER

PERPEN-DICULAR

The steering wheel is the operator control that permits turning the vehicle's wheel(s). Sometimes it's round (like in cars) and sometimes it's just a tiller-type affair. Whichever, it's also a lever arm. As well, it may turn around several times for just ten degrees of steer-angle at the wheels. There may be a small gearbox that the steering wheel is attached to, which increases the mechanical advantage. This gives you the ability to overcome 40 pounds worth of wheel resistance (when the vehicle is parked) with only, say, 5 pounds of force on the steering wheel. As well, the steering (gear) box translates the rotary motion of the steering wheel into the back-and-forth movement necessary to turn the wheel. The mechanical advantage also works for you in reverse; when you hit a bump in the road that exerts, say 5 pounds of deflection to the wheel, only a small portion of that reaches you. For our previous example (5 to 40), this amounts to 1/8th of 5 pounds, or (a quick punching of the calculator), 0.625 pounds. Easy enough to handle. We've used an 8-to-1 ratio in our example; for most cars on the road today, 20-to-1 is common. The higher the ratio, the more times you will need to rotate your steering wheel to affect the same steering angle. Trucks have steering wheels which requires more turns 'lock to lock' than passenger cars. VWs have less. If you've got a tiller attached to your single-wheel steering system, it may be one-to-one. You can extend the length of the lever arm, but then you get into a funny place with needing a lot of room to swing the tiller. There's a way to get around this (see Fig. 4-8) but, alas, it's just a gearbox in disguise of the tiller.

SUSPENSION

The function of the suspension system is to 'suspend' the vehicle, carrying its weight, and that of the driver, passengers, and load. There's front suspension and rear suspension, each carrying its share of the weight, but different in type because each does a different job. The front suspension must allow for unrestricted motion of the steering, irrespective of terrain; should there be interference under rough conditions, you'd be in real trouble. The rear suspension must deal with rear-end torque movements (during acceleration) and help keep the vehicle level, particularly if a straight-axle, differential-type drive is being used. But let's consider some types of sus-

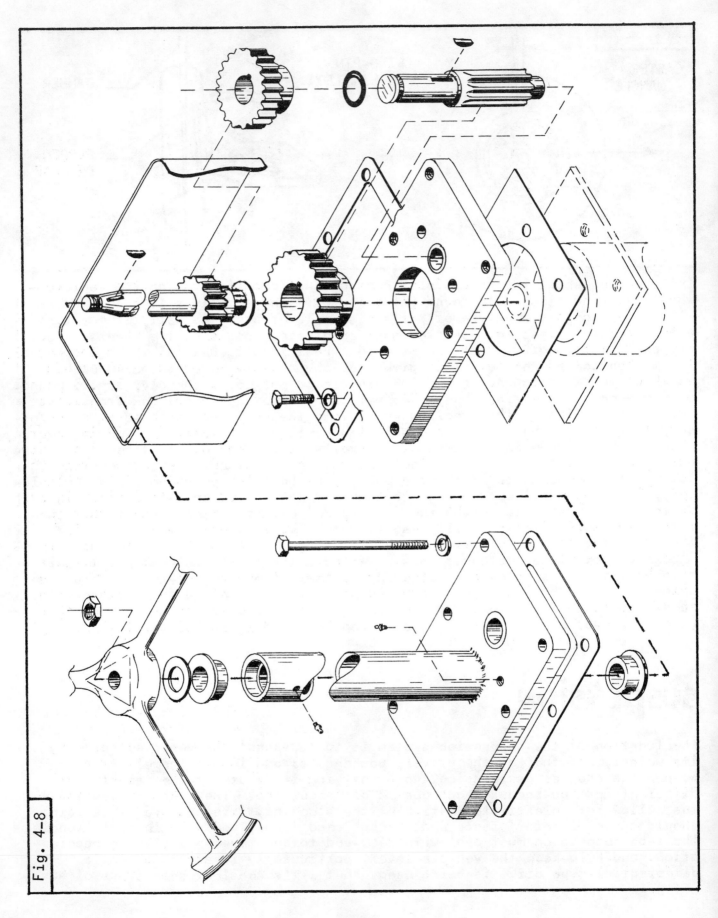

Fig. 4-8

130

pension before we choose one of them for the front or rear. There are leaf springs, coil springs, and torsion bars, but I'll only deal with the first two.

LEAF SPRINGS

This is the first type of suspension that was used when man went mobile. Exceptin' fanny fat, maybe. Anyway, leaf springs made of spring steel are used to connect the axle to the vehicle frame (see Fig. 4-9). Like the name implies, they 'spring', absorbing what the wheel's reaction to surface irregularities won't (the tire will distort to absorb this, too). They're elastic, so once pushed or pulled in a given direction, they will try to return to where they were. An undesirable effect of this is that they go <u>past</u> the original position and then recoil, much like a pendulum. But there are ways of dealing with that, as we shall soon see.

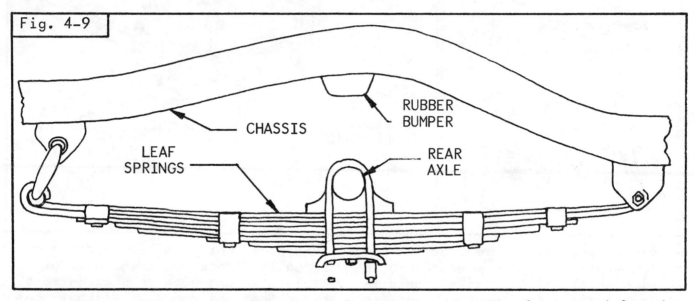

Fig. 4-9

CHASSIS

RUBBER BUMPER

LEAF SPRINGS

REAR AXLE

Leaf springs come in long, flat bars of spring steel. The fewer used for the job and the longer they are, the more the spring action and the 'softer' the spring. Put on more, or decrease the length of the ones you use, they get 'stiffer'. Too soft, you get seasick; too stiff, and you develop callouses on your behind.

COIL SPRINGS

Coil springs are a more recent type of spring, and used extensively in cars now, particularly in the front suspension (see Fig. 4-10). Whereas leaf springs absorb shock by bending, coil springs do it by compressing. Coil springs are made from spring steel rod which is formed in coils, and tempered (heat-treated) for the proper amount of spring. The kind that you'll find in the retractable ball point of your pen is a softie; automotive suspension springs are thick, short, and stiff.

Like the leaf spring, which is secured on flexible joints to the frame, coil springs must be limited in their travel. That is, if your front right wheel went into a chuckhole, the spring might pop out, and then where would you be?

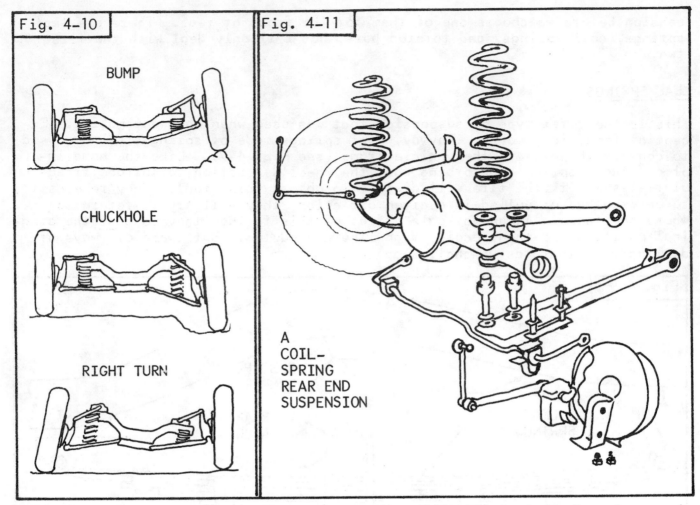

Fig. 4-10

BUMP

CHUCKHOLE

RIGHT TURN

Fig. 4-11

A COIL-SPRING REAR END SUSPENSION

Retainers and guides are used to hold it in place. For both leaf springs and coil springs, rubber bumpers are often used on the frame where the axle or wheel assembly might strike should the vehicle's weight come down exceptionally hard; this is the pronounced experience called 'bottoming out'. Without that little backup, the axle (or something) would break for sure.

COIL OR LEAF SPRINGS

Excepting four-wheel drive, or other straight-axle front end systems which will use the leaf spring, most vehicles today use the independent front suspension (see Fig. 4-10) and, necessarily, a coil spring. Rear end suspension is usually leaf springs for straight axle and differential (see Fig. 4-9), although coil springs can be used (see Fig. 4-11). Independent rear suspension will use coil springs or torsion bars, with equal popularity. If you're home-building these systems for you EV, you'll find it easier to work with the leaf springs than with coil springs or torsion bars. You can add or subtract leaf spring sections as use dictates, whereas with the other, you may need to replace the assembly should your initial design prove unsatisfactory.

SHOCK ABSORBERS

Springs by themselves --- whether coil, leaf, or torsion bar --- are elastic, and must do something with the energy that they're continuously absorbing. So,

they do. Boing, boing, boing, boing, boing. Remember, they have elastic
memory, only they just can't seem to stop at the right place. And, if you
make them stiffer, they won't do it a whole lot less, and now traveling is a
bone-jarring experience. Enter the shock absorber. This is almost a misnomer;
'spring dampener' would be better. Because that's what they do. But they do
it by taking out of the spring what made it 'boing' (compress) in the first
place: some kind of shock.

With a properly-mounted shock absorber, the spring still takes the initial
shock. It flexes fast, so the shock does not travel through the frame and,
ultimately, your body. But, when the spring (leaf or coil) starts to return, the shock absorber comes into action, slowing down this motion, absorbing the shock, and dampening the spring. So, the spring only goes past its
original position a little bit, and quickly settles down. Shock absorbers
serve other purposes too. Like, absorbing lateral as well as vertical motion
(if they're mounted to do so). They also help to reduce body sway, dampening
the jerky movements of an amateur or poor driver. This not only makes for a
more comfortable ride, but a safer one, too; steering control is greatly affected by good 'shocks'.

How do shock absorbers do what they do? They're cylinders filled with a
fluid (normally a light oil). There are two chambers and a small check-valve
in between them. In one direction, they pass the oil very easily, limited
only by the size of the hole in the check-valve (during the compression stroke,
or upward movement). But, when the spring starts to come back and the shock

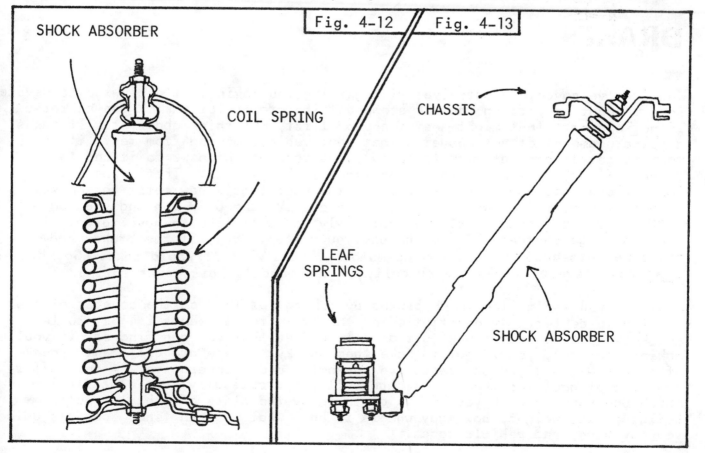

SHOCK ABSORBER

Fig. 4-12   Fig. 4-13

COIL SPRING

CHASSIS

LEAF
SPRINGS

SHOCK ABSORBER

absorber is pulled apart, the check-valve comes into action, and the oil is forced to go back into the cylinder through a much smaller hole. It's under pressure, so the oil and shock absorber get hot when this happens. And <u>that</u> is where the energy goes. Good workin' shocks get hot, and dissipate the heat into the environment. Yep, another source of heat pollution in cars; I wonder if anyone has calculated how much?

There are, by the way, double-acting shock absorbers; they restrict motion in both directions, providing a much stronger dampening effect. That's the heavy duty kind. In a lightweight PASEV, a soft spring and a good shock absorber will make for a comfy ride. In the UTLEV, get beefy springs and good shocks, or medium spring and double-acting shocks. And, don't forget to allow for the one-in-a-thousand chance that you'll bottom the vehicle at some point. Get rubber bottom bumpers.

In rear suspension, the shock absorbers are mounted at an angle (see Fig. 4-12). While even vertically-mounted shock absorbers will reduce body sway, these angle-mounted shocks really minimize lateral motion. Don't get them at too much of an angle, though; their spring dampening capability will be weakened. For front suspension with leaf springs, they'll also be mounted at an angle, but more vertical than lateral. If you've independent suspension in front and it's using coil springs, you'll probably find the shock absorbers mounted inside the coil spring (see Fig. 4-13) but they're occasionally alongside the springs, also.

brakes

While we've concerned ourselves with getting you moving, it'd be wise to devote some thought to getting your EV stopped. The brakes for the EV can be rated in horsepower. That might seem funny at first, but think about it. It takes a certain amount of horsepower to get your vehicle moving from rest; if we want to get it back at rest (stopped), the rate at which we do it and the amount of work done can also be described in horsepower. That's where the term 'brake-horsepower' comes from, by the way; that's how motor horsepower is determined. If we were to accelerate our EV from 0-30 mph and you had a kid run out in front of you, you certainly wouldn't like to have to wait 10 seconds or go another 220 feet before you'd stop. But, if the brakes had the same horsepower rating as the motor, that's what it would take. So, brakes <u>must</u> have several times the capacity of the motor's horsepower rating.

However, you won't find 15 HP brakes by asking for them at the counter of the local auto center. My description of the brake requirements is just to let you know that you can't use just any ole brakes that you can find or, if you're making your own, you've got to make them Chunky. There are different types of brakes --- drum, disc, resistive, dynamic, and regenerative --- and different ways of applying them --- mechanically, hydraulically, and electrically. Which one you use with your EV is dictated by the class of vehicle you're building, its weight, how many wheels it has, what you can find, some prejudices you may have, and vehicle codes.

If your farm is the only place your EV will be operated, for all the vehicle codes care, you can press a stick against the wheel, or throw a rock (secured by a rope attached to the frame) out the back. Take it on the streets, though, and that's not enough. Codes 26301.5, 26311, 26450 --- 26454, 26456, and 26457 spell it out. Here's the synopsis of all that information:

1. You must have service brakes on all wheels.
2. You need service brakes that will stop your vehicle in 25 feet from 20 miles per hour. If you can swing getting into the exempt class, you will need to stop in 32 feet from 15 mph, or not operate at a speed higher than one from which you can stop in 32 feet.
3. The service brake system, if hydraulic, must be rendered only partially inactive if any single portion of the system, other than master cylinder, wheel assembly, or drum assembly, fails. Manufacturers today meet this requirement through the use of a dual-master cylinder. With this setup, the front wheels are isolated from the rear wheels; a failure in either will leave the other still operative. Without it, it's 'four-wheels-and-no-brakes' time with a single-component failure.
4. A separately-applied parking brake must be installed in addition to the service-braking system. It _may_ activate the same brakes, but must be so engineered that it does not interfere with the service brakes, and, yet, it will stop the vehicle if required to do so.
5. The service brakes should be pedal-applied. The parking brake may be pedal-applied as long as it is not the same pedal as that used for the service brakes. Or, the parking brake may be applied by muscular effort, springs, or electrically.

Well, if you're still somewhat confused, you should be. The term 'service brake' is not really defined in its usage. And, at only one point is there a mention of its being pedal-operated. But it should be sufficient to say that you're going to play hell trying to brake a vehicle via a handbrake when you need both hands on the wheel. Motorbikes solved this problem (partially) by installing the brake lever on the handlebar. Service brakes, therefore, should be pedal-operated. This applies to all classes of vehicles excepting (perhaps) Class 5 or 6.

Before we consider some possible combinations to minimize the hardware we'll need to have a safe and serviceable brake system, and still meet the codes, let's look at the different types of brakes. There are four in all, if we leave out the rope-and-rock trick: drum, disc, resistive, and dynamic.

DRUM BRAKES

This is one of the older types, but you'll find that most vehicles today use the drum brake. That's because it's been around a long time, it's pretty good, they've got a lot of parts stocked for the wearable portions of drum-type brakes, and they're fairly simple mechanisms (see Fig. 4-14). The service brake portion of the drum brake is usually hydraulically-operated. When you trounce on the brake pedal, you pressurize some hydraulic lines and, at each wheel, brake shoes are forced against the inner drum wall. The resistive surface of the brake shoe (much like the clutch plate) against the steel drum wall gives us heat, which is where the vehicle's inertia goes as we stop.

If you go shopping for drum brakes, get the single-tailing kind. This means

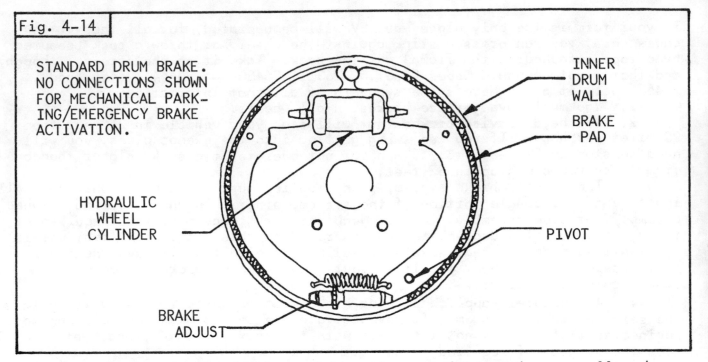

Fig. 4-14

STANDARD DRUM BRAKE.
NO CONNECTIONS SHOWN
FOR MECHANICAL PARK-
ING/EMERGENCY BRAKE
ACTIVATION.

INNER
DRUM
WALL

BRAKE
PAD

HYDRAULIC
WHEEL
CYLINDER

PIVOT

BRAKE
ADJUST

that there is one wheel cylinder and it pushes on the two shoes equally; depending on which direction the wheel's rotating (whether you're in forward or
reverse), only one of the two brake shoes is truly 'active'. Sure, you've
got only half the braking power at each wheel compared to what you might have,
but you've got good brakes then in <u>both</u> directions. Other type of drum brakes
--- double-tailing included --- will give you better brakes in the most frequently traveled direction (forward) but, in reverse, you've got nothing to effectively stop you. The single-tailing kind of brakes are easy to identify; they
have only one wheel cylinder!

The parking brake for the drum-type brakes is an activation of only the rear
brakes in the vehicle. This is a mechanical linkage, which is pulled taut by
steel cables when you apply the parking brake. As it applies the same brakes
that the hydraulic lines operate, it must be designed for the parking brake
hookup without interference to the functioning of the service brakes. There
is nothing in the codes that specifies that the rear brakes must be activated
by a parking or 'emergency' brake, but if you intend to do it, and you get
front wheel assemblies which have no provisions for a mechanical brake attach-
ment, you're going to be a mite irritated when you try to connect the parking
brake!

DISC-TYPE BRAKES

Disc-type brakes are the newer class of brakes, and they're designed for larger
and faster vehicles because they have better over-all braking performance than
drum-type brakes. This is due primarily to their greater cooling capacity;
under heavy use, drum-type brakes 'fade' (the drums and shoes getting so hot
that effective braking is reduced). When a vehicle is braked, most of its
weight shifts to the front wheels. And that's where you'll want to have super-
good, heavy-duty brakes. It's one reason that newer cars have disc brakes on
the front only. If they put them on the back, too, your back wheels would
be forever locking up when you braked; remember that whatever weight is shift-

ed forward is shifted from the back, so there's less traction on the rear wheels and they'll lock easier.

There may not be a parking brake adaptor on the standard disc brakes you find, so look for it, if you expect to incorporate it in a system other than just service brakes. Even if you can't find that feature in car disc brakes, realize that motorcycles nowadays use them, and they're mechanically activated. Good luck!

RESISTIVE BRAKES

Actually, drum and disc brakes would be included in this category, except that I specifically wanted to mention the type of brakes used on bicycles, and couldn't figure out what else to call them. When you operate the hand-brake on a bicycle, a pincer-type motion brings two separate rubber 'shoes' into contact with both sides of the bicycle wheel's rim. Great for bicycle and rider alike. Add a motor and a couple of batteries, and it might not be so hot a braking system. Warning to Class 5 and 6 EVs: What works for 200 pounds of bicycle and rider may not stop a 450-pound converted-bicycle EV. Or, at least, don't assume it will!

DYNAMIC AND REGENERATIVE BRAKING

Dynamic and regenerative braking systems are confined to vehicles using some kind of electrical motor. A similar method of braking without hitting the brake pedal is used in internal-combustion engine'd cars; this is 'compressive' braking and stems from the characteristics of the engine itself (it slows itself down when the accelerator pedal is let up). Because of the relative complexity or impracticality of regenerative braking, few individuals may be able to use this form of braking. Dynamic braking, however, is quite feasible for most electric vehicles, and it's fortunate that it is; I predict that the vehicle codes will eventually (if not immediately) require it in electric vehicles. Why? The codes are very specifically against 'coasting' a vehicle, but there are 'efficiency' reasons for doing it in an electric vehicle. Which will win out remains to be seen but, until the laws come into effect, it will only be local jurisdiction that can require the use of dynamic braking any time the accelerator pedal is not depressed. Both dynamic and regenerative braking are extensively covered in the Control section of Chapter 3 (Practical Control Circuits and Special Circuits subsections).

APPLYING BRAKES

Disc and drum brakes are applied hydraulically, although they could be activated mechanically. Resistive brakes (bicycle type) are always mechanically-applied. Regenerative and dynamic brakes are electrically-applied. The codes don't specify hydraulic brakes for EVs or any other vehicles, but you can't beat the hydraulic system for pure braking power, so don't balk at the idea of using one.

There are lots of master cylinders to be had, steel brake lines can be had by stripping them from junked cars, and flexible fittings for the steered-wheel brake connections are just as readily available.

AN EV BRAKING SYSTEM

To get the most from the least, and still abide by the codes, first check your state's codes to see if there are any appreciable differences from the California vehicle codes. If not, here's one possible system:

A. For a three-wheeled, single rear wheel drive EV:
1. Install hydraulic, drum-type brakes on all three wheels.
2. Using a dual master cylinder, separate the front and rear brakes. This meets the hydraulic brake specification (partial brakes with component failure) and the emergency brake requirements.
3. Install a ratchet mechanical brake, using the drum-type brake assembly of the front or rear wheel(s) for connection; or install a band brake on the drivetrain (if possible) on the wheel's side of the gearbox. This brake will serve as a parking brake and a secondary emergency brake.

B. For the same vehicle another system is:
1. Install hydraulic, drum-type wheels and brakes on the front only. Install a mechanically-activated drum or disc brake on the single rear wheel.
2. Install a single master cylinder for activating the front brakes (as service brakes) and install linkage for normal application of the rear brake as well. Should some part of the hydraulic system fail, you're still left with a pedal-operated, mechanical brake on the rear wheel.
3. Install a standard ratchet hand-pulled parking brake to also engage the rear brake.

C. Still another system for the same type of vehicle:
1. Install mechanical, pedal-activated drum or disc brakes for each wheel.
2. Install a hand-pulled ratchet parking brake with mechanical linkage to one or more of those wheels (see Fig. 4-15 for non-interfering linkages).

There are other combinations which will be just as good, and quite possibly legal. But whichever method you finally decide upon should be checked with the vehicle codes. If the authorities get the feeling that you're trying to put one over on them, they may rule against you. That's no great loss, unless you've built the vehicle and installed the proposed system in the meanwhile! To illustrate the point, consider this: If you install a service brake system such as that outlined in the first combination example, your parking brake could be something as simple as a bolt shoved through a hole in the driveshaft and holes in the frame. This will undoubtedly 'lock the braked wheels to the point of traction' (see 26451). The highway patrol might be skeptical about it, but it might be approved because it does meet all the requirements listed for the parking brake. So you smugly slip the bolt through when you park the EV on a hill. Only, when you come back, you can't get the vehicle out of 'park' because the bolt is pinched. Or, what happens if you apply power with that bolt still engaged? Or, what happens if you accidently engage it while driving down the road? By the time you figure out a fail-safe way to keep from applying power while it's engaged, or to prevent activation when you're operating the vehicle, you could have installed a nice, simple parking brake.

OPERATOR LINKAGE

Linkage connects operator controls to the devices which need some kind of mechanical movement. Most linkage is designed for more than just moving the required device through the required distance; in many cases, mechanical advantage is incorporated in the design to keep you from having to develop

138

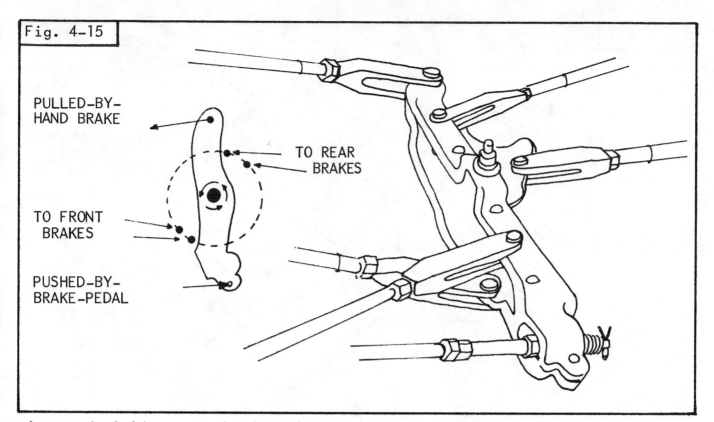

Fig. 4-15

PULLED-BY-
HAND BRAKE

TO REAR
BRAKES

TO FRONT
BRAKES

PUSHED-BY-
BRAKE-PEDAL

sixteen-inch biceps to do the job. How this is done is simple in principle,
but sometimes difficult to apply if you haven't a working knowledge of it.
Sometimes the process is a matter of what portion of the 'swing' the linkage is secured to (see Fig. 4-16). If the advantage in this drawing is not
immediately evident to you, I'd suggest some further reading on the subject.

To keep it all 'sanitary' when you finally determine the number of foot-oper-
ated pedals you'll have --- accelerator, brake, clutch (if used) and emergency/
parking brake (whether foot- or hand-operated) --- diagram it all out, and insure non-interference in linkage, amount of pedal travel, etc. There are many
tricks to this scheme, but they're all variations on the theme (note the rhyme)

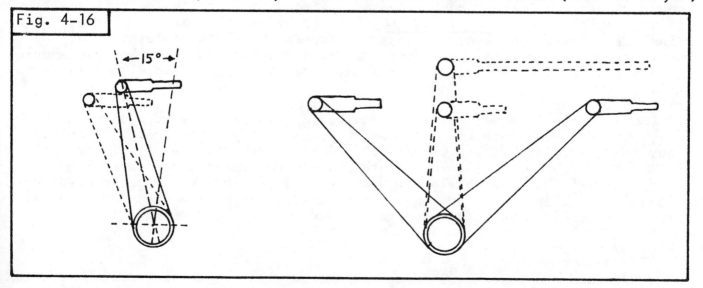

Fig. 4-16

15°

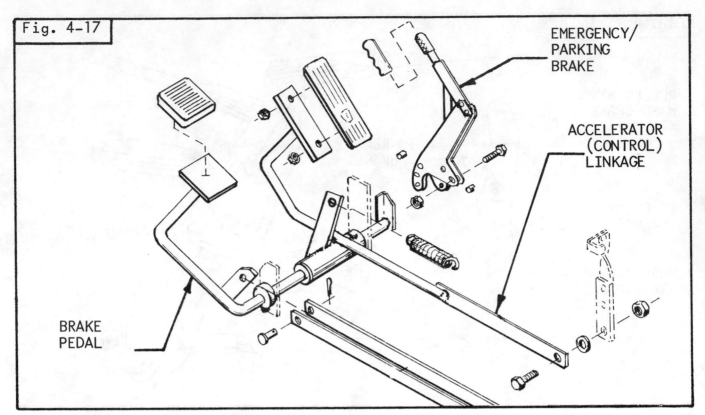

Fig. 4-17

EMERGENCY/
PARKING
BRAKE

ACCELERATOR
(CONTROL)
LINKAGE

BRAKE
PEDAL

of good common sense. Don't get 'psyched' at the apparent complexity; you can have a lot of fun designing your own. A floor plan of sorts, with sample pedal and linkage assembly, is provided in Fig. 4-17.

wheels/tires

A decision on some other parts of assemblies might determine the wheels you end up with, but if it hasn't come to that, there are a few things to ponder over about wheels. We've already discussed the need to minimize the rolling friction of the vehicle (see Determining μ, Chapter 2) and the parts that the tire's diameter, width, type and air pressure play in the final computation of the coefficient of friction. But there are other factors as well that you should be aware of before firming up what kind, size, and type of wheel and tires to get.

If you select a large-diameter, narrow-width, lightweight, hard tire, it probably came off your bother's ten speed bicycle. If you get enough to outfit your three-wheeler EV, you've got both of his tires and one off his friend's bike. You might as well take the other while you're at it; after all you <u>will</u> need a spare! But, seriously now, this will do for a Class 6 , and maybe a Class 5 if you're strict on keeping the vehicle weight low, but that's about it. Why? Let's investigate traction, load ratings, and wheel support.

TRACTION

Whatever we do to lessen the 'drag' on the EV with respect to rolling friction, also reduces the desirable effect of traction, unfortunately. Fortunately, however, even the sliding friction of rubber over concrete is several multiples of the tire's coefficient of friction (μ) or we'd be forced to go to real high-friction, power-gulping tires on any kind of vehicle. But, we can't ignore the relatively small difference between the rolling friction and sliding friction (where the wheels are locked up because you've got the brake pedal to the floor). In larger vehicles, there is usually horsepower to spare for the increased friction of the wide tires you'll find on many cars. Because we have to concern ourselves with this friction in a homebuilt EV, we must also make doubly sure that we're still able to maintain the grip with the road. This is essential in braking, and in negotiating turns; after all, when you 'round the bend', it's only the friction which keeps you from continuing in a straight line --- off the road, over a cliff, or up onto someone's lawn.

Fortunately, when we increase the wheel and tire diameter, we increase our traction. A wider tire would also increase the traction, but here, we compromise; a narrow tire gives us a lessened coefficient of friction. A hard tire (solid, or pneumatic with a high air pressure) gives us less friction and, consequently, less traction. If you select and use a solid tire, you're stuck with whatever coefficient of friction it demonstrates. But, in a pneumatic tire, tire pressure (and, therefore, the coefficient of friction) can be varied to account for increased traction needs. In this way, we provide for the best overall performance under a variety of loads, road surfaces, and other circumstances.

WHEEL LOAD RATINGS

Wheels have load ratings. Some wheels have bearings mounted in them and, when a shaft is inserted through the bearings, they'll rotate about the shaft. Other wheels have no bearings; they're connected directly to a shaft which, in turn, must be mounted in external bearings to facilitate rotation. Most wheels must take at least radial loads. Others will also be rated for side-thrust, or axial loads. If it's a radial load, the wheel will use ball, roller, or needle bearings. If the wheel will be subjected to side-thrust (axial loads), the bearings will need to be tapered-roller bearings. If the wheel will be subjected to axial loads from both directions, dual tapered-roller bearings are called for.

Bicycle wheels are designed for radial loads. The weight of the bicycle and rider bear down directly perpedicular to the wheel's axle. Or, in another way of speaking, the forces on the wheel are directed through the center and rim to rim. Even when the bicycle takes a corner (except at extremely low speeds), the bicycle leans into the turn, and the forces still tend to direct themselves through the center of the wheel and rim to rim. The ball bearings used in the wheels would take some side-loading, but normally they don't experience it.

However, if you put the bicycle wheel on a three-wheel (or four-wheel) vehicle, the wheels will not be able to lean in corners as they do with a two-wheel'ed vehicle. So, axial loads (side-thrusts) will be placed on the tire, wheel, bearings, and axle. At low speeds, it seems that the ball bearings would probably handle this side-thrust --- but, at higher vehicle speeds, it's doubtful. Furthermore, it's almost irrelevant whether the bearings can or can't handle

141

the load; we are now faced with the question of whether the wheel itself can survive. A long-spoked, rimmed wheel designed for bicycles simply cannot handle side-thrust.

Motorcycle wheels offer some relief from this problem; they're much beefier than the bicycle equivalent, and designed for higher speeds, greater vehicle weights, and some side-thrust. How much in the way of axial loads they will take is questionable but, with larger ball bearings, the capacity of the bearing to survive is increased. But, again, the wheel will collapse long before the bearings give out.

Automobiles use wheels that are designed for very heavy radial and axial loads --- single or double-taper roller bearings, and solid, no-spoke wheels. However, this is a bit of overkill for a lightweight EV; these wheels are heavy, wide, and will only bolt up to a large drum-and-wheel assembly. If your EV is really small and lightweight, fat bicycle wheels might be just the thing to use. Anything that doesn't gross over 1000 lbs. might use the better motorcycle wheels, provided that the vehicle doesn't exceed speeds of 30 mph. Anything over that weight or speed, and you'd better look around for some thin, lightweight (compact) automotive wheels and tires. Foreign cars use smaller wheels, but they're not only thin; they're also usually small in diameter. It's not going to be easy to find what you need, but take your time and get something that will pay for itself in ease of adaptation to your EV's design, and waste as little energy as possible in use. If they weren't so prohibitively expensive, the kind of wheels and tires used on the old Model A and other cars-of-the-past would be ideal!

You should know where your EV's wheels come from, by the way. This will be an indicator of what they were and weren't designed to do. You can't just look at the wheel and say, "Yep, that'll work just fine." That's because wheels don't fail when they're parked at the curb. Nope, they fall apart or disintegrate when we need them the most, which is also the absolutely wrong time. If you get a wheel off a motorbike, it's not difficult to at least estimate what it will do. Figure the weight of the motorbike, add 200 pounds for the driver, another 150 pounds for a passenger, give it a safety factor of two (that might be generous for some motorbikes), and then divide by two (it's not a unicycle, right?). That's what each of its two wheels will take (in forces). Note that I didn't say "in weight". Don't forget that when you brake hard, the forces acting on the wheels may be several times what they experience sitting under the load at the curb.

WHEEL SUPPORT

Another thing to consider about the use of particular wheels with the EV is wheel support. A motorcycle wheel is supported (as in a bicycle wheel) close-in, on both sides of the wheel, by the fork (front or rear). A fork support is ideal for the rear, single wheel drive in a three-wheeler, and perhaps the single front wheel in a twin-wheel rear drive 3-wheeler --- but forks just won't make it for the other wheels. And if the wheels are supported on just one side, like most automotive wheels, they're just not going to be strong enough with that small diameter axle mounting. There will be exceptions to this, particularly if the wheels were designed for some punishing use, but most of the standard hardware won't be tough enough.

142

To use motorcycle or large bicycle wheels in an EV will require the replacement of the wheels' axle with a larger one. After removing the old axle --- by dissembly, punching it out, or drilling out the centermost portion --- the wheel can be made to accept a larger axle. While you're at it, install some beefy ball bearings or tapered-roller bearings. Either job, axle or bearings, is not going to be an easy one; everything is going to depend upon the quality of metal in the wheel hub, the tools you have access to, and the experience you have to call upon, whether yours or someone else's. Conversions mean work --- it may not make sense to spend a few less dollars on something you think you can adapt. In this case, try for something you can install outright.

PRACTICAL WHEEL ASSEMBLIES

For below-10-mph EVs, a simple single-wheel assembly can be used (see Fig. 4-18). For higher speed EVs, the single wheel assembly should approximate the design for a motorcycle. If you're using two wheels up front, whether you've got a single or two wheels in the rear for drive, the final assembly will be a little more involved (see Fig. 4-19). Here, the suspension (leaf springs and shock absorbers), steering, and wheel assemblies are combined into an integral unit. The rear wheel assembly, if involving two wheels and a differential, might eventually appear as drawn in Fig. 2-20, although this assembly does not include wheel-brakes; instead, it uses a band-brake around part of the power train.

Whichever design you choose to build, don't forget about wheel fenders, or skirts; these are not 'customizing' items. Rather, they will keep rocks, dust, and mud from slinging about, striking other parts of the vehicle. And they'll keep rocks or other road debris from being flung rearward, striking vehicles that are following you. For wheels that are steerable, allow a deep

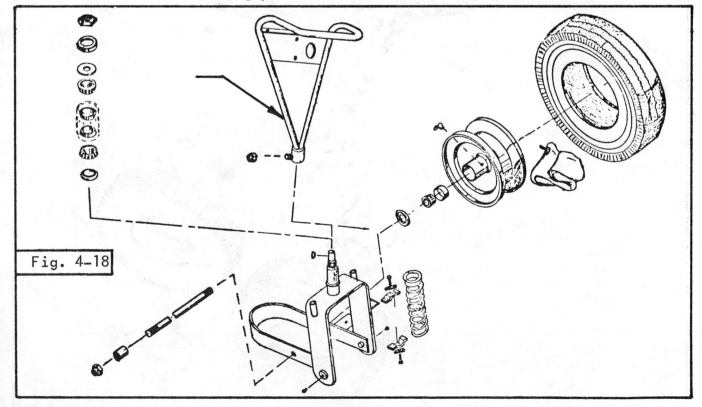

Fig. 4-18

Fig. 4-19

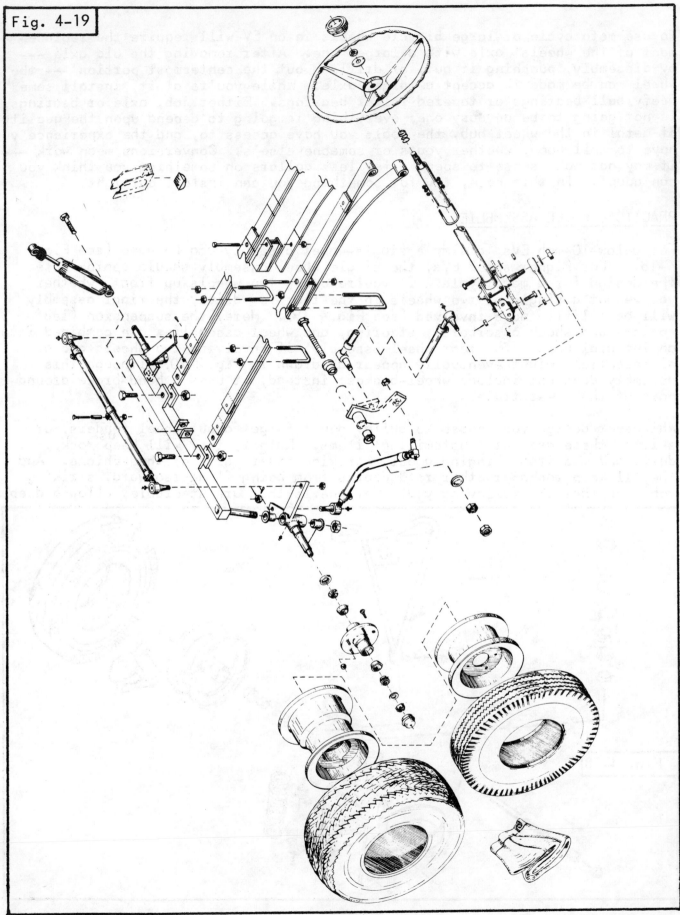

wheel well, or affix the fender so that it moves with the wheel itself. You must 'screen' the fronts of the wheels too. Mud or spray flung forward off the spinning tire gets caught in the wind, and is driven back onto the windshield. I'm the proud owner/rebuilder of a vintage jeep which has straight fenders. They do add to its neat appearance, but they sure don't stop that flung mud. It's bloody maddening when you're plowing through the stuff; the first time it happened to me, I didn't even have my windshield up. Lucky I wear glasses!

FRAME

The frame is what holds things together and determines the shape of the beast. It's a skeleton onto which you'll hang the various assemblies --- powertrain, battery bank, steering, suspension, axles, wheels, people and other knicknacks. It won't do to have our assemblies separating from one another as we take corners or bounce along a rough road. So, rigidity and strength are two of the first prerequisites of the frame.

The frame can be made of a number of materials. Of those that are available, I figure that it's all limited to three materials --- steel, aluminum, and plastic. In steel, what's used depends on what part of the EV we're concerned with. The front axle, the main frame members, or bumpers may use heavy angle iron, or I-beams. General support structures, braces, and ribs will be made of lighter materials -- angle iron or even metal tubes. Whether you use low-cost steel or more expensive aluminum, the difference will not be discernable once a coat of paint is applied. If plastic is used, the frame will look more like a molded body (dune buggy-type, maybe). For most situations, there will be an individualistic blend of the three --- steel, aluminum, and plastic --- determined by fate (oh, gee, a little red wagon nobody's using!) more than design. Wood won't be of much use as a frame material; without special workmanship, it doesn't have the high strength per pound that the other materials offer.

Considerable thought must be given to what material is going to work best with the tools, skills, and experience you possess. Are things to be bolted together, or welded? Where are things located? With less experience behind you, things may be a bit more difficult --- we tend to get all jammed up in the head when close tolerances are called for. Look at somebody's homebuilt vehicle; looks great, doesn't it! I mean everything seems to be in its proper space, evenly proportioned, no waste, clean lines, etc. Now, turn your back and sketch it out as you saw it. Or go home and make a model. Not too easy, is it? It's a shame that all of us don't possess that very unique ability of forming the picture in the mind's eye, and then forming it from the clay of materials about us. That comes from talent or painstakingly-acquired skills. The rest of us must labor at the drawings, and curse as we bungle and put two things into the same space. The problem is not 'what to do' so often as it is 'how to do it' without inadvertently messing everything up, all the way down the line. At the same time, we must place braces and ribs where they will provide the required structural strengthening.

If this scares you off, check into the fiberglas-reinforced plastics (composites) that are being developed for EV body/frames (see Sources). These are attractive even to the homebuilder because they have a good cost-benefit ratio. As well, because they are so basic, there is much you can do to have the completed EV appear very different from any other EV made from the same 'base'. And they are extremely lightweight. Don't feel that you'd be 'cheating' on the building-your-own part; you'll have plenty of other decisions to make for your EV. Being practical means choosing your route toward the goal. If you easily disregard an off-the-shelf item because you want to rough it, maybe you ought to think about smelting the ore for the steel you use!

There are a few things which will help the frame plan. First, don't try to do it all at once. The first part calls for putting down the number of wheels that you plan to use and where they go. If it's four, it's easy. If it's three, you've got to make that decision that you have been putting off. Is it going to be one in back or one in front. (Of course, there are other arrangements --- see Fig. 4-1.) If you believe my arguments (see the 3-wheeled EV, Chapter 1), then it'll be a single wheel in front for the UTLEV and a single wheel in back for the PASEV.

Use graph paper to do the initial layout; it's easier to keep everything to scale. If you know the approximate tire diameters, sketch those in to scale. Once you start the process, you will be amazed at how much you can do with what little you may know about such things. For example: If you decide to build a single wheel forward, you plan on using a tiller instead of a steering box, and attach it directly to the wheel, then the wheel must be located very close to where the driver is. On the other hand, if you decide to use the gearbox idea or the regular steering wheel, you can have the wheel in one place and the driver in another. Things start falling into place. How about tiller swing? You'll want to keep the tiller fairly short or you'll run into a problem with it (actually, you'll probably run into your passenger's stomach with it). What about the wheel --- will it clear framework and fenders as it swings? Etc., etc. etc.

A limiting factor of the floor plan, where the view is supposed to be looking straight down on the vehicle, is that it's hard to figure relative height in the vehicle. Is this piece of pipe that's part of the main framework level, or angling upward or downward as it travels from front to back? Gee, if my batteries are there, how can the motor be there, too? The answer is simple. It's there if you can see through it --- like in the drawing --- but in reality, the batteries are under the motor, and you've experienced your first height problem. This will cause you to do some side views. First, draw in anything that you can from the 'hanging up in the tree' view. Then, proceed to arrange more of the EV's assemblies. If you find this too confusing to work with, maybe you can build a model. Whatever happens, keep redoing it until you find something that you really like and won't depart from in design. Only then should you toss out all of the other stuff. Until trees are recognized for the priceless things they are, paper is cheaper than the aluminum and many other expensive materials that you will buy for your EV.

Wiring, mounting the locations of solenoids, and that sort of stuff comes later. In fact, it may never see a place on your drawings, because it fits very well into the nooks and crannies that will abound in your EV. This is not to say to ignore it; it's just that your drawings don't need to have it artistically added. But bigger jobs, like venting for the battery compartment, are something that you must think out, or they'll be real hassles later on.

The next thing is to identify the main structural members of the framework. Some will be big stuff --- large diameter pipes or I-beams or angle iron --- and some will be the small angle iron or tubing that rigidizes the vehicle's framework. Then there's the superstructure. This is what you may attach a roof to, or hang a windshield in, or slap a seat onto. It may also provide a higher profile, so that you don't sit quite so close to the ground, obscured from the vision of other drivers. Make sure that you get things labeled right on your plans. Then, it's easy to determine how much material you'll need by adding up the various lengths you've specified for the frame.

Other points:
1. If you're using large diameter wheels in your EV, don't forget that the framework can extend down below the axles. How far depends on what kind of road surfaces you must traverse, but it seems a bit ridiculous to have the bottom of the battery compartment as far as fifteen inches off the ground when the EV is using thirty-inch wheels. The law says that no portion of the vehicle may extend below the lowermost portion of the rim of the wheel (#24008), but that's usually a <u>long</u> way from the axle. If you're a bit worried about this, design it low and make the bottom material tough; this skid plate will protect the vehicle's vital parts from road, rock, or water damage.

2. Keeping the vehicle codes in mind, be careful to give the vehicle really adequate width and length. A narrow wheel base means the vehicle has a propensity to roll, unless it's got an extremely low center of gravity. A low-profile EV is dangerous to others and to its passengers. The sports car enthusiasts among EV'ers will like to style their EV after the Lotus, but this is asking for trouble. Reasons like 'it's just streamlining' don't hold up for speeds under 30 mph.

3. Since the greatest threat to the small EV will be a rear-end collision, make sure the rear end is adequately reinforced for this possibility. High-back or head-rest type seats are highly recommended.

skin

This is what others see when they look at your vehicle from the outside --- the skin. If you don't cover its skeleton, your EV will look like an incomplete vehicle or a dune buggy. For the wetter seasons, a skin is nice. For the colder environments, a skin is nice. And to cover up sometimes-ugly framework, components, and bubble-gum jobs, a skin is a must. It serves other functions as well. It keeps road dust out of the EV's innards (and yours, too). It keeps out the noise or, at least, some of it. It keeps the wind from rustling through your shining tresses, or trying to blow anything and everything that isn't tied down out of the EV.

If you finally decide to put on a skin after a few days, months, or years of driving your homebuilt EV, there's not much that you can do to change the overall shape of the vehicle. However, if this is something that you plan to do from the start, design for it if you can. I say "if you can" because sometimes it's a lot more effort than it's worth to "frame" an EV to look exactly the way we want it to. An Excalibur, it ain't never gonna be. Some folks think that 'utility' means 'ugly', and there's no argument that's going to change that feeling. But I like the looks of Land Rovers and the early jeeps, and if ever there were vehicles built for utility, those were.

Tubing is nice framing stuff to use when you've got to skin something, particularly if you can pop-rivet whatever it is that you wish to attach to it. That's because it has lots of angles and you don't have to be in a particular plane like you do with flat-stock or angle iron. If you like square corners, you can use square pipe; it's more expensive than tubing, but it's neater sometimes.

One thing you should ask yourself: What it is that you intend to 'skin'? The passenger compartment? All of the EV's assemblies? The battery compartment? All of the above? None of the above? No answer? No opinion? If you checked 'Don't understand the question', understand that, unless the EV is completely open to air and meant to be that way forever, you must isolate the battery compartment from the passenger compartment. Particularly if you have the batteries in the forward part of the vehicle. Otherwise, you get what the old dual-wing pilots of the early days of aviation got --- lots of fumes to breathe. They used castor oil for the engines then, and if breathing it has any of the same effects as swallowing it, it wasn't difficult to figure out the first thing the pilot was going to do when he landed his plane. Bet those guys had clear digestive systems. Anyhow, your batteries won't be using castor oil, and the hydrogen won't cause you frequent pit stops, but it will sure choke your throat something fierce! So, skin the passenger compartment, or if you like plenty of fresh air, skin only the battery compartment. You'll definitely want to get it buttoned up securely---no leaks.

A skin for weatherproofing is different than a skin for cutting down road noise (and keeping the wind and cold out and the warmth and calm air inside). Metal is great for all-around performance and durability under all types of weather, but it's lousy for road noise and is, of course, a great conductor of heat. Bad. Wood is less tough for the same job, but it does have some insulative value and it will dampen some noise. But, with a certain design, it could act like the wood in a fine guitar, resonating that much-hated motor whine to a hair-pulling crescendo. And, without treatment, it won't be too great for most weather conditions.

Fiberglas or plastics can be rigid and thin, weatherproof, sound-dampening, and quite inexpensive. But it takes a lot of skill to work with these materials. You can buy pre-molded plastic bodies or skins for the EV carcass but, of course, those don't leave you much leeway in filling the interior.

DEPARTMENT OF ECOLOGICAL WARFARE BULLETIN NO. 29-6

THE M-78 SOLAR-HEATED WIND-ELECTRIC TANK WITH M-117 METHANE GUN

5 vehicles

It's getting down to the end of the book and, unless you peeked, nary an EV to be seen that's for real and actual. Well, you get the full concentration here; this chapter has all of the photos to be found in the book, save one. And besides the featured UTLEV we operate, there's some discussion on the PASEV and UTLEV that we're going to be building soon. But a look at OX first.

earthmind's UTLEV

This story begins in, of all places, a Goodwill Industries resale yard in Orange County in 1973. A friend of mine dragged me there to get my expert opinion on some electronic stuff he'd previously spotted. Once we got there, he ignored my comments, so I wandered off to see what else I could find. My eye caught hold of a strange-looking vehicle only partially visible admist rubble, clothes, and old toasters. It didn't look any less odd as I cleared away debris; it kinda reminded me of one of those things short-skirted meter maids drive around in while defacing tires with chalk, so I kept on poking about. Finally, I lifted one of the two plywood sections on the rear bed, and to my complete surprise, I was looking down on six huge lead-acid batteries. Well! An electric Something! A quick check under the rearmost plywood panel confirmed that it still has its electric motor, and an oil-bath gearbox, to boot! This was interesting!

Half an hour later, I was looking at it and wanting it. I guess I'm just a kid about some things. I figured I was the only one who could truly appreciate its 'possibilities'. Despite the somewhat blinding enthusiasm, I did manage to see that the tires were good, the motor and gearbox were free of smoke or oil deposits, the front end was dented, and the frame solid. Oh, and the batteries looked salvagable. It didn't really look used, just rejected. The yardman said that he couldn't take less than $200, but he took $95.

Getting the ole hunk home (across Los Angeles) was anything but fun, but we managed. First thing, I started working on those batteries. At the time I thought myself to be the Guru of tired, exhausted batteries; I only had to look at them and they would provide another 20 years of grueling service. Well, I spent a month on 'em trying to breathe life back into those plates. Seems like they just wanted to make gas, converting electricity into hydrogen and oxygen; they never ceased to bubble and gurgle! Finally, on the umpteenth go-round, one of the battery charger leads sparked at a terminal. The battery sucked flame, ignited its gas-filled innards, and blew up! Mercy, what a sound!

The whole side of the battery came off; fortunately, I was on the opposite side. And then there were gallons of sulphuric acid gushing across the floor. When I'd cleaned up that mess, I still couldn't find the battery wall. Minutes later I found it --- 20 feet away and embedded in some shelves! The other five batteries and the remains of the one that exploded were hauled to a battery-salvage yard a few days later.

In the next month, I wrote to Taylor-Dunn; what looked to be their emblem was just barely readable on the side of the vehicle. They were very helpful. They sent me a specifications sheet and let me know that the last owners of the vehicle has been a costume rental place. And, if I could locate a certain number stamped in the body or frame somewhere, they would be able to help get the vehicle street-legal. I never did find that number!

Some months later Earthmind purchased some used batteries --- twenty, 6-volt, 180-ampere hour truck batteries --- for its wind-electric systems, and I managed to sneak six of 'em away to put in the electric vehicle (or Ox, as we'll refer to it). I needed to test out the motor; there wasn't much point in doing any other work on Ox until I had. So, I jacked up the rear wheels and connected the batteries. In both reverse and forward, it spun those wheels beautifully. Elated with this discovery, I let down the jacks, and proceeded to disconnect the batteries. I didn't get too far. When I pulled on one of the long motor leads, something flashed, and it was all I could do to climb aboard for one of the wildest rides of my life!

It was about one o'clock in the morning. Earlier, I had pushed Ox into our garage, lowered the hinged door (to keep out the cold and keep in the noise), and proceeded with the test. Now, for some reason, there was power to the motor, evidenced by the scream of tires spinning on smooth concrete and billowing blue smoke. I was trying desperately to rip off one of the battery connectors, but Ox got traction before I'd succeeded, and I half-jumped, half-fell, across the rear bed as it kamikazeed for the garage door. It hit, only slightly hesitated as the massive door swung up on its hinges, and we were out into the night --- flat out! I'd stopped trying to rip loose a connector; I was hanging on for dear life! Ox hit a refrigerator sitting in the driveway, which went flying through the air in one direction while I, from that impact, went flying off in the other. And that crazy Ox was still going! And then I heard it crash to a stop. It had found our parked Dodge 4x4, a massive, ex-World War II ammunitions carrier. And the batteries, in falling from the bed on impact, pulled loose the wire connectors, and Ox's wheels ground to a halt. Neighbors were awakened by the din of that wild ride, but I was okay; it was at an end, and I picked up the strewn batteries before calling it quits for the morning.

Later the same day, I discovered why the whole thing had happened. Insulation on one of the motor wires had frayed and, by sufficient movement, could be brought in contact with the frame. This was the required polarity, when the Fwd-Neutral-Rev switch was in the Fwd position, to put the full battery bank across the motor, bypassing the accelerator pedal. It made me wonder. The front end of Ox had been dented when I got the vehicle. Could this have happened before, to the previous owners? Maybe they hadn't been able to figure out what did it! Assuredly, I had not had the vehicle long enough to have frayed that wire.

Now that I knew the motor was good, and that the vehicle had plenty of torque, I had to make a few basic decisions about what Ox was going to be, and what kind of modification would be required. So, I'd sit down on the front seat and fantasize. How about an electric sports car? I could peel out at traffic signals in blazing silence! Or, an off-road vehicle? Climbing high into the back country --- an electric mountain-goat! When I finished with all of that nonsense, I looked at the facts. A lot of vehicle weight. With the present gear ratio, a mighty 8-10 mph top speed. A series-field motor, which shot down any chance of installing regenerative braking (to put energy back into the batteries). And that heavy front end.

Look --- I can sit down with the best of 'em and design an electric vehicle. Just tell me what you want it to do. And how well, or how fast, or with what budget, with what range, etc. But when you already have something, you have to be careful about what you choose to change it into. Without some deft strokes of realism, you'd soon end up replacing some major parts --- at some major cost --- and you'd have been better off starting from scratch. So, I saw what I had to work with, and concentrated on clearing away some of the more obvious cobwebs. A heavy front end, huh? Well, out came the torch and off with it! And the brakes didn't work very well, so I Maltby'ed the bolts and springs and adjusted them tight. Bolted in a new seat. Rigged up a tiller for steering until I could get a universal joint to rig up the steering wheel again (the original got torched off with the cab --- who said all the changes were also improvements?). And just generally got the vehicle running. If you use it, you get folks used to it --- and besides the thrill it brings, you quickly learn what doesn't work, or what you'd like to have on it.

Around January of 1976, we moved our belongings and Earthmind into temporary quarters in Acton, California. The Ox came in handy for hauling around junk, and we even started using it to pick up our mail at the local post office, about a mile away. This was always an exciting event, watching people watch us as we bopped along. And we weren't street-legal, so we had to keep a sharp eye out for the CHP (California Highway Patrol). But it was fun, until we learned one of the disadvantages of a ground-hugging vehicle. On one trip, I almost became a statistic when somebody backed out of a parking space when I was directly behind their car. I missed getting crushed by doing some fancy steering, but I collided with the post office building, missing their big front window by less than I'd care to remember! And the brick wall wrapped the accelerator linkage into a pretzel. With a bit of jury-rigging, I limped home.

Soon, I was at work on Ox, welding together a front frame assembly out of EMT (electrical thin-walled conduit). Not only would the framework protect the passenger and driver, but as well the steering, brake and accelerator linkages. The higher profile served to make us a bit easier to see and gave us something to which we could stick paneling when we eventually installed a windshield, cab, and doors.

It wasn't until we came to Mariposa that we were able to begin charging Ox from one of our wind-machines. We installed a regular wall receptacle into the front to aid in plugging Ox into the electrical system. When the household batteries are charged, the switches connect Ox directly to our windplant, and back again when we need to use the vehicle.

Top left and clockwise: * Our farmdog, Pumpkin, guards Ox during charging from our wind-machine. * Ox's front end is welded EMT (conduit); note the tiller steering. * Shooting from midway up our tower, and with the plywood bed removed, Ox's innards are laid bare. Battery spacing is affected by small wood blocks. * A close-up of the accelerator pedal linkage shows a pivot point and the return spring. * The forward-neutral-reverse switch is located temporarily behind the driver/passenger seat.

Top left and counter-clock-wise: * An undershot of the brake and accelerator linkage. * The control system is neatly snuggled in Ox's framework; note the slide-switch (right) and resistive coils (left). * A close-up of the 24-volt, 41-amp, series motor with lead-outs for motor reversing. * Stepping back, a clearer shot of the gearbox, transaxle, and suspension. * A mechanically-braked rear wheel.

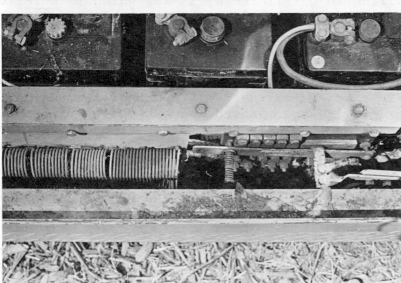

Furthermore, we found a new place for Ox --- out in the 'field'. Because our windplants produce 32 volts DC, we have acquired motors, appliances, light bulbs, and tools which use this voltage directly. If we have holes to drill or wood to cut, we run the vehicle out to the site and use our 32 volt drill or skillsaw. How about welding together that broken trailer hitch down in the canyon? No problem. Drive the Ox down there, attach the leads for our antique 32 volt arc welder (or the electrodes directly to the batteries if you're a good welder) and soon the sparks are flying. Need some lights in a hurry way out there? Use some standard sockets, screw in some 32 volt bulbs, drive Ox to the place you need the light, and plug 'em in. If you've ever used a gas-powered standby generator for the same jobs, you'll appreciate the wonderful silence that Ox affords, whatever situation comes up.

Once we caught on to this idea, we worked another arrangement. We'd been using just 32 volts out there. Why not 60 cycle, 110 volts AC? So we stuck our inverter on the vehicle to try out the soldering gun on some wiring in my jeep. And believe it or not, someone else obviously thought a lot of the idea, becuz within the hour our area experienced a blackout (the farm we are leasing has utility power). For that wiring to get finished, it was going to have to be done with Ox and the inverter. And it was! Our inverter (which is 30 years old) has a 200 watt limit, but larger units are available for the same applications.

We like driving around on wind-watts, but we do have other ways to charge Ox. First, we have a homemade battery charger that delivers 7.5 amps from 0-110 volts DC; this is operated on utility power. Second, we can charge Ox from a small lawnmower engine-powered alternator whipped together from auto parts; it delivers 35 amps at 0-45 volts DC. A third possibility is to use the existing alternator in your car (voltage regulator bypassed); we've not used this method yet. If you can find one, there are inverters which are also battery chargers. Or, if you're competent in electronics, re-wiring a standard inverter to obtain charging capacity is possible.

Although this vehicle would be classified as modified, not homebuilt, it seems like a homebuilt with all the work that we've done on it. And, while it ain't fancy, it does the job for us. We've taken this vehicle over about every kind of terrain; it may go slow, but it makes it. The tiller-type steering may never be replaced with a steering wheel; it has proven adequate for the low speed and loads we've carried on the EV around the farm. The same goes for the dashboard monitor panel; it may remain non-existent. The few simple controls we do have make using the vehicle a snap. Because it's not used on the street, it doesn't have lights or a horn. Since the vehicle is plugged into our windmachine whenever it's not being used, its state of charge is always high. A monthly water and hydrometer check, equalizing charge, and battery washdown is sufficient for our needs.

Two major changes for this vehicle are slated. One is to re-locate the slide-switch, resistive control unit rearward and out of the battery compartment; I'm really alarmed to see the flash of an arc as this disconnects, especially after heavy battery discharging. Second, because there is sufficient room, we'll be installing two other batteries, in addition to the six already used. Then, we'll series four batteries and put them in parallel with a series arrangement of the other four. Although this only provides 24 volts instead of the 36 we've been running, it will double the AH capacity of the batteries. This will eliminate the overvoltage condition for our motor (which is 24 volts) and lessen the discharge rate of any one battery to one-half the total motor draw. This should increase the life of our batteries and the motor as well. Besides, the only time we have the pedal to the floor on our UTLEV is when we're climbing hills and need the extra oomph. With a high-AH 24v pack instead of a low-AH 36-volt pack, we should keep right on going and going and going.......

A plaNNed PASEV

Earthmind plans to build a PASEV. We've listed some of the parameters and have several designs on the drafting board, but there's no telling what we'll end up with. Sometimes EVs are like paintings --- you only know what you've got when you're finished.

But we have made some decisions. First, we're going to try for the MB classification (see Motorized Bicycles, Chapter 1). This automatically means 'under two horsepower for the motor'. Which limits our top speed to around 25 mph. One of the other prerequisites for the motorized bicycle class is that the device have two or three wheels --- we'll use three. This will be the C design previously discussed (see A Three-Wheeled PASEV, Chapter 1) --- one drive wheel in the rear and two steerable wheels in the front. We'll hold the vehicle weight under 1000 pounds, and we expect that fully three-quarters of that will be batteries.

We may use a VW front end, or we may fabricate our own if we run into problems adapting that to large diameter (30-inch) motorcycle wheels. We'll have a large motorcycle wheel in the rear; if we really run into trouble with distributing vehicle weight, we may run two wheels within a few inches of each other back there. The current plan calls for hydraulically-applied disc brakes up front, and a mechanically-activated drum brake in rear; a mechanical parking/emergency brake will have a hand-lever in the cab, mechanically-linked with the rear brake (see Fig. 4-15). The vehicle will also have an electrically-activated mechanical solenoid which will secure the driveshaft. We'll wire the thing so that it will be impossible to power the vehicle without its being released.

We intend to power the EV with a 36-volt or 48-volt battery pack; this will be decided primarily by the voltage rating of the motor we get. The drive motor will be either a compound motor, wound for near-series motor operation, or a permanent magnet motor. We intend to use at least dynamic braking (dashboard-controlled), if not regenerative braking for those mountain passes near our home. We'll use a two-speed gearbox. The controller may be of any type. I'm personally in favor of a slide-switch-type resistive coil control (see Fig. 3-19), but a discrete voltage tap method (Fig. 3-14) or a solenoid-switched resistive coil (Fig. 3-20) may be satisfactory. I guess it will mostly depend on our ability to acquire the solenoids at a reasonable cost. Otherwise, we stay very simple.

We'll have full monitor on the dashboard. An ammeter to read motor current, regenerative-charging current, and charger current. A voltmeter to read the pack voltage or individual batteries, as desired (see Fig. 3-32). An odometer for EV miles; this will be essential to our maintenance charts, and to determining the efficiency of our EV. A speedometer or a tachometer, so that we'll know how fast we are going. A temperature gauge to read three things: the battery compartment (air) temperature, a pilot battery temperature, and motor temperature. We'll imbed thermistors to take these readings.

We'll have lots of operator controls to keep the driver of our EV busy. A steering wheel, of course. Brakes, too; hand-and pedal-operated. No clutch, though. A Fwd-Neutral-Rev switch on the dash. A key-operated (safety) switch for battery-lockout. Headlight switch. Brake light switch. Turn signal switch. A dynamic-braking switch. A regenerative-braking mode switch. A battery blower switch; this will be a manual override for the automatic starting of this blower when the EV is under power. An emergency flasher switch. A horn button. An interior light switch. A battery compartment light switch. Yep, it'll look like the cockpit of a 747.

We'll use the same windmachine to charge our EV at home. So that we can do charging on non-windy days, we'll use our homebuilt lawnmower-engine-powered alternator unit, which only weighs about 35 pounds. And, if we have to make a long run in the EV, we'll tuck it away so that we can charge enroute or at our destination for the return trip. We do not plan to rig the vehicle up for charging from utility power. We're gonna write 'wind-watts' on the side, and I'd like it to be as truthful as possible.

In a cooperative venture with some other folks who want to build small EVs for sale, we'll build this and several other types and sizes of EVs. Further down the line, we even plan to build a UTLEV from the ground up. While these other folks are concerned with kits and readymade EVs, I like the kind you build from plans tailored to fit the variety of EV subassemblies someone is likely to scrounge. The EVs we'll build will be designed with the homebuilder in mind, and I intend to write about their design, construction, testing, and use. Book Two in this series on electric vehicles will concern itself with the PASEV story. Book Three will deal exclusively with UTLEVs. If you don't build or buy your own EV right away, keep in touch; you may find either or both of the upcoming books helpful.

A plaNNed UTLEV

Sometime after we finish the intended PASEV, we'll start working on Ox II, or another UTLEV. That's not to say that we find the need for one, but just that we'd like to see certain things in a UTLEV which we'd be foolish to try to incorporate into Ox. Ox has been a great help --- I think that, because of our experience with this vehicle, we have a better feel for which of our ideas are far-fetched, and which ones will work.

It would be foolish to suggest that what I'll say about it now, and what it'll eventually end up being, are one-and-the-same. I only suggest what might happen

SHE WAS DOING FINE THERE, UNTIL I SUDDENLY LOST POWER!

if we were to start construction on it tomorrow.

It will definitely have the workhorse motor --- a series field motor. I'm satisfied with the performance of the one we have in Ox, but would like to make it 2-3.5 HP to handle just about everything on the farm. A 24-volt rating seems okay. A fixed gear ratio sounds best and Ox's rated speed --- 8 mph --- also seems okay.

The basic frame would be tubing, instead of the heavy and expensive angle iron in Ox. If three wheels are used, it will be the A design layout --- one wheel in front for steering and two in back for the drive and supporting the load. I'll use a transaxle if I can find a lightweight with the exact ratios I need, but I may otherwise fabricate a non-differential rear end for the vehicle. The wheels will be no larger than the ones Ox sports --- 8-inch wheels, which give an 18-inch tire diameter. I do intend to have the rear ones spread wider than those in Ox.

Battery power will be paralleled sets of 24 volts (or the motor's voltage rating, if it's not 24 volts). This gives the AH capacity without over-voltage to the motor or pulling too much current from any one battery. For light loads, I'll be able to select one pack or the other, but the dashboard switch will bring both on-line for heavy stuff. The Fwd-Neutral-Rev switch in Ox will be replaced with a simple toggle on the dash which has solenoids do the switching for reverse; in the forward position, then, no solenoid current will be drawn.

I'm playing with the idea of four wheels for this around-the-farm UTLEV. I know the extra wheel would add some stability, and two wheels aren't all that much harder to rig than a single wheel up front. As well, the steering of two wheels is not extraordinarily complex, so it's a thought I can't dismiss.

159

Main motor control will probably end up being the good ole standby --- a slide-switch, resistive setup for armature control. I'm intrigued by the challenge of solenoid controls, but just can't beat down the idea of low-cost, simple, easily-fixed resistive controls. Besides, I'm cheap; I'd rather build my own and save that solenoid-money for rare moments of madness.

One definite change from Ox will be the battery compartment. It will be located in the same place (under the workbed), but I intend to make it easy to hose down the batteries. Beats the sponge bath everytime!

Although we've learned to live without monitoring stuff in Ox, I intend to equip our new UTLEV with the basics --- voltmeter, ammeter, and temperature gauge. The voltmeter will be wired for pack or individual battery readings (see Fig. 3-32) and the ammeter will be able to monitor charging and discharge of the EV's battery pack. The temperature gauge will monitor battery compartment (air) temperature, as well as a single battery's temperature.

We'll make some changes in the frame; whereas Ox has a lot of heavy angle iron, the new beast will be made of light, thin-wall steel tubing (EMT). This is stuff that I'm not only familiar with, but it's easier on the budget. I don't expect to approach the strength of Ox but, for our application, I think Ox is a bit of overkill. We'll see!

Suspension will remain the same in the new EV --- coil springs and shocks for the rear end, and coil springs (for a single wheel) or leaf springs (for a twin-wheel) up front for the steered-wheels. Steering will not be a tiller, as in Ox, but a wheel with a gearbox (similar to Fig. 4-8). And, when we've got everything bolted/welded/baling wire'd together, we'll skin at least the cab of the new UTLEV; this will mostly be for all-weather operation.

We'll firm up decisions on this UTLEV after we've built the new PASEV; the latter should pave the way for the former. And, of course, we intend to write a book on each. They'll include discussions among the persons involved, so that it becomes clear who decided what, and why. We'll describe problems encountered and how/if they're solved. They'll be good manuals to have on the bench when you're building your own EV, if you don't do it in the meantime!

Cubbyhole

The Cubbyhole is the place where I've stuck the few things that might have interfered with the smooth flow of text in the main part of the book. It's broken up into several sections, to keep things tidy. Section A contains the California Vehicle Codes which are applicable to EVs; it begins with an alphabetical list for your easy reference. Section B describes how to find the resistance and wattage ratings required for field coils, while Section F does the same thing for resistive coils in armature current applications. Sections C and D have the answers for problems posed in the text. Section E gives some other battery wiring schemes for voltage-tap motor control. Last, but certainly not least, Section G discusses safety in the design, construction, operation, and maintenance of your EV.

A   CALIFORNIA VEHICLE CODES APPLICABLE TO EVS

DEFINITIONS

bicycle, 21200
darkness, 280
golf cart, 345
motorcycle, 400
motor-driven cycle, 405
motorized bicycle, 406
motor vehicle, 415
new vehicle, 430
passenger vehicle, 34710
pneumatic tire, 485
safety glazing material, 535
solid tire, 560
specially-constructed vehicle, 580
street/highway, 590
vehicle, 670
vehicle verifier, 675.5, 675.6

EQUIPMENT

backup lights, 24606
beam indicators, 24408
beams, multiple, 24409
bicycle, reflectorized, 21201.5
bicycle requirements, 21201
brake, parking, standards, 26451

brake, required, 26450
brakes, after engine failure, 26453
brakes, condition of 26454
brakes, emergency, 26301.5
brakes, service, 26311
bumper, 28071
bumper projection, 35408
bumper testing, 39715
center of gravity, unsafe, 24008.5
federal safety standards, 24011
fenders/mudguards, 27600
glazing material, replacement, 26703
golf cart, 24001.5
headlamps, 24400
headlamps on motor-driven cycles, 25651
height, 35250
horn, 27000
inner tubes, 27455
lamps on other vehicles, 25803
length, 35400
license plate light, 24601
lighting requirements, 24252
manufacturer's name, gvw rating, 24009
mirrors, 26709
parking lights, lit, 24800
reflectors, 24607
reflectors, vehicle, 24609
reflecting material, 25500

280.   "Darkness" is any time from one-half hour after sunset to one-half hour before sunrise and any other time when visibility is not sufficient to render clearly discernible any person or vehicle on the highway at a distance of 1000 feet.

345.   A "golf cart" is a motor vehicle having not less than three wheels in contact with the ground, having an unladen weight of less than 1300 pounds which is designed to be and is operated at not more than 15 miles per hour and designed to carry golf equipment and not more than two persons, including the driver.

400.   A "motorcycle" is any motor vehicle other than a tractor having a seat or saddle for the use of the rider and designed to travel on not more than three wheels in contact with the ground and weighing less than 1500 pounds, except that four wheels may be in contact with the ground when two of the wheels are a functional part of a sidecar.

405.   A "motor-driven cycle" is any motorcycle, including every motor scooter, with a motor which produces less than 15 gross brake horsepower, and every bicycle with motor attached. A motor-driven cycle does not include a motorized bicycle, as defined in Section 406.

406.   A "motorized bicycle" is any two-wheeled or three-wheeled device having fully operative pedals for propulsion by human power, or having no pedals if powered solely by electrical energy, and an automatic transmission and a motor which produces less than 2 gross brake horsepower and is capable

of propelling the device at a maximum speed of not more than 30 miles per hour on level ground.

415.   A "motor vehicle" is a vehicle which is self-propelled.

430.   A "new vehicle" is a vehicle that has never been sold and operated, or registered with the department, or registered with the appropriate agency of authority, or sold and operated upon the highways of any other state, District of Columbia, territory or possession of the United States or foreign state, province or country. The word "sold" shall not be deemed to include or extend to any sale made by a manufacturer or a distributor to a dealer or by a dealer to another dealer licensed under this code.

485.   A "pneumatic tire" is a tire inflated or capable of inflation with compressed air.

535.   Safety glazing material is any glazing material so constructed, treated, or combined with other materials as to reduce, in comparison with ordinary sheet, plate, or float glass, the likelihood of injury to persons by glazing material whether it may be broken or unbroken, and which complies with regulations adopted pursuant to Section 2402.5 and is of a type approved by the Department of the California Highway Patrol.

560.   A "solid tire" is a tire of rubber or other resilient material which does not depend upon compressed air for the support of the load.

580.   A "specially constructed vehicle" is a vehicle of a type required to be registered under this code not originally constructed under a distinctive name, make, model, or type by a generally recognized manufacturer of vehicles.

590.   "Street" is a way or place of whatever nature publicly maintained and open to the use of the public for purposes of vehicular travel. Street includes highway.

670.   A "vehicle" is a device by which any person or property may be propelled, moved, or drawn upon a highway, excepting a device moved exclusively by human power or used exclusively upon stationary rails or tracks.

675.5   A "vehicle verifier" is a person not expressly excluded by Section 675.6 who inspects, records, documents, and submits to the department, or its authorized representative, such proof of vehicle identification as may be required by the department for the purpose of registering or transferring the ownership of vehicles.

675.6   (a) "Vehicle verifier" does not include any of the following: (1) A peace officer, (2) An authorized employee of the department, (3) A special agent of the National Auto Theft Bureau, (4) An employee of an organization certified under the provisions of Part 5 (commencing with Section 12140) of Division 2 of the Insurance Code whose duties require or authorize the verification of vehicles.
        (b) Any person specified in subdivision (a) may perform the duties of a vehicle verifier without obtaining the special permit required in Section 11300.

2402.5   The commissioner shall, after he has considered motor vehicle safety standards adopted pursuant to the National Traffic and Motor Vehicle Safety Act of 1966 (15 U.S.C., Sec. 1381 et seq.), adopt and enforce regulations identical to such standards with respect to any motor vehicle or item of motor vehicle equipment applicable to the same aspect of performance of such vehicle or item of equipment.

Following adoption of such regulations, the commissioner may test vehicles and specify types of equipment for compliance with the federal standards. In formulating test procedures, the commissioner shall review and consider test procedures utilized for compliance with the federal standards. If such vehicle or equipment does not conform to regulations adopted by the commissioner, no person shall sell or offer for sale any such vehicle or equipment.

As used in this section, "motor vehicle safety standard" means a minimum standard for motor vehicle performance, or motor vehicle equipment performance which is practicable, which meets the need for motor vehicle safety and which provides objective criteria. A federal motor vehicle safety standard which conflicts with an equipment provision of this code applicable to the same aspect of performance shall supersede that specific provision of this code with respect to vehicles in compliance with the federal motor vehicle safety standard that was in effect at the time of sale.

It is the intent of the Legislature that the Department of California Highway Patrol shall continue to carry out the approval of lamps, devices, and equipment on new vehicles first sold in California. Testing requirements of this code and regulations adopted pursuant thereto shall be met by the manufacturer submitting a report from a laboratory approved by the department showing compliance with this code and such regulations. The test report shall contain a description adequate for positive identification of the particular item of equipment as prescribed by the Department of the California Highway Patrol and shall state the detailed data and measurements obtained to show compliance with each test requirement.

4001.   All vehicles exempt from the payment of registration fees shall be registered as otherwise required by this code by the person having custody thereof, and he shall display upon the vehicle a license plate bearing distinguishing marks or symbols, which shall be furnished by the department free of charge.

4019.   A golf cart operated pursuant to Section 21115 is exempt from registration.

4020.   A motorized bicycle operated upon a highway is exempt from registration.

4150.   Application for the original registration of a vehicle of a type required to be registered under this code shall be made by the owner to the department upon the appropriate form furnished by it and shall contain:
(a) The true name and business or residence address of the owner, and of the legal owner, if any.
(b) The name of the county in which the owner resides.
(c) A description of the vehicle, including the following data insofar as it may exist: The make, model, and type of body. The vehicle identification number or any other identifying number as may be required by

the department. The date first sold by a manufacturer or dealer to a consumer.

(d) Such information as may reasonably be required by the department to enable it to determine whether the vehicle is lawfully entitled to registration.

4153.   In the event the vehicle to be registered is a specially constructed or reconstructed vehicle, the application shall also state such fact and contain such additional information as may reasonably be required by the department to enable it properly to register the vehicle.

11505.   (a) The department, upon granting a license, shall issue to the applicant a license containing the applicant's name and address and the general distinguishing number assigned to the applicant.

(b) When the department has issued a license pursuant to subdivision (a), the licensee may apply for and the department shall issue special plates which shall have displayed thereon the general distinguishing number assigned to the applicant. Each plate so issued shall also contain a number or symbol identifying the plate from every other plate bearing a like general distinguishing number.

(c) The department shall also furnish books and forms as it may determine necessary, which books and forms are and shall remain the property of the department and may be taken up at any time for inspection.

11506.   Except where the provisions of this code require the refusal to issue a license, the department may issue a license restricted by conditions to be observed in the exercise of the privilege. The terms and conditions to be attached to the exercise of the privilege under such restricted license shall be such as may, in the judgement of the department, be in the public interest and suitable to the qualifications of the applicant as disclosed by the application and investigation by the department.

21114.5 Notwithstanding section 21663 or any other provision of this code, local authorities may, by ordinance, authorize the operation of electric carts by physically disabled persons, or persons 50 years of age or older, or, while in the course of their employment, by employees of the United States Postal Service, state and local governmental agencies, or utility companies, on public sidewalks. Any such ordinance shall, however, contain provisions requiring any such disabled person or person 50 years of age or older who owns an electric cart to apply to the local authority for a permit and an identification sticker to so operate the cart, and requiring such person to affix such sticker to the cart in order to operate it on the sidewalk.

21115.   If a local authority finds that a highway under its jurisdiction is located adjacent to a golf course and between the golf course and the place where golf carts are parked or stored or is within or bounded by a real estate development offering golf facilities and is designed and constructed, so as to safely permit the use thereof of regular vehicular traffic and also the driving of golf carts thereon, the local authority may by resolution or ordinance designate such highway or portion thereof for such combined use and prescribe rules and regulations therefor which shall have the force of law. No such highway shall be so designated for a distance of more than one-half mile from the golf course if such highway is not located within such a development or beyond the area of such development, provided, the findings of the local authority in this respect shall be conclusive. Upon such designation becoming effective it shall be lawful to drive golf carts upon such highway in accordance with the rules and regulations prescribed as aforesaid. Such rules and regulations may establish speed limits and other operating standards but shall not require that the golf carts conform to any requirements of this code with respect to equipment, registration, or licensing.

The rules and regulations shall not be effective until appropriate signs giving notice thereof are posted along the highway affected.

A "real estate development offering golf facilities," for purposes of this section, means an area of single-family or multiple-family residences with a security gate, the owners or occupants of which are eligible for membership in, or the use of, one or more golf courses within such development by virtue of their ownership or occupancy of a residential dwelling unit in such development.

21200.   Every person riding a bicycle upon a roadway or any paved shoulder has all the rights and is subject to all the duties applicable to a driver of a vehicle by this division and Division 10 (commencing with Section 20000), except those provisions which by their very nature can have no application.

A bicycle is a device upon which any person may ride, propelled exclusively by human power through a belt, chain, or gears, and having either two or three wheels in a tandem or tricycle arrangement.

21201.   (a) No person shall operate a bicycle on a roadway unless it is equipped with a brake which will enable the operator to make one braked wheel skid on dry, level, clean pavement.

(b) No person shall operate on the highway any bicycle equipped with handlebars so raised that the operator must elevate his hands above the level of his shoulders in order to grasp the normal steering grip area.

(c) No person shall operate upon any highway a bicycle which is of such a size as to prevent the operator from safely stopping the bicycle, supporting it in an upright position with at least one foot on the ground, and restarting it in a safe manner.

(d) Every bicycle operated upon any highway during darkness shall be equipped (1) with a lamp emitting a white light which, while the bicycle is in motion, illuminates the highway in front of the bicyclist and is visible from a distance of 300 feet in front and from the sides of the bicycle; (2) with a red reflector, of a type approved by the department, on the rear which shall be visible from a distance of 500 feet to the rear when directly in front of lawful upper beams of headlamps on a motor vehicle; (3) with a white or yellow reflector, of a type approved by the department, on each pedal visible from the front and rear of the bicycle from a distance of 200 feet; and (4) with a white or yellow reflector on each side forward of the center of the bicycle and with a white or red reflector on each side to the rear of the center of the bicycle, except that bicycles which are equipped with reflectorized tires on the front and the rear need not be equipped with these side reflectors.

(e) A lamp or lamp combination, emitting a white light, attached to the operator and visible from a distance of 300 feet in front and from the sides of the bicycle, may be used in lieu of the lamp required by clause (1) of subdivision (d).

21201.5 (a) No person shall sell or offer for sale a reflex reflector or reflectorized tire for use on a bicycle unless it is of a type approved by the department.

(b) No person shall sell or offer for sale a new bicycle that is not equipped with a white or yellow reflector, of a type approved by the department, on each pedal visible from the front and rear of the bicycle during darkness from a distance of 200 feet, and with a white or yellow reflector on each side forward of the center of the bicycle, and with a white or red reflector on each side to the rear of the center of the bicycle, except that bicycles which are equipped with reflectorized tires on the front and rear need not be equipped with these side reflectors.

(c) No person shall sell or offer for sale a bicycle unless it is equipped with a red reflector, of a type approved by the department, on the rear of the bicycle.

(d) Area reflectorizing material meeting the requirements of Section 25500 may be used on a bicycle.

21207.5 Notwithstanding Sections 21207 and 23127 of this code, Section 5079.7 of the Public Resources Code, or any other provision of law, no motorized bicycle may be operated on a bicycle path or trail, bikeway, equestrian trail, or hiking or recreational trail, unless it is within or adjacent to a roadway or unless the local authority or the governing body of a public agency having jurisdiction over such path or trail permits, by ordinance, such operation.

21654. (a) Notwithstanding the prima facie speed limits, any vehicle proceeding upon a highway at a speed less than the normal speed of traffic moving in the same direction at such time shall be driven in the right-hand lane for traffic or as close as practicable to the right-hand edge or curb, except when overtaking and passing another vehicle proceeding in the same direction or when preparing for a left turn at an intersection or into a private road or driveway.

(b) If a vehicle is being driven at a speed less than the normal speed of traffic moving in the same direction at such time, and is not being driven in the right-hand lane for traffic or as close as practicable to the right-hand edge or curb, it shall constitute prima facie evidence that the driver is operating the vehicle in violation of subdivision (a) of this section.

(c) The Department of Transportation, with respect to state highways, and local authorities, with respect to highways under their jurisdiction, may place and maintain upon highways official signs directing slow-moving traffic to use the right-hand traffic lane except when overtaking and passing another vehicle or preparing for a left turn.

21656. On a two-lane highway where passing is unsafe because of traffic in the opposite direction or other conditions, a slow-moving vehicle, including a passenger vehicle, behind which five or more vehicles are formed in line, shall turn off the roadway at the nearest place designated as a turnout by signs erected by the authority having jurisdiction over the highway, or wherever sufficient area for a safe turnout exists, in order to permit the vehicles following it to proceed. As used in this section, a slow-moving vehicle is one which is proceeding at a rate of speed less than the normal flow of traffic at the particular time and place.

21663.   No person shall operate or move a motor vehicle upon a sidewalk except as may be necessary to enter or leave adjacent property.

21710.   The driver of a motor vehicle when traveling on down grade upon any highway shall not coast with the gears of such vehicle in neutral.

21716.   No person shall operate a golf cart on any highway except in a speed zone of 25 miles per hour or less.

21960.   (a) The Department of Transportation and local authorities may, by order, ordinance, or resolution, with respect to freeways or designated portions thereof, under their respective jurisdictions, to which all rights of access have been acquired, prohibit or restrict the use of freeways or any portion thereof by pedestrians, bicycles, or other non-motorized traffic or by any person operating a motor-driven cycle or a motorized bicycle. Any such prohibition or restriction pertaining to either bicycles or motor-driven cycles, or to both, shall be deemed to include motorized bicycles; and no person may operate a motorized bicycle wherever such prohibition or restriction is in force. Notwithstanding any provisions of any order, ordinance, or resolution to the contrary, the driver or passengers of a disabled vehicle stopped on a freeway may walk to the nearest exit, in either direction, on that side of the freeway upon which the vehicle is disabled, from which telephone or motor vehicle repair services are available.
     (b) Such prohibitory regulation shall be effective when appropriate signs giving notice thereof are erected upon any freeway and the approaches thereto.
     (c) No ordinance or resolution of local authorities shall apply to any state highway until the proposed ordinance or resolution has been presented to, and approved in writing by, the Department of Transportation.

22400.   (a) No person shall drive upon a highway at such a slow speed as to impede or block the normal and reasonable movement of traffic, except when reduced speed is necessary for safe operation or because on a grade or in compliance with law.
     (b) Whenever the Department of Transportation determines on the basis of an engineering and traffic survey that slow speeds on any part of a state highway consistently impede the normal and reasonable movement of traffic, the department may determine and declare a minimum speed limit below which no person shall drive a vehicle, except when necessary for safe operation or in compliance with law, when appropriate signs giving notice thereof are erected along the part of the highway for which a minimum speed limit has been established.
     Subdivision (b) of this section shall apply only to vehicles subject to registration.

22409.   No person shall operate any vehicle equipped with any solid tire when such vehicle has a gross weight as set forth in the following table at any speed in excess of the speeds set forth opposite such gross weight:

When gross weight of vehicle and load is:	Maximum speed in miles per hour:
10,000 lbs. or more but less than 16,000 lbs.	25
16,000 lbs. or more but less than 22,000 lbs.	15
22,000 lbs. or more	12

22503.5 Notwithstanding any other provision of this code, any local authority may, by ordinance or resolution, establish special parking regulations
for two-wheeled or three-wheeled motor vehicles.

23330. Except where a special permit has been obtained from the Department
of Transportation under the provisions of Article 6 (commencing with Section
35780) of Chapter 5 of Division 15, none of the following shall be permitted
on any vehicular crossing:
    (a) Animals while being led or driven, even though tethered or
harnessed.
    (b) Bicycles or motorized bicycles, unless the department by signs
indicates that either bicycles or motorized bicycles are permitted upon all
or any portion of the vehicular crossing.
    (c) Vehicles carrying explosives in any amount or carrying more
than 10 gallons of corrosive liquids.
    (d) Vehicles having a total width of vehicle or load exceeding 102
inches.
    (e) Vehicles carrying items prohibited by regulations promulgated
by the Department of Transportation.

24001.5 A golf cart as defined in Section 345 shall only be subject to the
provisions of this division which are applicable to a motorcycle.

24002. It is unlawful to operate any vehicle or combination of vehicles
which is in an unsafe condition, which is not equipped as required by this
code, or which is not safely loaded.

24008. It is unlawful to operate any passenger vehicle, or commercial vehicle under 4000 lbs., which has been modified from the original design so
that any portion of such vehicle other than the wheels has less clearance
from the surface of a level roadway than the clearance between the roadway
and the lowermost portion of any rim of any wheel when in contact with such
roadway.

24008.5 An "unsafe condition" within the meaning of Section 24002 includes,
but is not limited to, the raising of the center of gravity or other modification of a vehicle so as to unsafely affect its operation or stability.

24009. No person shall sell or offer for sale a new motor truck, truck
tractor, or bus that is not equipped with an identification plate or marking
bearing the manufacturer's name and the manufacturer's gross vehicle weight
rating of such vehicle.

24011. Whenever a federal motor vehicle safety standard is established under the National Traffic and Motor Vehicle Safety Act of 1966 (15 U.S.C.,
Sec. 1381, et seq.) no dealer shall sell or offer for sale a vehicle to
which the standard is applicable, unless:
    (a) Such vehicle or equipment conforms to the applicable federal
standard.
    (b) The vehicle or equipment bears thereon a certification by the
manufacturer or the distributor that it complies with the applicable federal
standards. The certification may be in the form of a symbol prescribed in

the federal standards or, if there is no federal symbol, by a symbol acceptable to the department.

24252. (a) All lighting equipment of a required type installed on a vehicle shall at all times be maintained in good working order. Lamps shall be equipped with bulbs of the correct voltage rating corresponding to the nominal voltage at the lamp socket.

(b) The voltage at any tail, stop, license plate, side marker or clearance lamp socket on a vehicle shall not be less than 85% of the design voltage of the bulb. Voltage tests shall be conducted with the engine operating.

(c) Two or more lamp or reflector functions may be combined, provided each function required to be approved meets the specifications determined and published by the department.

(1) No turn signal lamp may be combined optically with a stoplamp unless the stoplamp is extinguished when the turn signal is flashing.

(2) No clearance lamp may be combined optically with any taillamp or identification lamp.

24253. (a) All motor vehicles manufactured and first registered after January 1, 1970, shall be equipped so all taillamps are capable of remaining lighted for a period of at least one-quarter hour with the engine inoperative. This requirement shall be complied with by an energy storing system which is recharged by energy produced by the vehicle.

(b) All motorcycles manufactured and first registered after January 1, 1971, shall be equipped so all taillamps, when turned on, will remain lighted automatically for a period of at least one-quarter hour if the engine stops.

24400. During darkness, every motor vehicle other than a motorcycle shall be equipped with at least two lighted headlamps, with at least one on each side of the front of the vehicle, and, except as to vehicles registered prior to January 1, 1930, they shall be located directly above or in advance of the front axle of the vehicle. The headlamps and every light source in any headlamp unit shall be located at a height of not more than 54 inches nor less than 24 inches.

24408. (a) Every new motor vehicle registered in this state after January 1, 1940, which has multiple-beam road lighting equipment shall be equipped with a beam indicator, which shall be lighted whenever the uppermost distribution of light from the headlamps is in use, and shall not otherwise be lighted.

(b) The indicator shall be so designed and located that when lighted it will be readily visible without glare to the driver of the vehicle so equipped. Any such lamp on the exterior of the vehicle shall have a light source not exceeding two candlepower, and the light shall not show to the front or sides of the vehicle.

24409. Whenever a motor vehicle is being operated during darkness, the driver shall use a distribution of light, or composite beam, directed high enough and of sufficient intensity to reveal persons and vehicles at a safe distance in advance of the vehicle, subject to the following requirements and limitations:

(a) Whenever the driver of a vehicle approaches an oncoming vehicle within 500 feet, he shall use a distribution of light or composite beam so aimed that the glaring rays are not projected into the eyes of the oncoming driver. The lowermost distribution of light specified in this article shall be deemed to avoid glare at all times regardless of road contour.

(b) Whenever the driver of a vehicle follows another vehicle within 300 feet to the rear, he shall use the lowermost distribution of light specified in this article.

24600. During darkness every motor vehicle which is not in combination with any other vehicle and every vehicle at the end of a combination of vehicles shall be equipped with lighted taillamps mounted on the rear as follows:

(a) Every such vehicle shall be equipped with one or more taillamps.

(b) Every such vehicle, other than motorcycles, manufactured and first registered on or after January 1, 1958, shall be equipped with not less than two taillamps, except that trailers and semitrailers manufactured after July 23, 1973, which are less than 30 inches wide, may be equipped with one taillamp which shall be mounted at or near the vertical centerline of the vehicles. If such a vehicle is equipped with two taillamps, they shall be mounted as specified in subdivision (d).

(c) Every such vehicle or vehicle at the end of a combination of vehicles, subject to subdivision (a) of Section 22406 shall be equipped with not less than two taillights.

(d) When two taillamps are required, at least one shall be mounted at the left and one at the right side respectively at the same level.

(e) Taillamps shall be red in color and shall be plainly visible from all distances within 1000 feet to the rear.

(f) Taillamps on vehicles manufactured on or after January 1, 1969, shall be mounted not lower than 15 inches nor higher than 72 inches.

24601. Either the taillamp or a separate lamp shall be so constructed and placed as to illuminate with a white light the rear license plate during darkness and render it clearly legible from a distance of 50 feet to the rear. When the rear license plate is illuminated by a lamp other than a required taillamp, the two lamps shall be turned on or off only by the same controls switch at all times.

24603. Every motor vehicle which is not in combination with any other vehicle and every vehicle at the end of a combination of vehicles shall at all times be equipped with stoplamps mounted on the rear as follows:

(a) Every such vehicle shall be equipped with one or more stoplamps.

(b) Every such vehicle, other than a motorcycle, manufactured and first registered on or after January 1, 1958, shall be equipped with two stoplamps, except that trailers and semitrailers manufactured after July 23, 1973, which are less than 30 inches wide, may be equipped with one stoplamp which shall be mounted at or near the vertical centerline of the trailer. If such vehicle is equipped with two stoplamps, they shall be mounted as specified in subdivision (d).

(c) Stoplamps on vehicles manufactured on or after January 1, 1969, shall be mounted not lower than 15 inches nor higher than 72 inches.

(d) Where two stoplamps are required, at least one shall be mounted at the left and one at the right side, respectively, at the same level.

(e) Stoplamps shall emit a red or amber light and shall be plainly visible and understandable from a distance of 300 feet to the rear both during normal sunlight and at nighttime, except that stoplamps on a vehicle of a size required to be equipped with clearance lamps shall be visible from a distance of 500 feet during such times.

(f) Stoplamps shall be actuated upon the application of the service (foot) brake and the hand control head for air, vacuum, or electric brakes. In addition, all stoplamps may be activated by a mechanical device designed to function only upon sudden release of the accelerator when the vehicle is in motion. Such mechanical device shall be approved by, and comply with specifications and regulations established by, the department.

(g) Any vehicle may be equipped with supplemental stoplamps mounted to the rear of the rearmost portion of the driver's seat in its rearmost position in addition to the lamps required to be mounted on the rear of the vehicle. The supplemental stoplamp on that side of a vehicle toward which a turn will be made may flash as part of the supplemental turn signal lamp.

24606. (a) Every motor vehicle, other than a motorcycle, of a type subject to registration and manufactured on or after January 1, 1969, shall be equipped with one or more backup lamps either separately or in combination with another lamp. Any vehicle may be equipped with backup lamps.

(b) Backup lamps shall be so directed as to project a white light illuminating the highway to the rear of the vehicle for a distance not to exceed 75 feet. A backup lamp may project incidental red, amber, or white light through reflectors or lenses that are adjacent, or close to, or are a part of the lamp assembly.

(c) Backup lamps shall not be lighted except when the vehicle is about to be or is backing or except in conjunction with a lighting system which activates the lights for a temporary period after the ignition system is turned off.

24607. Every vehicle subject to registration under this code shall at all times be equipped with red reflectors mounted on the rear as follows:

(a) Every vehicle shall be equipped with at least one reflector so maintained as to be plainly visible at night from all distances within 350 to 100 feet from the vehicle when directly in front of the lawful upper headlamp beams.

(b) Every vehicle, other than a motorcycle, manufactured and first registered on or after January 1, 1965, shall be equipped with at least two reflectors meeting the visibility requirements of subdivision (a), except that trailers and semitrailers manufactured after July 23, 1973, which are less than thirty inches wide, may be equipped with one reflector which shall be mounted at or near the vertical centerline of the trailer. If such vehicle is equipped with two reflectors, they shall be mounted as specified in subdivision (d).

(c) Every motor truck having an unladen weight of more than 5000 lbs., every trailer coach, every camp trailer, every vehicle or vehicle at the end of a combination of vehicles subject to subdivision (a) of Section 22406, and every vehicle 80 or more inches in width manufactured on or after January 1, 1969, shall be equipped with at least two reflectors maintained so as to be plainly visible at night from all distances between 600 feet to 100 feet from the vehicle when directly in front of lawful upper headlamp beams.

(d) When more than one reflector is required, at least one shall be mounted at the left side, and one at the right side, respectively, at the same level. Required reflectors shall be mounted not lower than 15 inches nor higher than 60 inches. Additional reflectors of a type approved by the department may be mounted at any height.

(e) Reflectors on truck tractors may be mounted on the rear of the cab. Any reflector installed on a vehicle as part of its original equipment prior to January 1, 1941, need not be of an approved type provided it meets the visibility requirements of subdivision (a).

24609. Any vehicle may be equipped with white or amber reflectors upon the front of the vehicle, but they shall be mounted not lower than 15 inches nor higher than 60 inches.

24615. It is unlawful to operate upon a public highway any vehicle or combination of vehicles, which is designed to be and is operated at a speed of 25 miles per hour or less, unless the rearmost vehicle displays a "slow-moving vehicle emblem," except upon vehicles used by a utility, whether publicly or privately owned, for the construction, maintenance, or repair of its own facilities or upon vehicles used by highway authorities or bridge or highway districts in highway maintenance, inspection, survey, or construction work, while such vehicle is engaged in work upon a highway at the jobsite. Any other vehicle or combination of vehicles, when operated at a speed of 25 miles per hour or less, may display such emblem. The emblem shall be mounted on the rear of the vehicle, base down, and at a height of not less than three nor more than five feet from the ground to base. Such emblem shall consist of a truncated triangle having a minimum height of 14 inches with a red reflective border not less than 1 3/4 inches in width and a fluorescent orange center.

This emblem shall not be displayed except as permitted or required by this section.

24800. No vehicle shall be driven at any time with the parking lamps lighted except when the lamps are being used as turn signal lamps or when the headlamps are also lighted.

24951. (a) Any vehicle may be equipped with a lamp-type turn signal system capable of clearly indicating any intention to turn either to the right or to the left.

(b) The following vehicles shall be equipped with a lamp-type turn signal system meeting the requirements of this chapter.

(1) Motor trucks, truck tractors, buses and passenger vehicles, other than motorcycles, manufactured and first registered on or after January 1, 1958.

(2) Trailers and semitrailers manufactured and first registered between December 3, 1957, and January 1, 1969, having a gross weight of 6000 pounds or more.

(3) Trailers and semitrailers 80 or more inches in width manufactured on or after January 1, 1969.

(4) Motorcycles manufactured and first registered on or after January 1, 1973, except motor-driven cycles whose speed attainable in one mile is 30 miles per hour or less.

The requirements of this subdivision shall not apply to special mobile equipment or auxiliary dollies.

(c) Turn signal lamps on vehicles manufactured on or after January 1, 1969, shall be mounted not lower than 15 inches.

24952. A lamp-type turn signal shall be plainly visible and understandable in normal sunlight and at nighttime from a distance of at least 300 feet to the front and rear of the vehicle, except that turn signal lamps on vehicles of a size required to be equipped with clearance lamps shall be visible from a distance of 500 feet during such times.

25500. (a) Area reflectorizing material may be displayed on any vehicle provided: the color red is not displayed on the front; designs do not tend to distort the width or length of the vehicle; and designs do not resemble official traffic control devices, except that alternate striping resembling a barricade pattern may be used.

No vehicle shall be equipped with area reflectorizing material contrary to these provisions.

(b) The provisions of this section shall not apply to license plate stickers or tabs affixed to license plates as authorized by the Department of Motor Vehicles.

25651. The headlamp upon a motor-driven cycle may be of the single beam or multiple-beam type, but in either event, when the vehicle is operated during darkness, the headlamp shall comply with the requirements and limitations as follows:

(a) The headlamp shall be of sufficient intensity to reveal a person or a vehicle at a distance of not less than 100 feet when the motor-driven cycle is operated at any speed less than 25 miles per hour and at a distance of not less than 200 feet when operated at a speed of 25 not to exceed 35 miles per hour, and at a distance of 300 feet when operated at a speed greater than 35 miles per hour.

(b) In the event the motor-driven cycle is equipped with a multiple beam headlamp, the upper beam shall meet the requirements set forth above and the lowermost beam shall meet the requirements applicable to a lowermost distribution of light as set forth in subdivision (b) of Section 24407.

(c) In the event that the motor-driven cycle is equipped with a single-beam lamp, it shall be so aimed that when the vehicle is loaded, none of the high-intensity portion of light at a distance of 25 feet ahead, shall project higher than the level of the center of the lamp from which it comes.

25803. (a) All vehicles not otherwise required to be equipped with headlamps, rear lights, or reflectors by this chapter shall during darkness be equipped with at least one lighted lamp exhibiting a white light visible from a distance of 500 feet to the front of the vehicle and with a lamp exhibiting a red light visible from a distance of 500 feet to the rear of the vehicle.

(b) Such vehicle shall also be equipped with an amber reflector on the front near the left side and a red reflector on the rear near the left side. The reflectors shall be mounted on the vehicle not lower than 16 inches nor higher than 60 inches above the ground and so designed and maintained as to be visible during darkness from all distances within 500 feet from the vehicle when directly in front of a motor vehicle displaying lawful lighted headlamps undimmed.

(c) In addition, if such vehicle or the load thereon has a total
outside width in excess of 100 inches there shall be displayed during darkness at the left outer extremity at least one amber light visible under normal atmospheric conditions from a distance of 500 feet to the front, sides,
and rear. At all other times there shall be displayed at the left outer extremity a red flag or cloth not less than 16 inches square.

26301.5 Every passenger vehicle manufactured and first registered after January 1, 1973, except motorcycles, shall be equipped with an emergency brake
system so constructed that rupture or leakage-type failure of any single
pressure component of the service brake system, except structural failures
of the brake master cylinder body or effectiveness indicator body, shall not
result in complete loss of function of the vehicle's brakes when force on the
brake pedal is continued.

26311.   (a) Every motor vehicle shall be equipped with service brakes on
all wheels, except as follows:
          (1) Trucks and truck tractors having three or more axles need not
have brakes on the front wheels, except when such vehicles are equipped with
at least two steerable axles, the wheels of one such axle need not be equipped with brakes.
          (2) Any vehicle being towed in a driveway-towaway operation.
          (3) Any vehicle manufactured prior to 1930.
          (4) Any two-axle truck tractor manufactured prior to 1964.
          (5) Any sidecar attached to a motorcycle.
          (6) Any motorcycle manufactured prior to 1966. Such motorcycle
shall be equipped with brakes on at least one wheel.
          (b) Means may be used for reducing the braking effort on the front
wheels of any bus, truck, or truck tractor, provided that the means for reducing the braking effort shall be used only when operating under adverse road
conditions, such as wet, snowy, or icy roads.
          (c) Vehicles and combinations of vehicles exempted in subdivisions
(a) and (b) from the requirements of brakes on all wheels shall comply with
the stopping distance requirements of Section 26454.

26450.   Every motor vehicle shall be equipped with a service brake system
and every motor vehicle, other than a motorcycle, shall be equipped with a
parking brake system. Both the service brake and parking brake shall be
separately applied.
          If the two systems are connected in any way, they shall be so con-
structed that failure of any one part, except failure in the drums, brake-
shoes, or other mechanical parts of the wheel brake assemblies, shall not
leave the motor vehicle without operative brakes.

26451.   The parking brake system of every motor vehicle shall comply with
the following requirements:
          (a) The parking brake shall be adequate to hold the vehicle or
combination of vehicles stationary on any grade on which it is operated under all conditions of loading on a surface free from snow, ice, or loose material. In any event the parking brake shall be capable of locking the
braked wheels to the limit of traction.
          (b) The parking brake shall be applied either by the driver's mus-
cular efforts, by spring action, or by other energy which is isolated and

175

used exclusively for the operation of the parking brake and emergency stopping system.

  (c) The parking brake shall be held in the applied position by mechanical means, spring devices, or captive air pressure in self-contained cells, which self-contained cells do not lose more than five pounds of air pressure during a 30-day period from their standard operating potential as established by the manufacturer. The force to hold the vehicle parked shall be applied through mechanical linkage to the braked wheels when a spring device or captive air pressure in self-contained cells is used.

26453. All motor vehicles shall be so equipped as to permit application of the brakes at least once for the purpose of bringing the vehicle to a stop within the legal stopping distance after the engine has become inoperative.

26454. (a) The service brakes of every motor vehicle or combination of vehicles shall be adequate to control the movement of and to stop and hold such vehicle or combination of vehicles under all conditions of loading on any grade on which it is operated.
  (b) Every motor vehicle or combination of vehicles, at any time and under all conditions of loading, shall, upon application of the service brake, be capable of stopping from an initial speed of 20 miles per hour according to the following requirements:

		Maximum stopping distance (feet)
(1)	Any passenger vehicle	25
(2)	Any single motor vehicle with a manufacturer's gross vehicle weight rating of less than 10,000 lbs.	30
(3)	Any combination of vehicles consisting of passenger vehicles or any motor vehicle with a manufacturer's gross vehicle weight rating of less than 10,000 lbs. in combination with any trailer, semitrailer, or trailer coach	40
(4)	Any single motor vehicle with a manufacturer's gross vehicle weight rating of 10,000 lbs. or more, or any bus	40
(5)	All other combinations of vehicles	50

26456. Stopping distance requirement tests shall be conducted on a substantially level, dry, smooth, hard-surfaced road that is free from loose material and where the grade does not exceed plus or minus 1%. Stopping distance shall be measured from the instant brake controls are moved and from an initial speed of approximately 20 miles per hour. No test of brake performance shall be made upon a highway at a speed in excess of 25 miles per hour.

26457. Special mobile equipment, logging vehicles, equipment operated under special permit, and any chassis without body or load are not subject to stopping distance requirements, but if any such vehicle or equipment cannot be stopped within 32 feet from an initial speed of 15 miles per hour, it shall not be operated at a speed in excess of that permitting a stop in 32 feet.

26700.   Every passenger vehicle, other than a motorcycle, and every bus, motortruck or truck tractor, and every firetruck, fire engine or other fire apparatus, whether publicly or privately owned, shall be equipped with an adequate windshield.

26703.   (a) No person shall replace any glazing materials used in partitions, doors, or windows in any motor vehicle, or in the outside windows or doors of any camper, with any glazing material other than safety glazing material.
         (b) No person shall replace any glazing material used in the windshield, rear window, wind deflectors, or windows to the left and right of the driver with any material other than safety glazing material.

26706.   (a) Every motor vehicle, except motorcycles, equipped with a windshield shall also be equipped with a self-operating windshield wiper.
         (b) Every new motor vehicle first registered after December 1, 1949, except motorcycles, shall be equipped with two such windshield wipers, one mounted on the right half and one on the left half of the windshield.
         (c) This section does not apply to snow removal equipment with adequate manually operated windshield wipers.

26707.   Windshield wipers required by this code shall be maintained in good operating condition and shall provide clear vision through the windshield for the driver. Wipers shall be operated under conditions of fog, snow, or rain and shall be capable of effectively clearing the windshield under all ordinary storm or load conditions while the vehicle is in operation.

26709.   (a) Every motor vehicle registered in a foreign jurisdiction and every motorcycle subject to registration in this state shall be equipped with a mirror so located as to reflect to the driver a view of the highway for a distance of at least 200 feet to the rear of such vehicle.
         Every motor vehicle subject to registration in this state, except motorcycles, shall be equipped with not less than two such mirrors, including one affixed to the left-hand side.
         (b) The following described types of motor vehicles, of a type subject to registration, shall be equipped with mirrors on both the left- and right-hand sides of the vehicle so located as to reflect to the driver a view of the highway through each mirror for a distance of at least 200 feet to the rear of such vehicle.
         (1) A motor vehicle so constructed or loaded as to obstruct the driver's view to the rear.
         (2) A motor vehicle towing a vehicle and the towed vehicle or load thereon obstructs the driver's view to the rear.
         (3) A bus or trolley coach.
         (c) The provisions of subdivision (b) shall not apply to a passenger vehicle when the load obstructing the driver's view consists of passengers.

27000.   Every motor vehicle when operated on a highway shall be equipped with a horn in good working order and capable of emitting sound audible under normal conditions from a distance of not less than 200 feet, but no horn shall emit an unreasonably loud or harsh sound. An authorized emergency vehicle used in responding to fire calls may be equipped with, and use in conjunction with the siren on such vehicle, an air horn which emits sounds which do not comply with the requirements of this section.

27450.   When any vehicle is equipped with any solid tire, the solid tire shall have a minimum thickness of resilient rubber as follows:
          (a) If the width of the tire is three inches but less than six inches, one inch thick.
          (b) If the width of the tire is six inches but not more than nine inches, 1 1/4 inches thick.
          (c) If the width of the tire is more than nine inches, 1 1/2 inches thick.

27451.   The rubber of a solid tire shall be measured between the surface of the roadway and the nearest metal part of the base flange to which the tire is attached at the point where the concentrated weight of the vehicle bears upon the surface of the roadway.

27452.   The required thickness of rubber shall extend evenly around the entire periphery of the tire. The entire solid tire shall be securely attached to the channel base and shall be without flat spots or bumpy rubber.

27455.   (a) On and after January 1, 1975, no person shall sell or offer for sale an inner tube for use in a radial tire unless, at the time of manufacture, the tube valve stem is colored red or is distinctly marked in accordance with rules and regulations adopted by the department, taking into consideration the recommendations of manufacturers of inner tubes.
          (b) No person shall install an inner tube in a radial tire unless the inner tube is designed for use in a radial tire.

27465.   (a) No dealer or person holding a retail seller's permit shall sell, offer for sale, expose for sale, or install on a vehicle for use on a highway a pneumatic tire when the tire is so worn that less than 1/32 of an inch tread remains in any two adjacent grooves at any location on the tire. This subdivision shall not apply to any person who installs on a vehicle, as part of an emergency service rendered to a disabled vehicle upon a highway, a spare tire with which the disbled vehicle was equipped.
          (b) No person shall use on a highway a pneumatic tire when the tire is so worn that less than 1/32 of an inch tread depth remains in any two adjacent grooves at any location on the tire.
          (c) The measurement of tread depth shall not be made where tiebars, humps, or fillets are located.
          (d) The requirements of this section shall not apply to those vehicles defined in Sections 322, 323, 545, and 36000, and those listed in Section 34500.

27600.   No person shall operate any motor vehicle having three or more wheels, any trailer, or semitrailer unless equipped with fenders, covers, or devices, including splash aprons, or unless the body of the vehicle or attachments thereto afford adequate protection to effectively minimize the spray or splash of water or mud to the rear of the vehicle and all such equipment or such body or attachments thereto shall be at least as wide as the tire tread. This section does not apply to those vehicles exempt from registration, trailers, and semitrailers having an unladen weight of under 1500 pounds, or any vehicles manufactured and first registered prior to January 1, 1971, having an unladen weight of under 1500 pounds.

28071. Every passenger vehicle registered in this state shall be equipped with a front bumper and with a rear bumper. As used in this section, "bumper" means any device designed and intended by a manufacturer to prevent the front or rear of the body of the vehicle from coming into contact with any other motor vehicle. This section shall not apply to any passenger vehicle that is required to be equipped with an energy absorption system pursuant to either state or federal law, or to any passenger vehicle which was not equipped with a front or rear bumper, or both, at the time that it was first sold and registered under the laws of this or any other state or foreign jurisdiction.

34710. As used in this division, "passenger vehicle" means any motor vehicle defined in Section 465, except any of the following motor vehicles:
     (a) Motorcycles.
     (b) Housecars.
     (c) Specially constructed vehicles.
     (d) Motor vehicles equipped with four-wheel drive.
     (e) Motor vehicles constructed on a truck chassis.
     (f) Motor vehicles operated for hire, compensation, or profit.
     (g) Makes of motor vehicles of a model year manufactured or sold in California in quantities of less than 2000 units for each such model year.
     (h) Motor vehicles designed and constructed by the manufacturer of such vehicles, for off-highway use, as determined by the Department of Motor Vehicles.

34715. (a) No new passenger vehicle, except a vehicle certified by its manufacturer as having been manufactured prior to January 1, 1973, shall be sold or registered on or after September 1, 1973, unless it has a manufacturer's warranty that it is equipped with an appropriate energy absorption system so that it can be driven directly into a standard Society of Automotive Engineers (SAE J-850) test barrier at a speed of five miles per hour without sustaining any property damage to the front of the vehicle and can be driven at a speed of five miles per hour into such barrier without sustaining any property damage to the rear of such vehicle.
     (b) Property damage, within the meaning of this section, shall not include abrasion to surfaces at the point or points of contact of the vehicle with the test barrier when undergoing such testing.

35100. (a) The total outside width of any vehicle or the load thereon shall not exceed 96 inches, except as otherwise provided in this chapter.
     (b) Notwithstanding the provisions of subdivision (a), the total outside width of any load may exceed a width of 96 inches, but shall not exceed a width of 100 inches, except as otherwise provided in this chapter.
     (c) The amendments to this section enacted at the 1973-1974 Regular Session of the Legislature increasing the permissible width of loads from 96 to 100 inches shall have no application to highways which are a part of the national system of interstate and defense highways (as referred to in Section 108 of the Federal Aid Highway Act of 1956) when such application would prevent this state from receiving any federal funds for highway purposes, and in such event the provisions of law applicable to the maximum per-

missible width of any such load in effect on December 31, 1974, shall remain applicable to such load.

35250. No vehicle shall exceed a height of 13 feet and 6 inches measured from the surface on which the vehicle stands, except as follows:

(a) The boom or mast of a forklift truck may not exceed a height of 14 feet.

(b) A double-deck bus may not exceed a height of 14 feet, 3 inches. Any double-deck bus which exceeds a height of 13 feet, 6 inches shall only be operated on those highways where such operation is deemed safe by the entity operating the bus.

35400. (a) No vehicle shall exceed a length of 40 feet.

(b) This section does not apply to:

(1) A vehicle used in a combination of vehicles when the excess length is caused by auxiliary parts, equipment, or machinery not used as space to carry any part of the load, except that the combination of vehicles shall not exceed the length provided for combination vehicles.

(2) A vehicle when the excess length is comprised by any parts necessary to comply with the fender and mudguard regulations of this code.

(3) An articulated bus, except that such bus shall not exceed a length of 60 feet.

(4) An articulated trolley coach, except that such trolley coach shall not exceed a length of 50 feet.

(5) A semitrailer while being towed by a truck tractor, if the distance from the kingpin to the rearmost axle of the semitrailer does not exceed 38 feet, provided that the semitrailer does not, exclusive of attachments, extend forward of the rear of the cab of the truck tractor.

(6) A bus when the excess length is caused by the projection of a front safety bumper or a rear safety bumper, or both. Such safety bumper shall not cause the length of the vehicle to exceed the maximum legal limit by more than one foot in the front and one foot in the rear. For purposes of this chapter, "safety bumper" means any device which may be fitted on an existing bumper or which replaces the bumper and is so constructed, treated, or manufactured so that it absorbs energy upon impact.

35408.   In no event shall a front bumper on a motor vehicle be constructed or installed so as to project more than two feet forward of the foremost part of either the fenders or cab structure or radiator, whichever extends farthest toward the front of such vehicle.

35413.   No person shall drive a motor vehicle upon a highway with any tire fastened in front of the vehicle, unless such tire is securely mounted in a tire carrier firmly attached to the vehicle in a manner approved and specified by the California Highway Patrol.

b FINDING RESISTANCE AND WATTAGE VALUES FOR RHEOSTATS

1.   So, you're ready to find the values of rheostats or tapped-resistors --- resistance and wattage --- for control of the current in the shunt field of shunt and compound motors. (Read that one _slowly_.) First, determine the voltage rating of the motor. Then, once you've found which leads are those of the field coils (and not the armature or series windings), you'll be able to discover the precise field current by one of two methods. You can connect the motor's rated voltage in batteries, and read the current draw on an ammeter. The other is to measure the DC resistance of the winding with an ohmmeter; since a small VOM (volt-ohmmeter) is handy for all kinds of things when doing the EV's electrical system, may I suggest that you think about getting one? Once you've got the ohm value of the field coils, you simply divide that into the rated voltage, and that's the number of amps the field draws.

2.   The field current is usually about 1/20th of the armature's current requirements and about 1/3rd to 1/4th the motor's rated voltage. At worst, a 48-volt motor will draw about 4 amps (in the 2-5HP range). Let's assume that's our finding when we conduct one of the two tests described above for finding the field current requirements.

3.   It's a characteristic of most motors that you do not need to reduce the field current very much to affect a _lot_ of change in the field flux (and a corresponding change in the motor speed, horsepower, current, etc.). In other words, decreasing the field current to one-half of what it normally draws may bring the motor to a stop under normal load. That's as good a place to start as any.

RESISTANCE

If we have a 48-volt motor rating, and we determine through testing that the field current draw is normally 4 amperes, we can determine the coil's own DC resistance thus:

$$48 \text{ volts} \div 4 \text{ amps} = 12 \text{ ohms, because Volts} = \text{Amps} \times \text{Ohms}$$

Since the field coils have a DC resistance of 12 ohms, all we need to do is add another 12 ohms of resistance. Or, more specifically, a 12-ohm rheostat. Wired in series (as shown in the figure), that totals to 24 ohms.

181

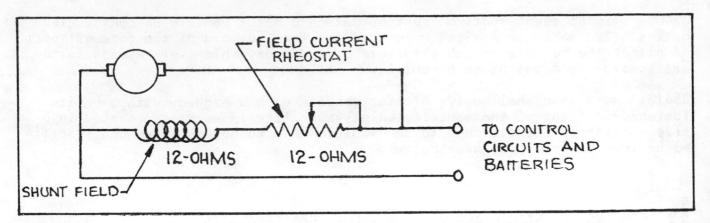

WATTAGE

We will need to find the wattage rating of the rheostat if we expect it to stay 'cool' in use. First, let's find the wattage rating of the field coils without a rheostat added:

Watts = Volts times Amps

Watts = 48 volts X 4 amperes

= 192 watts

The wattage of the field coils with the rheostat in-line and set at its full value (12 ohms) comes to:

Watts = 48 volts X 2 amps

= 96 watts

Since each of the resistances --- field coils and rheostat --- are identical, and both are sharing the 96 watts of heat dissipation, we have:

$R_{coil} + R_{rheostat}$ = 2R = 96 watts

Therefore, R = 96 ÷ 2 = 48 watts

Therefore, for this shunt field, you will need a rheostat with a minimum value of 50 watts and a resistance of at least 12 ohms. I'd get one with values of 75 watts and 15 ohms (if possible), so that I might be able to cut down the field current just a little bit more. But, be careful if you extend the ratings. An increased resistance rating without a substantially increased wattage rating spells trouble. A rheostat set halfway between full resistance and no resistance cannot dissipate but a portion of the wattage rating (heat) for the whole rheostat.

C SOLUTIONS TO PROBLEMS

Here are the solutions to the problems posed on page 42. The basic information given for all four problems follows. George is driving a 1600-lbs. (curb weight) EV. Toupee and all, he weighs 180 lbs. With George in the EV, we have 1780 lbs. of operating weight. The EV is sporting 6 by 16 tires, properly inflated, I might add, to 20 PSI. The EVs efficiency is 25% and it's running a 15HP motor. Now to the problems!

PROBLEM ONE

Here we find George trying to figure out if he can do 35 mph on a level concrete surface. To find this solution, let's drag one of the aforementioned formulas back out of the bin:

$$(1) HP_m = \frac{(\mu)\ (W)\ (k)\ (V)}{550\text{-ft lbs/sec}}$$

It should be obvious that we need to find μ and we need to find 'k'. μ is easy; we look at the chart (Fig. 2-6 on page 24) under 16 x 6 tires. I come up with .027 for concrete. The value of 'k' is determined also from its chart (see Fig. 2-8 on page 26); for 25%, that's a 'k' value of 4. So, by filling in the respective values, we have:

$$15HP = \frac{(.027)\ (1780\text{-lb})\ (4)\ (V)}{550\text{ ft-lbs/sec}}$$

Let's do two things to rearrange the formula so that we can easily solve to find 'V'. First, multiply 550 ft-lbs/sec by 15HP; this puts the HP 'tag' into its corresponding expression of ft-lb/sec. Comes to 8250 ft-lb/sec by my calculator. Next, let's solve for 'V':

$$V = \frac{8250\text{ ft-lbs/sec}}{(.027)\ 1780\text{-lb})\ (4)} = \frac{8250\text{ ft-lbs/sec}}{192.24\text{-lb}} = 42.9\text{ ft/sec}$$

Note that 'V' is expressed in ft/sec. We can look at Fig. 2-9 on page 27 for an approximation of that figure in MPH, but let's use the conversion factor for ft/sec to MPH. That's .682, or:

$$MPH = (.682)\ (42.9\text{ ft/sec}) = 29.3\text{ MPH}$$

The question was: Could George do 35 MPH? The answer is: NO!

PROBLEM TWO

In this next problem, nothing changes except that George is confronting a hill with a 9% grade; here's where the hillclimbing horsepower chart (see Fig. 2-10 on page 30) comes in handy. A quick look at a 9%-grade and at 30 mph (which his top speed of 29.3 MPH EV approaches) indicates the need for an additional 7+ HP. How do we go about finding at what speed the EV can take this hill?

Without getting into a 'fit-all' expression to account for the EV's HP requirements for both level and hillclimbing horsepower, let's simply check out some things. First, we know that everything else about this vehicle that's expressed in formula (1) is constant --- the efficiency, weight, and motor horsepower remain the same. Therefore, we can deal with the speed given in Problem One (29.3 mph) on level ground and the EV climbing a hill of known grade at an unknown speed, expressing differences as a ratio. We know:

$$\frac{15HP \text{ (level)}}{29.3 \text{ MPH}} = \frac{XHP \text{ (level)} + YHP \text{ (hillclimbing)}}{Z \text{ mph}}$$

It may seem that we have 2 knowns and 3 unknowns, but not true; we have:

$$XHP \text{ (level)} + YHP \text{ (hillclimbing)} = 15HP$$

Rather than try to derive one more relationship and sub-solve the 'three-equations/three-unknowns' malarky, let's take a look at that chart again (page 30). Picking at random, we see that at 20 MPH for a 9% grade, the EV would need an additional 4.8 HP over that required to propel the EV at the same speed on level ground. Finding that value is easy because, if all else remains constant, a lower speed requires less horsepower, or:

$$15HP/29.3MPH = X \text{ HP}/20 \text{ mph}$$

With a quick cross-multiply, I get:

$$X \text{ HP} = 10.2 \text{ HP}$$

Since it's a combination of the two --- level and hillclimbing --- that determines the amount of horsepower we need to climb the hill at 20 MPH, we add them:

$$10.2 \text{ HP} + 4.8 \text{ HP} = 15 \text{ HP}$$

This is what we need, and this is what we've got. So George can make it up that slope at 20 mph, provided that he has a gear ratio which will develop that horsepower at that speed. And, believe it or not, when I wrote that problem, I didn't know that it would come out that easily. If the required HP figure had come out being more than the actual horsepower available, you'd have to check out another speed below the one we tried.

PROBLEM THREE

George goofs on his turnoff and finds himself, as I'm sure you have at times, in the wrong place. George can go across a field instead of back-tracking, only it's loam instead of concrete. We find that his μ will be increased considerably; looking at the chart (Fig. 2-6 on page 24), we find that his tires will have a μ of .319 through that stuff. But George remembers that by deflating the tires a bit, he can decrease that value of μ. So he does, and it does; he doesn't have a way of finding out, but the good fairy told me he decreased the μ by 25%. Since 25% of .319 is .080, he's now got a μ of .239, which is still tough.

At this point, you could enter this figure into formula (1) but, since nothing else has changed since Problem One, let's just set up a ratio. We know that with an increased μ, we are going to be moving a lot slower than the 29.3 mph on concrete. That will be our doublecheck if we get the ratio expressed incorrectly. Here it is:

$$\frac{29.3mph}{.239} = \frac{Xmph}{.027}$$

Or,   X mph = 3.3 MPH

Slow going, for sure. But, we're not finished yet. The problem asks for the amount of time that it will take to cross the field. And, since we can go 3.31 miles in one hour, we can go one mile in

$$\frac{3.31\ miles}{hour} = \frac{1\ mile}{X\ hours}$$

     X hours = .3 hours or, approximately, 18 minutes.

PROBLEM FOUR

George is going to have to do some fast calculating on this one, or he may make the trip into town in vain. Let's do it for him. A few things have changed here. Mertha is in the vehicle now, and that's another 350 lbs; total operating weight of the EV, including George (Mertha doesn't drive, or she'd probably leave him behind), is now 2130 lbs. The question is: Can they make it into town (5 miles away) in 13 minutes? First, let's translate that into MPH by a simple ratio:

$$\frac{5\ miles}{13\ minutes} = \frac{X\ miles}{60\ minutes}$$

Or,   X miles = 23.1 mph

We know that he could do 29.3 mph with 1780-lbs of weight, so now we have:

$$\frac{1780-lb}{2130-lb} = \frac{X\ mph}{29.3\ mph}$$

Which is how fast they can go and, since we see that they can make it if they average 23.1 MPH, there's no question that they can make it, barring blown fuses, stray golf-balls, and bursting A-bombs.

As an exercise, you might work out the problems by using formula (1); they should be identical. I won't check them, so it may be one way to catch me in an error!

d MORE SOLUTIONS TO PROBLEMS

Okay, before we work out the solutions to the problems posed in Figures 2-16 through 2-19 (page 50), let's look at a couple of rules for working with gear ratios to keep things from getting too confused.

RULE ONE ---Ratios in gears/sprockets/pulleys are commonly expressed as the ratio of input speed to output speed. That is:

> ratio = input/output or Input: Output.

RULE TWO ---To keep things tidy, it's best to consider the output speed as unit one (1) and let the input side of the expression represent the ratio. Or:

> 1:2 is incorrect but .5:1 is correct.

RULE THREE ---Reduce the ratio until the output side is reduced to unit one.

RULE FOUR ---Proper ratio expression (as in TWO above) is particularly important when computing multiple ratios to determine the overall ratio. To quickly get a gear ratio into the proper expression, divide the output gear size (or driven shaft) by the input gear size (or drive shaft). This is the correct lefthand figure (to the left of the colon); the righthand expression will be unit one (1).

RULE FIVE ---To find an overall gear ratio if multiple ratios are involved, simply multiply all of the lefthand figures together. The product of the lefthand figures --- all those ones multiplied by other ones --- will be one.

If for whatever reason you need to reverse the unit one in the expression without messing up the ratio expression, divide the figure which is not one into one. Or:

> To reverse .5:1 means 1/.5, which is 2, or 1:2 is the same ratio.

> To reverse 1:4.5 means 1/4.5, which is .22 or .22:1 is the same ratio.

Okay, now the problems!

PROBLEM ONE

1. From Fig. 2-16, we have a 1-1/2 inch diameter gear turning at 1000 RPM and spinning a 24-inch bicycle wheel and we need to determine its RPM. First, let's get the gear ratio. Using rule #4, we divide the 24-inch wheel by the 1-1/2 inch one.

> $\frac{24}{1.5} = 16$ The ratio is then 16:1.

Since this expression says that the little wheel is turning 16 times faster than the big one, we can find the RPM of the bicycle wheel by:

$$\frac{1000 \text{ RPM}}{16} = 62.5 \text{ RPM}$$

If we sneak a look at Fig. 2-13, we'll see that the bicycle is doing less than 5mph.

PROBLEM TWO

In Fig. 2-17, we've got two ratios to concern ourselves with; they are:

a. $\frac{12''}{2''} = 6$, or 6:1 for the first gear ratio, and

b. $\frac{4''}{3''} = 1.3$, or 1.3:1 for the second gear ratio.

Now, let's multiply the two ratios together for the overall ratio:

6 times 1.3 = 7.8

Since the driveshaft is turning at 30 rpm and it's turning 7.8 times faster than the final, driven shaft, the latter must be turning at:

$$\frac{30 \text{ RPM}}{7.8} = 3.85 \text{ RPM}$$

PROBLEM THREE

This is an easy one, because the ratios are already given for us --- 2.1:1 and 4.5:1 ---so we apply Rule 5:

2.1 times 4.5 = 10.5:1

We know the input to the transmission is 1800 rpm and, by looking at the ratios, we see that the output shaft (or wheel) is turning at:

$$\frac{1800 \text{ RPM}}{10.5} = 171.4 \text{ RPM}$$

PROBLEM FOUR

Don't get blown away by the appearance of this one; it just looks complicated. Let's take it piece by piece:

a.   3/2= 1.5:1
b.   4/7= .57:1
c.   5/2= 2.5:1
d.   4/10= .4/1

Multiply the left side together and you'll get:

1.5 times .57 times 2.5 times .4 = .855, or .855:1

Whoa! That's not the answer. I asked for the ratio of output to input, which is backward to the normal way. And, I won't accept 1:.855 either. Apply Rule 2, or:

1:.855 is the same as 1/.855:1 or 1.17:1.

E <u>BATTERY COMBINATIONS</u> (from page 78)

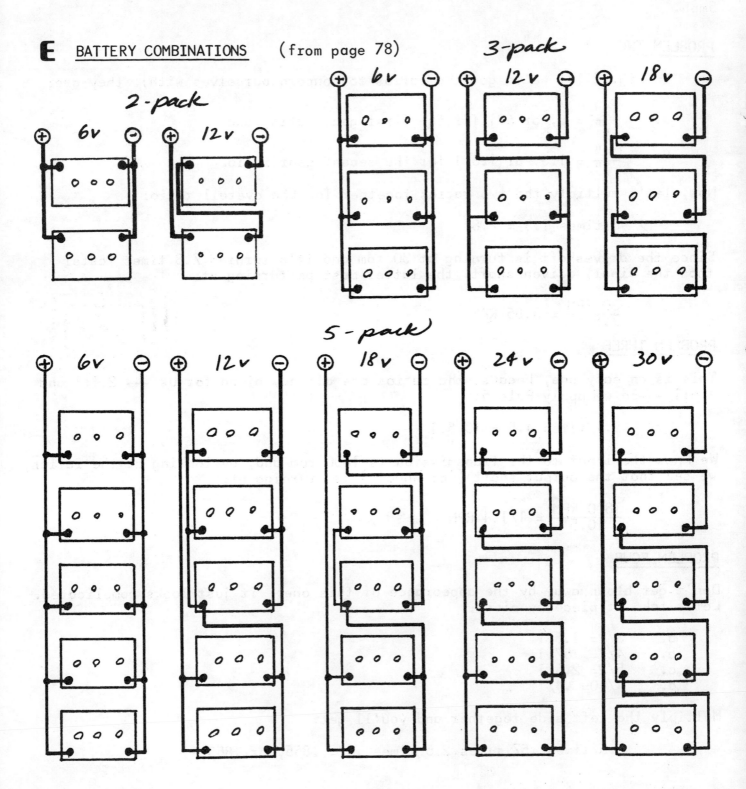

6-pack

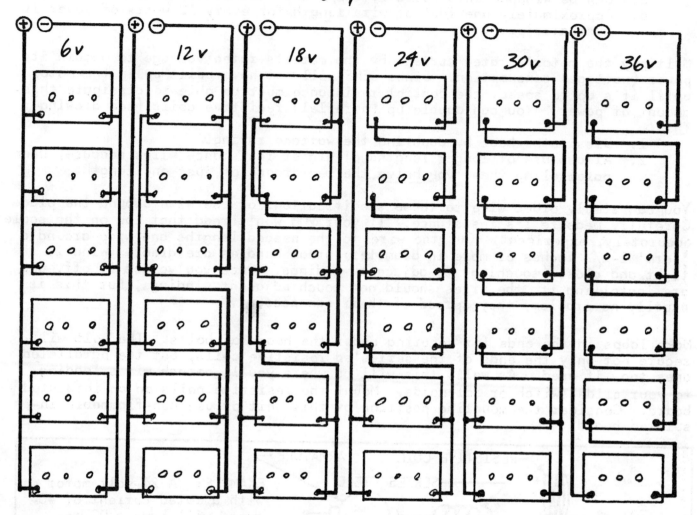

f RESISTIVE COILS FOR ARMATURE CURRENT CONTROL

To find the values of resistive coils used to limit armature current you'll need to know, or find (by experimentation) what the motor's rated current is. Divide the motor's rated voltage by its rated current; this gives you the motor's DC resistance. The total resistance you'll need for control should equal the motor's DC resistance. Determine the number of discrete steps you wish to use (usually around 5) and ADD one to this number. Divide this figure into the total resistance figure. Distribute the resistance as in the drawing.

Resistor coils are made from resistive wire, having the following general characteristics:
1. High melting point.
2. Non-corroding with applied heat.
3. 1/8" diameter or larger.

4. Resistance somewhere around 48 ohms per 1000 feet.
5. Can be wrapped into coils of 1-1/2 inch diameter without breaking.
6. Approximately one foot of wire length for every 12 watts of power it must dissipate.

Multiply the motor's rated current by the motor's rated voltage to obtain its power (wattage) consumption. Since CEMF will not have built up in the motor until it's up to speed, the control resistance must be able to dissipate this amount of power. You can double up (parallel) resistive coils (see drawing). This:
1. Dissipates heat by doubling the wattage rating.
2. Allows use of longer lengths of higher resistance wires because, when paralleling them, you <u>halve</u> the resistance of just one length.

You can simply order wire to these specifications or use wire around the place. Carefully measure its resistance. If your VOM won't read that low on the scale accurately, experiment. Cut the wire to the needed lengths and wrap around a 'form' 1-1/2 inches or more in diameter; broom handles are great. Wind it tight and close (touching) to adjacent windings. Once you've got it off, and are installing it, the wires should not touch adjacent windings, but this is usually no problem; they spread of their own account.

Make loops in the ends for securing under the heads of bolts. The bolt will secure not only the ends of the series'ed resistive coils, but the paralleled ones too, if used. As well, this will be where you'll attach wires leading to your slide-switch or solenoids. Mount the resistive coils on an insulated board. Consider the mounting position of this unit or use non-flammable insulated board.

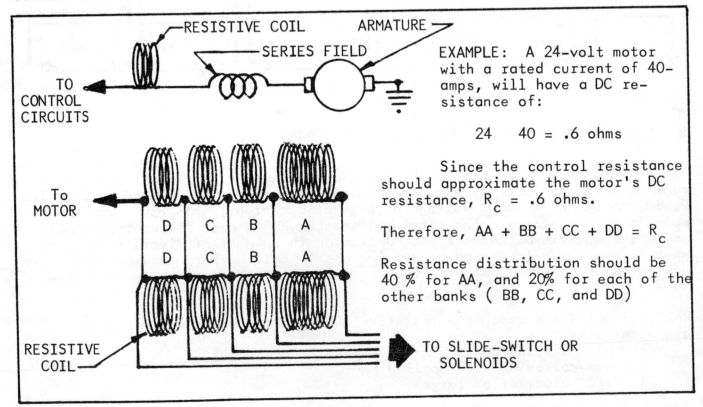

TO CONTROL CIRCUITS — RESISTIVE COIL — SERIES FIELD — ARMATURE

To MOTOR

RESISTIVE COIL

TO SLIDE-SWITCH OR SOLENOIDS

EXAMPLE: A 24-volt motor with a rated current of 40-amps, will have a DC resistance of:

$$24 \quad 40 = .6 \text{ ohms}$$

Since the control resistance should approximate the motor's DC resistance, $R_c = .6$ ohms.

Therefore, $AA + BB + CC + DD = R_c$

Resistance distribution should be 40 % for AA, and 20% for each of the other banks (BB, CC, and DD)

G   SAFETY

Safety usually gets a lot of lip-service --- particularly right after a grue-some accident. That's because we tend to forget such things as maintenance or monthly checks, letting schedules and little irritating noises 'go' be-cause we don't have time just at the moment, but 'maybe tomorrow'. And, most of us are very lucky. We get trouble when it really isn't. What I mean is: something happens and we are able to pull over to the side of the road and have our troubles towed away. Those folks who could really tell the story about safety are dead. It's not a statistically-supported fact but, if we had investigative teams for car accidents like we have for airplane crashes, I think a lot of those 'lost control of the vehicle'-categorized accidents would end up being classed as 'mechanical failure' or 'poor design'. All of which means: Trouble comes from many directions at different times. You only have to be unsafe one time to make it your last time.

Periodic maintenance and care of an EV will go a long way toward spotting potential hazards, which shouldn't have the chance to bloom into real dangers. Since maintenance tends to get boring for some folks after a while, I suggest that you 'design-in' safety wherever you can. That's the way I'll treat the subjects dealt with in this section --- safety in design, installation, oper-ation, and maintenance. Your EV can only be as safe as you make it!

BATTERY DESIGN SAFETY

When designing the battery compartment, provide for battery strap-down. This will keep the batteries in place, whether you're climbing hills or bouncing along a rough road. You don't need to have a ruptured battery case or spill-ed acid from the caps. Should you ever (cringe!) 'roll' your EV, you certain-ly don't need to be swimming in sulphuric acid along with all of your other troubles!

Keep spark-producing items --- switches, relays, solenoids, lights, etc. --- out of the battery compartment. That goes for any conductor of electricity that might, through on-the-road antics, be brought into contact with the battery posts or associated wiring.

Pretend that the batteries are a bunch of two-year-old kids left in a room by themselves. That means no loose objects they can get hold of, and no sharp (edge or point) protrusions that might puncture the little darlings.

Place the batteries where they will do minimal harm if a case should rupture. If this is impossible, put them wherever they get lots of protection, even if you have a 'fender-bender' with someone.

You don't need any vented gases in either the passenger compartment or anywhere they might be ignited. Even if you install blowers, watch out where you vent the gases. This is not going to be an accidental thing; you must design proper venting for your EV.

Batteries get hot, too, during excessive consumption or prolonged use. This should not happen; temperatures above 125°F will destroy a battery. Make sure that you provide for ventilations around, across, and even under the batteries. This will pay double dividends. It will keep things cool, and also make it easier to hose down the batteries when you need to clean them.

BATTERY INSTALLATION SAFETY

Watch what you set the batteries down on as you install them. Sure, you may have installed 'whoopee cushions' in there, but if you don't look, you might find that little sheet-metal screw you dropped yesterday the rough way.

Wirebrush battery posts and connector terminals until you get bright, shiny surfaces (lead or copper). Then, using lockwashers, tighten down the connectors. Doublecheck the polarity of the batteries, shifting batteries around if you stuck 'em in there wrong. When you've got good, 'sanitary' connections, smear vaseline about the lead or copper surfaces of posts and terminals alike. Gook it on there if you can't be sure that you're getting it into the crevices. Then, wipe off the excess, leaving a thin coat.

Do not install the batteries' connectors until you have checked out the control system entirely, and you know the EV will not start as you make the last connection. At the least bit of sparking or 'hot' smell, disconnect what you've just done, and re-check everything. If you inadvertently short out a battery, don't use your hands to rip off the connector; burned hands only compound the problem. A lead-acid battery will not be destroyed by shorting it out; its internal resistance prevents destructive current flow. It's only if a spark or glowing-red wire ignites battery gases that you've got trouble. If it shorts but doesn't blow, you've got some time. More than enough if you have a pair of wire cutters with you and can cut the offending wires; they'll be so hot, they'll cut easily. Since this may cause a spark, try to cut into a portion of the wire not immediately above the battery's vent caps.

Never use tools around the batteries which can physically short out one or more terminals. The best scheme is to buy an extra open-end or closed-end wrench just for the battery pack, and tape it up with electrical tape. The rubber stuff gets sticky in hot weather, so use friction tape if possible. Cover the other end of the wrench entirely and the handle, too; leave only a little bit of the 'working' end exposed. This way you can't short from any post to another, or from a post to ground. Always disconnect the grounding wire for the batteries before you work on them. If you don't know which is which, or if your EV's electrical circuit reverses this in operation, disconnect both of the 'end' wires to the battery pack (positive and negative) before working on the batteries.

BATTERY MAINTENANCE

If you should ever short one or more batteries, however temporarily, you'll notice that there are now little hollows in the posts or connectors. That's where current melted the lead to slag and 'blew' it out of there. Maybe you didn't notice it, but maybe you got blinded by it. Get my point? Get some plastic glasses which completely 'cup' your eyes --- side, top, and bottom as well as the front --- and use them whenever you must work on the batteries. That includes when you're adding water to the batteries, too. Did you know that adding water to batteries is a flagrant violation of the most basic safety rule in a chemistry lab? ("Never add water to acid.") It's true! But, because the solution is weak and because the water hits the acid down inside the vent holes, it's not particularly dangerous here. This is still playing games with your eyes, though.

When working on the powerpack, it might be a good idea to remove a ring, necklace, or watch; if they're metal, they're conductors, and you don't want them near batteries. It's a painful jig you'll be dancing, trying to get them off after they've been turned red-hot in a few seconds.

No smoking or open flame is the rule when working around batteries. So everyone knows, post this message at the charging station and in the cab of your EV. Sure, it can be safe if you do it at the proper time, in the proper way, and if you've taken the necessary precautions. But during or after charging, and during or after some heavy EV use, are <u>not</u> proper times. Pocketed gas in the battery compartment can be a real danger.

Besides the aforementioned water and hydrometer checks (see <u>Batteries</u>, pg. 61), you must clean the batteries of dust, debris, and sprayed battery acid. There will be wet or splotchy-looking areas on the battery surface. If you don't believe you've got acid spilled there, dust a little common baking soda over the batteries, and listen to it hiss and foam! A tablespoon per quart of water will be enough solution to clean the tops of the battery. Your cleaning kit should contain a toothbrush and a small artist's brush; these will help you clean around the battery connectors and vent holes. Under <u>NO</u> circumstances should you remove the vent caps while you're cleaning the battery top. You may brush some of that debris into the cells and contaminate the solution, and you'll neutralize the battery acid in the cell if you're using baking soda.

Cleaning the batteries is done whenever the need arises. Along with the hydrometer and water checks, it can be part of a schedule. At least, you'll be able to see if the batteries need cleaning when you perform the other checks. If you've given some design thought to hosing down the batteries, this will be a quick and painless job.

Do yourself a favor while you're performing checks. Look at the battery connectors. Look at the wiring. Pull on 'em, touch them. Any discrepancies of any sort, note them. If they need work, do it or note when you will.

When the batteries have been scrubbed and rinsed clean, don't forget to apply a new, thin coat of vaseline around the connectors. Usually, the positive post of the battery is the one that gets corroded or has deposits --- but do them all. Wipe off the excess vaseline; it's just a dust-catcher.

Battery acid will eat your clothes; like the weevil, it likes cotton. It won't do it at first contact, but within 18 hours, the cloth disintegrates. Even if it's a few drops of the stuff, you'll have holes. Be careful where you brush your sleeve, or what you wipe your hands on, or where those drops falling from the hydrometer are landing. Even at your best behavior, those darn drops find their way to your clothes. So, if you can afford to put those jeans and that shirt (or suit and tie if you do your work spiffied up) in the washing

24 HOURS LATER...

machine a little early, do it. If you won't immediately run the load, rinse the clothes under water, which dilutes the acid.

The hydrometer deserves some attention before you put it away for next time. First, rinse it with water. Then, remove the tip or the ball (whichever comes off the easiest) and carefully remove the float. Now, run some paper toweling up through the tube, cleaning the inner surface. Do the same for the outside surface and use baking soda on the bulb and tip to remove as much of the acid as possible. Rinse the whole affair with lots of water. If you leave any baking soda in there, it will neutralize the next sample of battery acid that you take, and screw up your reading.

Electrical shock is possible in an EV, particularly if voltages above 36 volts are present. Heck, 1-1/2 volts can kill you under the right conditions! Don't have exposed wiring. If you must get into the innards of your EV, disconnect the ground lead of the batteries. Check potential powered points with a voltmeter, not your hand or finger.

OTHER SAFETY STUFF

A book could be written on the safety aspects of just about anything. If I want to attempt that now, I'd better go to a new book because this one is getting full! I'm feeling like I've pretty well included safety in a lot of my comments throughout the book. Here are a few more pointers.

Always put the Fwd-Neutral-Rev switch in neutral when stopped, parked, charging the EV, etc. This way, accidental depression of the accelerator pedal

will not cause the EV to start. If there are children about, go one step
further; install a key-switch which prevents accidental or intentional EV
operation.

Always apply the emergency brake on an EV; it doesn't have the 'compressive
brake' a stopped car engine has, to hold the vehicle. If you've installed a
dynamic braking circuit (see Special Circuits, page 96), flip on the (manual
activation) toggle on the dashboard.

Do not put your EV into traffic for the first time before you've given it a
'workout' on a flat plain without trees, cars, people, dogs, and ditches.
If your trial surface is a bit bouncy, that's good; if it doesn't take much
to break something on a bouncy trial run, it'd only take it a little longer
to come apart on the smooth road. Of special concern are steering and brakes
--- a loss of either of these on the road is usually fatal.

Noise is energy. _Wasted_ energy. A quiet EV is an efficient EV. Lots of
whines, growls, jerks, rattles, etc., mean possible trouble --- something's
rubbing where it's not suppose to, there's a misalignment somewhere, etc.
Check it out when it occurs and try to isolate it. Repair and proceed.

Know the limitations of your EV. Don't drive it over terrain it wasn't de-
signed to handle. Don't operate it at its maximum speed without first driv-
ing it at lower speeds, until you're sure that you can handle its antics.
There are many idiosyncrasies to vehicles. Some take us back to the draw-
ing board, because they cannot be tolerated. Others, we simply live with.
A little wheel chatter at precisely 26 mph. License plate wiggle at 19 mph.
A propensity for the vehicle to lift, as if trying to take off, at 123 mph.
Irritating, yes. Dangerous, no.

Linkage is what connects the operator controls --- pedals, brake levers,
steering wheel, etc. --- to the things we're trying to affect: brakes, transmission gears, clutch, wheel assembly. And, since any system is only as good
as the weakest part of that system, make sure your linkage works! It's lousy
to have bad brakes, but it's worse to have good brakes that you can't activate.
Let's hear it for stiff linkage with steel pivots and cotter pins! And, since
brakes wear, or you may want to change the amount of pedal travel, allow for
some adjustment --- install a nut-and-bolt arrangement or drill additional
holes in the levers for more (or less) distance from the pivot.

Bibliography/Sources/References

We've put together a list of <u>some</u> of the information sources of which we are aware; a full listing would take nothing less than a whole chapter, and would unnecessarily duplicate the bibliographies of other groups.

A few words about respect and sensitivity. Many of the references or sources of information/literature/hardware are small groups, and you deserve a no-answer if you write without thinking. Always enclose a SASE (self-addressed, stamped envelope) when asking for information; it's most likely to be the right size if it's a 9 x 12 mailer. Enclose a dollar or a check for same. Most folks will return this to you, but if they're operating on a shoestring budget, it'll get you more than a weary sigh and your letter cast into the nearest trashcan. This courtesy applies to big companies, too, because most of them are staffed by real-live people, who like neat letters and don't like demands or two pages of questions. When writing and asking for info, use the KISS principle (keep it simple . . . stupid) and you'll have a good chance of getting an answer. And, while most manufacturers have departments to answer specific questions about applications of their parts, DON'T BUG THEM. They've got plenty of work to do without having to try designing an <u>EV</u> for you. Do your homework, exhausting every angle, before you run someone down on your problem. Don't ask for handouts, and you'll be surprised at how much help you'll get. Before long, you'll have accumulated a very meaty library, made contact with some knowledgeable people, and be off to a good start.

BATTERIES

Aid Equipment, 11722 S. Mayfield Ave., Alsip Industrial District, Worth, IL 60482

ABC Battery, Inc., 2709 Davison Rd., Flint, MI 48506

American Battery Co., 1520 McGavock St., Nashville, TN 37203

Atlantic Battery Co., 80-86 Elm St., Watertown, MA 02172

Barrett Battery, Inc., 3317 LaGrange St., Toledo, OH 43608

Batteries Mfg. Co., 14694 Dequindre, Detroit, MI 48212

Battery Builders Supply Co., 21 W. 238-91 St., Naperville, IL 60540

Battery Service Co., 8628 "I" St., Omaha, NB 68127

Battery Systems, Inc., 2601 S. Garnsey St., Santa Ana, CA 92707

Bright Star, 602 Getty Ave., Clifton, NJ 07015

Burgess Div. of Clevite Corp., P. O. Box 3140, St. Paul, MN 55101

Carr Battery Mfg., 634 State St., Bridgeport, CT 06603

C & D Batteries, Eltuce Corp., Washington & Cherry St., Conshohocken, PA 16428

Chloride, Inc., P. O. Box 1124, Tampa, FL 33601

Copperstate Mfg. Co., Inc., 550 S. Central, Phoenix, AZ 85004

Crescent Battery & Light Co., Inc., 818 Camp St., New Orleans, LA 70130

Crown Battery Mfg. Co., 1071 N Fifth St., Fremont, OH 43420

C & W Lektra-Battery Co., 24600 Crestview Court, Farmington, MI 48024

Delatron Systems Corp., 20370 Rand Rd., Palatine, IL 60067

Delco-Remy, Div. of GM, P. O. Box 2439, Anderson, IN 46011

Dual-Lite Co., P. O. Box 468, Newtown, CT 06470

Dyno Battery Co., 4248-23 Ave. W, Seattle, WA 98199

East Penn Mfg. Co., Inc., Lyon Station, PA 19536

Eggle-Pitchen Industries, Box 47, Joplin, MO 64801

Electro Battery, Inc., 3118-23 Ave. N, St. Petersburg, FL 33713

Electro Battery Mfg. Co., 12201 Dorsett Rd., Maryland Heights, MO 64043

Electro-Lite Battery, 1225 E. 40 St., Chattanooga, TN 37407

Elpower Corp., 2117 S. Anne St., Santa Anna, CA 92704

Empire Battery Co., 6833 Creek Rd., Cincinnati, OH 45242

ESB Batteries, Inc., P. O. Box 6949, Cleveland, OH 44101

Estee Battery Co., 2700 Carrier Ave., Los Angeles, CA 90040

Fairbanks Battery Div., North Slope Enterprises, 1/4 mile Richardson Hwy.,
     Fairbanks, AK 99701

General Battery Co., P. O. Box 1262, Reading, PA 19603

Gould, Inc., 485 Calhoun St., Trenton, NJ 08618

Great Lakes Battery Co., 6240 S. Transit Rd., Lockport, NY 14094

Gulton Battery, 212 T. Dorham Ave., Metnchen, NJ 08840

Hester Battery Co., 425 Fifth Ave. S, Nashville, TN 37203

Hydrate Battery Co., Box 4204, Lynchburg, VA 24502

Illinois Battery Mfg. Co., 2453 Irving Pk. Rd., Chicago, IL 60618

Internation Battery Mfg. Co., 1935 Woodville Rd., Oregon Branch, Toledo, OH 4551

Kansas City Battery Co., 744 Southwest Blvd., Kansas City, KS 66103

Keystone Battery Co., 16 Hamilton St., Saugus, MA 01906

KW Battery Co., 3555 Howard, Skokie, IL 60076

Marathon Battery Co., 8301 Imperial Dr., Waco, TX 76710

Moore Industrial Battery Co., 4312-20 Spring Grove Ave., Cincinnati, OH 45223

Moore Battery Co., 3860 Blake St., Denver, CO 80205

Mule Battery Co., 325 Valley St., Providence, RI 02908

New Castle Battery Mfg. Co., P. O. Box 5207, New Castle, PA 16105

Prestolite Battery Div., P. O. Box 931, Toledo, OH 43694

Ramak Industries, Inc., 3505 Winhoma Dr., Memphis, TN 38188

RCA Batteries, 415 S. 5th St., Harrison, NJ 07029

Simon Battery & Research Corp., Geidel Battery Div., 3040 Bigelow Blvd., Pittsburgh, PA 15219

Stockton Battery Mfg. Co., Inc., 1640 E. Pinchot St., Stockton, CA 95205

Surrette Storage Battery Co., Box 711, Salem, MA 01970

Texford Battery Co., 2002 Milby St., Houston, TX 77003

Trojan Battery Co., 9440 Ann St., Santa Fe Springs, CA 90670

Varta Batteries, Inc., 85 Executive Blvd., Cross Westchester, Executive Park, Elmsford, NY 10523

Wagstaff Battery Mfg. Co., 2124 N. Williams, Partland, OR 97227

Wolverine Battery Co., 1254 Phillips S.W., Grand Rapids, MI 49507

Yuasa Battery, 8108 S. Freestone Ave., Santa Fe Springs, CA 90670

Zan, David C., Inc., P. O. Box 153, Plainfield, IL 60544

ELECTRIC VEHICLES

Armco Composites, 333 N. 6th, St. Charles, IL 60174 (basic EV bodies)

Battronic Truck Corp., P. O. Box 30, Boyertown, PA 19512

Corbin Gentry, Inc., 40 Maple St., Somersville, CT 06072

Electric Fuel Propulsion Corp., 336 W. Eight Mile Rd., Detroit, MI 48220

Electric Vehicle Systems, P. O. Box 941, Danville, CA 94526

Pedalpower Bike Electrification, General Engines Co., 591 Mantua Blvd., Sewell, NJ 08080

F. J. Kielian, Specialty Merchandising, 130 Drake Ave., South San Francisco, CA 94080

Lead Industries Ass'n., 292 Madison Ave., New York, NY 10017

Sebring-Vanguard, Inc., Sebring Air Terminal, Sebring, FL 33870

Sunward Corp., 21414 Arase St., Canoga Park, CA 91304

ELECTRONIC/ELECTRICAL

Burstein-Applebee, 3199 Mercier St., Kansas City, MO 64111

Simpson Instruments, 853 Dundee Ave., Elgin, IL 60120

Surplus Center, 1000 W. "O" St., Lincoln, NB 68501

Tempo Products Co., 6200 Cochran Rd., Cleveland, OH 44139
West Wind, 309 1/2 W. Boyd Dr., Farmington, NM 87401
Zurn Industries, Inc., Recreational Prod. Div., 5533 Perry Highway, Erie, PA 16509

INVERTERS

Allied Electronics, 2400 W. Washington Blvd., Chicago, IL 60612
Basku, 603-5th, Highland, IL 60645
Creative Electronics, 221 N. LaSalle St., Suite 1038, Chicago, IL 60601
Eico Electronic Instrument Co., 283 Malta St., Brooklyn, NY 11207
Electro Sales Co., 100 Fellsway West, Somerville, MA 02145
Gauter Motor Co., 2750 W. George St., Chicago, IL 60618
Globe-Union, 5757 N. Greenbay Ave., Milwaukee, WI 53201
Gulton, 13041 Genise Ave., Hawthorne, CA 90250
Robert Hammond, 24 Tiffany St. W, Guelph, Ont. Canada N1H 1Y1
Heath Co., Benton Harbor, MI 49022
Interelectronics, 100 U.S. Hwy. 303, Congers, NY 10920
Lorain, 1122 F St., Lorain, OH 44052
Newark Electronics, 500 N. Pulaski Rd., Chicago, IL 60624
Northwestern Electric, 1752 N. Springfield Ave., Chicago, IL 60647
Nova Electric Mfg. Co., 263 Hillside Ave., Nutley, NJ 07110
Ratelco, Inc., 610 Pontius Ave. N, Seattle, WA 98109
Solar Corp., 5669 Elston Ave., Chicago, IL 60646
Systron-Donner Corp., 889 Galindo, Concord, CA 94518
Wilmore Electronics Inc., Box 2973, Durham, NC 27705
Windworks, Rt. 3, Box 329, Mukwonago, WI 53149

MAGAZINES

Alternative Sources of Energy, Rt. 2, Box 90A, Milaca, MN 56353
Electric Vehicle Council, 90 Park Ave., New York, NY 10016

POWERTRAIN

Armac Gears, 4401 N. Ravenswood Ave., Chicago, IL 60640
W. W. Grainger, Inc., 5959 Howard St., Chicago, IL 60648
Kohler, 421 High St., Kohler, WI 53044
Leese-Neville, 1374 E. 51st St., Cleveland, OH 44103

Palley Supply Co., 2263 E. Vernon Ave., Dept. M-70, Los Angeles, CA 90058

Reliance Electric, 24701 Euclid, Cleveland, OH 44117

Virden Perma-Bilt, Box 7160, Amarillo, TX 79109

Winsmith Power Transmissions, Div. of UMC Industries, Inc., Springville, NY 14141

REFERENCES

Alternator-gas engine power plants plans, $5, B-UR-O Co., 34161 B. Coast Hwy., Dept. C-2, Dana Point, CA 92629

"Alt-power" car alternator 110-V generator plans, $5, same as above.

Auto Parts & Accessories Catalog - $1.00 from J. C. Whitney & Co., 1917-19 Archer Ave., P. O. Box 8410, Chicago, IL 60680

ASE Magazine column: "Martin Answers:" Q & A with Martin Jopp, who has 55 years of daily experience with electrical systems, etc.

Basic Electricity, Bureau of Naval Personnel, 1970, 490 pp., $3.50 from Dover Publishing Co., 180 Varick St., New York, NY 10014

Basic Electricity, Vol. 1-5, 6 & 7, Van Valkenburgh, Hooger, & Neville, Inc., 1953, 700 pp., $13.75 from Hayden Book Co., 50 Essex St., Rochelle Park, NJ 07662

Batteries and Energy Systems, C. L. Mantell, Phd., 1970, 221 pp., $15 from McGraw Hill Book Co., 1221 Avenue of the Americas, New York, NY 10020

"Battery Information and Manufacturing Guide", $3.50, publishes The Battery Man @ $4.50/yr., from Independent Battery Mfgs. Ass'n., 100 Larchwood Dr., Largo, FL 33540

CoEvolution Quarterly, P. O. Box 428, Sausolito, CA 94965 - $8/yr. Back issues $2 each.

Electric Generating Systems, Loren J. Mages, 1970, 374 pp., $5.95 from Theodore Audel & Co., 4300 W. 62 St., Indianapolis, IN 46268

Electric Motors by E. Anderson, 1968, 432 pp., $5.95 from Theodore Audel & Co., same address as above.

Energybook I, $4.25, Energybook II, $5.25, from Running Press, 38 S. 19th St., Philadephia, PA 19103

Energy Primer - Solar, Water, Wind, & Biofuels, 1974, 200 pp., $4.50 from Portola Inst., 558 Santa Cruz, Menlo Park, CA 94025

Eveready Battery Applications Engineering Data, free from Union Carbide Corp., Consumer Prod. Div., 270 Park Ave., New York, NY 10017

"Facts About Storage Batteries" - $1.00 from ESB Batteries, Inc., P. O. Box 6949, Cleveland, OH 44101

The Homebuilt, Wind-Generated Electricity Handbook, Michael Hackleman, 1975, 200 pp., $8 from Earthmind, 5246 Boyer Rd., Mariposa, CA 95338

"Homemade Power Plants - 12V generator" - standby generators, John's Workshop, ASE #22, p. 36-37.

The Lead Acid Storage Battery - $1.00 from Exide, 5 Penn Ctr. Plaza, Philidelphia PA 19103

LeJay Manual, plans for electric gadgets, electric scooter, wind plants, etc., 1945, $1.70 from LeJay Mfg. Co., Belleplaine, MN 56011

"110-V Car Alternator" by Roswell Aga, ASE #22, p. 10-12.

SCR Manual-Chap. 9: Choppers, Inverters, & Cycloinverters, $2 from F. Gutzwiller Editor, 1964, G. E. Corp, W. Genesee St., Auburn, NY 13021

Simplified Electrical Wiring Handbook, Sears, Roebuck, Co., 1969.

"Storing Your Own Power" - battery systems, John's Workshop, ASE #23, p. 37-40.

Understanding Batteries, 15 pgs. - $3 from Earthmind.

Voltswagon: How to Convert a VW to Electric Power, ASE #18, p. 16-19, Jory Squibb

Wind & Windspinners, Michael Hackleman, 1975, 200 pp., $8 from Earthmind.

STANDBY GENERATORS

Belyea Co. Inc., 42 Howell St., Jersey City, NJ 07306

Empire Electric Co., 5200-02 First Ave., Brooklyn, NY 11232

Empire Generator Corp., W190, N11260 Carnegie Dr., Germantown, WI 53022

Howelite Generators, Rendale & Nelson Sts., Port Chester, NY 10573

Ideal Electric, 615 - 1st St., Mansfield, OH 44903

Katolight Corp., Mankato, MN 56007

McCulloch, 989 S. Brooklyn Ave., Wellsville, NY 19895

Onan Corp., 1400 73rd Ave NE, Minneapolis, MN 55432

Unigen, Inc., 194 W. Stone St., Almont, MI 48003

Winco Div. of Dynatech, P. O. Box 3263, Sioux City, IA 51102

Windpower Mfg. Co., Newton, IA 50208

I've been with Earthmind for 4 years now, and I'm self-taught in wind and solar energy and electric vehicles. I've no degrees in anything, but I had many college majors: physics, math, engineering, drafting, and welding. As well, I spent 4 years in the Navy and two at Scripps Institute of Oceanography --- both as an electronics technician. I'm presently teaching some classes in Alternative Sources of Energy and I spend a lot of time working on VW engines.

Now that the book is done, I intend to do a little backpacking in nearby Yosemite. And some fast-paced games of Frisbee. Stalking quail with my slingshot (I've not hit any yet, but probability is working in my favor). Sipping a few Heinekens. Maybe buying my sister's hangglider and doing some wind energy research of a different nature. Or turning out copious designs on a pedal-powered paddlewheel boat or the like. And, of course, spending a little more time with my ladyfriend!

Michael

I work with gardens, animals, graphic design, colors, books, languages... there are never enough hours in the day! I admire quality and subtlety --- in environments, in work, in people's lives --- and I'm angry to see so many things going in the opposite direction. I go crazy in stationary and office supply stores. I'm so excited by reams of fresh white paper, unused brushes, ink --- tools and materials in such abundance. I'm in love with California and that man on the other end of the string.

VANESSA

Earthmind is still looking for a home --- a place to set up a wind and solar energy-powered workshop for people to learn about these concepts and devices, build there own, and carry on research. As well, it'd be a place for us to live. We are looking for people as well as land. If you feel that you could make a positive contribution to our efforts, contact us and we'll let you know who we're looking for and how it all happens. You won't get rich (economically) but we do enjoy life here.

ABBREVIATION TEARSHEET

BC---bicycle

EV---electric vehicle

MB---motorized bicycle

MC---motorcycle

MV---motor vehicle

PASEV---passenger electric vehicle

SV---special vehicle

UTLEV---utility electric vehicle

Class 1---4 wheels; 2000+ lbs.; speeds over 30 mph; manufactured or conversion; PASEV.

Class 2---4 wheels; under 2000 lbs.; speeds over 30 mph; manufactured, conversion, or homebuilt; UTLEV or PASEV.

Class 3---3 wheels; 1000-2000 lbs.; speeds around 30 mph; manufactured or homebuilt; UTLEV or PASEV; using a motor which doesn't permit a MB classification.

Class 4---3 wheels; under 1000 lbs. operating, if PASEV with just under 30 mph speeds, or under 1500 lbs. if UTLEV with 15 mph top speed; MB classification.

Class 5---3 wheels; under 500 lbs.; 15-25 mph; PASEV resembling a beefed-up adult tri-wheel bike; MB classification.

Class 6---2 wheels; under 250 lbs.; around 15 mph; PASEV; modified bicycle with motor-assist.